S0-AGQ-777

Outstanding National Acclaim for
The Fruit Palace

"FAST-PACED, INFORMATIVE, AT TIMES GRIM AND MENACING, OTHER TIMES COMICAL . . . The Perilous quest to find the Colombian connection begins in Bogotá but soon is tramping through scruffy waterfront barrios, steamy jungle villages and desolate mountain towns, outlasting earthquake, fever and contrabandistas."

—UPI

"TRAVEL WRITING AT ITS BEST, and Nicholl's investigations into the drug trade lend the book a comedy and tension that give it the taste and pleasure of fiction."

—*Kirkus Reviews*

"AN UNFORGETTABLE FEAST OF INFORMATION, LAUGHS, AND SHEER TERROR."

—*Booklist*

"A GOOD, SOLID ADVENTURE YARN . . . nonfiction that shames the most escapist sort of fiction for its color, suspense, and most of all, characters."

—*Rocky Mountain News*

"AS EDGE-OF-THE-CHAIR AS ANY EPISODE OF *MIAMI VICE*."

—*Albuquerque Journal*

"SPELLBINDING."

—Pasadena, CA, *Star-News*

The Critics Raved Over

"UNDENIABLY, AN INTERESTING BOOK . . . It has a large cast of high-detailed characters and exquisitely described settings. A genuinely exciting tale."
—*Best Sellers*

"MORE THAN A BOOK WITH A COCAINE HOOK: it is a Third World odyssey and a personal account of human failings and determination, often laced with treading-upon-the-trapdoor humor."
—*Kansas City Star*

"Nicholl, with the help and hindrance of derelict journalists, coke-snorting jet setters and bartenders in fly-blown dives, goes after the powerful story . . . Nicholl does not preach; he simply tells us what is there."
—*Pittsburgh Press*

"READS LIKE A WELL-PLOTTED NOVEL, compelling the reader to the end."
—Jackson, Miss., *Clarion-Ledger/News*

"A story of adventure so fascinating, so intriguing, that it reads more like a novel than like a journalistic account."
—*Minnesota Daily Welcome*

The Fruit Palace

"ONE FINE PIECE OF WORK ... An impressionistic, though highly accessible, sense of Colombia itself, warts and all—or should I say, drugs and all."
—*Wichita Eagle-Beacon*

"SHAMELESSLY CANDID, RUEFULLY COMIC, PIERCINGLY OBSERVANT ADVENTURE STORY-CUM-TRAVELOGUE that paints Colombia in compelling prose ... The tale is a lively, earthy pageant; it is also a scary one."
—*Twin Cities Reader*

"WICKEDLY FUNNY, SUSPENSEFUL, packed with lore about cocaine and the trafficking in it. . . . A lovely travel book. THIS IS A ONE-OF-A-KIND BOOK—part Hunter Thompson, part William Burroughs ... In short, irresistible."
—Oakland, Mich., *Press*

"As thoughtful as it is funny, as harrowing as it is droll."
—Flint, Mich., *Journal*

"An exciting and lushly written picture of the insanity that is life in the post-cocaine Colombia."
—Charlotte, N.C., *Observer*

"LOOK OUT HUNTER THOMPSON!"
—*Columbus Dispatch*

THE FRUIT PALACE

Charles Nicholl

ST. MARTIN'S PRESS/NEW YORK

St. Martin's Press titles are available at quantity discounts for sales pro-
motions, premiums or fund raising. Special books or book excerpts can
also be created to fit specific needs. For information to write to special
sales manager, St. Martin's Press, 175 Fifth Avenue, New York, N. Y.
10010.

Lyrics from "Rosalita" reprinted by permission of Jon Landau Manage-
ment, Inc. © Bruce Springsteen Music 1974.

THE FRUIT PALACE

Copyright © 1985 by Charles Nicholl

All rights reserved. Printed in the United States of America. No part of
this book may be used or reproduced in any manner whatsoever without
written permission except in the case of brief quotations embodied in
critical articles or reviews. For information, address St. Martin's Press,
175 Fifth Avenue, New York, N.Y. 10010.

Library of Congress Catalog Card Number: 86-3779

ISBN: 0-312-90725-7

Printed in the United States of America

First St. Martin's Press mass market edition/November 1987

10 9 8 7 6 5 4 3 2 1

For Sally

99 SMATA CO

37 CARTAGENA C R 31 MAR 10 09A1

MAR 10 11 20
OFICINA
STA MARTA

CARLOS MICHELL
PALACIO DE FRUTAS
CALLE 10C NR 249
SANTAMARTA

PLEASE FIND OUT PRICE AND CONDITION OF LUIS'S GOLD BROGS

INDESCREETLY LET ME KNOW OBGM YOU COME ROOM 32

NANCY

37 10C 249 COHEN OK COHEN 32
909 OGEMA CO

33

CONTENTS

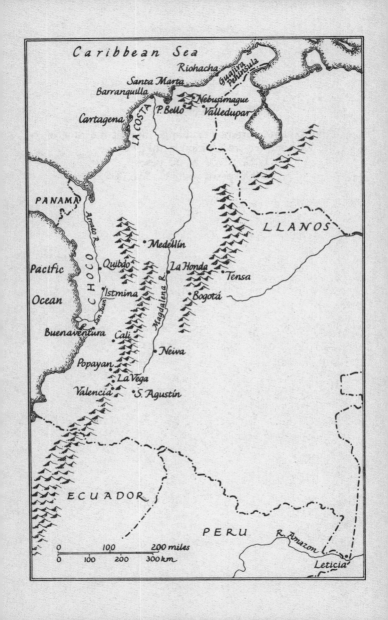

NOTE

Approximate currency exchange rates at the time of the author's trip to Colombia in 1983:

U.S. $1.00 = 60 pesos
1,000 pesos = U.S. $16.00

PREFACE

It is raining in Europe. There are no windows in this narrow, strip-lit room, but I know it's raining, as it was when the plane landed two, maybe three hours ago. One of the customs officers has just come back in. "It's pissing down out there," he says. The shoulder of his blue, vaguely naval uniform are wet. The other officer, the Scot, the one who asks all the questions, turns to me and says, "Looks like we're doing you a favour after all."

They have looked up my record, looked up my rectum, searched me from the heel of my boot to the lining of my hat. They have sifted through my baggage, deftly and patiently, like archaeologists. There remains the possibility that I'm body-packing—carrying cocaine inside my stomach, packaged up in condoms or the fingers of surgical gloves—but they are inclined to doubt it. It seems I am clean. They are dealing with a nuisance, an eccentric, a fool, but not a smuggler.

So the only problem is this handful of greenish-brown leaves, sitting on the pinewood desk in front of me, spilling out of a couple of pages of last Wednesday's edition of *El Bogotano*. They are coca leaves. To be precise, they are the leaves of *Erythroxylum novogranatense*, the sub-species of *Erythroxylum coca* that grows in the temperate mountain valleys of Colombia. I have explained it all carefully. I'm just a writer, a poor hack returning home from an assignment. I brought the leaves back as a souvenir. They were given to me by the Arhuacos, the mountain Indians of the Sierra Nevada. I stretch the point a little and say they were a 'ceremonial' gift. No, I was not aware they were illegal here. Such a mild stimulant, surely, no stronger than maté leaves or ginseng root. Yes, of course I knew that cocaine was extracted from coca leaves, but look, the leaves are old and stale. They are spotted with white mildew—*coca caspada*, they call it, dandruffy coca. Any self-respecting coca user would throw them away. The most diligent *cocinero* in the world couldn't get a grain of cocaine out of them.

My two interrogators, the dark Scot and his soft-spoken, curly-haired back-up man, would probably let the whole thing go. It has been an interesting morning for them. They had pulled a thousand people with Colombian stamps in their passport, but they had never seen a coca leaf before. "Most instructive," says the droll Scot. But the Senior Officer, one Liggett, has been summoned, and he has no doubts whatever. The law clearly states that the coca leaf is a Controlled Substance, a Class A drug as defined in Schedule Two of the Misuse of Drugs Act, 1971. I am consequently under arrest, and when they are good and ready I'll be taken down to Heathrow police station to be charged.

I am just tired now. At the beginning, when they stopped calling me "Sir" and brought me in here, I was scared. Then I was angry. Now I am as blank as this room. Above a washbasin, where a mirror might be, is a document headed "Notes for the Guidance of Arrested Persons". On the desk, among the leaves, are fragments of a Bogotá newspaper—the photograph of a kidnap victim, the winning numbers in the Cundinamarca lottery, a small ad proclaiming the amazing powers of Professor Johnny, *maestro en ciencias ocultas*.

Time passes slowly in Room 1094A. Smugglers call these the dead-end rooms.

The Scot settles down the other side of the desk, licks his finger, turns a new page of his notebook. "Right. Let's run through this story of yours from the beginning, shall we?"

1

AT THE FRUIT PALACE

If these things have a beginning I suppose this began at the Fruit Palace, some twelve years ago now. The Fruit Palace was a small, whitewashed café, much like thousands of others in Colombia. It stood a couple of blocks up from the waterfront in Santa Marta, a hot, scruffy sea-port on the northern coast. The wooden sign outside read, "EL PALACIO DE LAS FRUTAS, Cafetería Refresquería Residencias," the letters painted in bright, naïve colours, with a small study in fruit—oranges, mangoes, a half-sliced pineapple—in the bottom corner. The speciality of the house was the *jugo*, or tropical fruit juice, but you could also get the usual range of cheap meals, liquor, provisions, and of course the ubiquitous *tinto*, the small cup of black coffee that fuels the nation.

The Fruit Palace was always open and never crowded. People drifted in off the street, to trade a bit of gossip and rest from the weight of the sun. In the evenings a few dock-workers might come in for a game of *veinti-una*, with much shouting and slapping down of cards and tossing back of rum. I think Julio, who owned and ran the Fruit Palace, actually preferred business slow. He had dreams of getting rich, he had complex schemes for getting rich, but they were quite divorced from his day-to-day life. Whisking *jugos* was something to do while he waited for the big one to turn up. "With a little bit of sweet and a little bit of sour," he said, "a man is happy."

His favourite getting-rich dream at that time was focused,

though none too clearly, on selling insurance. Ever since he had heard of the Sistema No Claims Bonus, he had been sure that this was his true niche. "It's marvellous," he said. "It's like I sell you a five-peso *jugo*, and then I say: If you don't drink it, I'll only charge you four."

Julio was in his mid-thirties, but he looked older. He was not a Samario, as the natives of Santa Marta are known, but one of the town's floating population. Santa Marta is a honeytrap for hopeful prospectors from the interior, drawn by the promise of the good life by the Caribbean Sea, and of the rich pickings to be had from the town's various forms of contraband, mainly—but by no means exclusively—drugs. Julio was from Boyacá, 500 miles south in the Eastern Cordillera of the Andes. With his black stubble, bad teeth, sideburns and faded check shirts, he had the typical look of the Colombian *criollo*, the mixed Spanish-Indian type that forms the majority of the country's people. But he had something else—a certain finesse, a dapperness of manner and philosophy. His pointed nose and thick, slightly twirled moustache gave him an oddly *belle époque* air, a minor French dandy somehow adrift down a South American back-street.

Julio's contribution to Santa Marta's black economy was a little modest dealing in emeralds. His father had been an *esmeraldero*, first an emerald miner at Coscuez and then a small-time dealer. Some people have a way with animals: Julio had a way with emeralds. He always had a small consignment on the go, and whenever a new gringo face turned up at the Fruit Palace, it was not long before the talk was steered round to the fabulous virtues of the Colombian gem emerald, *la más famosa en el mundo*. Out would come the little fold of tissue paper, with a pair of Muzo stones or a thimbleful of uncut *canutillos* winking inside. He would rock a stone gently in his palm, like a tiny dice. *"Mire, mire, el fuego verde!"* Look at the green fire in it. His prices were always good, even by black market standards. I wondered if he sometimes sold fakes—he certainly spoke expertly about counterfeiting: rock candy, vanadium, doublets and triplets, and so on—but it wouldn't have done to ask him.

Also living at the Fruit Palace was a girl called Miriam, who did the cooking and the cleaning. Julio had a wife and a little daughter, but they were somewhere else for a while—the vagueness was Julio's—and in the meantime he was sharing his bed with Miriam. She was a plump, moody Caquetana girl in her twenties. She wore tight skirts and a man's wristwatch. As she worked she rendered current hit songs in a tuneless, hissing kind of whistle—her favourite was a tearjerker entitled *"Volver Volver Volver."* She was no great beauty, but like Lily in the song she had that certain flash every time she smiled. She flirted slyly with all the gringos. She visited me in my dreams, her breasts syncopating softly as they did when she danced to the songs on the radio. The quiet glint of machismo in Julio's eye was enough to keep it at that.

There was a small back room behind the café which Julio rented out—this was the *residencias* advertised on the sign outside. I had stumbled into the café one day for a beer, straight off the train from Barrancabermeja, a fifteen-hour haul across the Magdalena plains. The room was vacant. Too tired to look for a hotel, I took it for the night. The profound nonchalance of Santa Marta stole over me, and I was still there three months later. The bed had once belonged to Julio's grandmother and had a carved cedarwood headboard of which he was very proud, but it was bone-hard to lie on, and after a while I slept in the hammock out in the yard. When the tiny rent Julio charged for the room grew too onerous, I actually rented the hammock off him for something like 10 pesos a night. I kept my belongings in a large, rusty parrot-cage, procured by Julio for this purpose. I shared the yard with a small contingent of animals. Down at the end by the kitchen lived the hen, immured by night in its miniature shack of old fruit boxes. There was a guard dog pacing on the neighbour's roof, there were rats beneath the concrete walkway, and there was the cockroach—one of many, but definitely *the* cockroach, sleek and fat and shiny brown as a conker.

Julio was delighted with this new arrangement. It had the

magic smack of something for nothing. I paid less, he got more, the back room now being free for other gringos—or possibly even *gringitas*—to fill. There were always gringos in town, North Americans mostly, also French Canadians, Italians, the occasional Brit. The better class of tourist stayed at the sea-front hotels, or out at Rodadero, the modern hotel development hidden round the headland. They certainly didn't stay down on 10th Street, where the Fruit Palace stood. This was really the last of the "safe" streets. After that you were on your own, in the shanty-town *barrio* of San Martín which sprawled up the dusty hills above the docks. Only the more dubious, low-rent travellers, or those who had special reasons for being near the docks, sought their lodgings here. In those days there were plenty who fell into one or both of those categories, and Julio's back room was seldom vacant for long.

When I think now of the Fruit Palace I remember especially the sweet-scented nights. Julio always bought his fruit overripe. This was both cheaper and better for making *jugos*, yet another instance of those secret financial harmonies he loved to observe. The musk of sweating tropical fruit pervaded the café. By day it had to compete with the oily aromas of Miriam's cuisine, but at night, swaying in my hammock in the yard, the sweet smell of corruption lay over me like a blanket.

The nights were filled with noises, accordions duelling down in the dockside bars, dogs barking across the low roofs, trucks gunning their engines ready for the long haul south. The dockland seemed to buzz right around the yard walls, delicious and dangerous, a faint periphery of menace like in the nights of childhood. Even in the dead of night, after all the jacks were in their boxes and even the animals were asleep, I would sometimes be woken by a strange concert of groans and squeaks. It was the sound of the sea wind swinging the wooden signboards of the cafés and flophouses down 10th Street. That sudden north-easterly wind, rising off the Caribbean after hours or sometimes days of stillness, was called "La Loca," the madwoman.

It was at the Fruit Palace that I had my first taste of the Colombian drug trade. Illegal drugs were, and still are, the economic and cultural heartbeat of Santa Marta. In the early 1970s, when I was there, this still primarily meant marijuana. Marijuana—known locally as *baretta, marimba* or *mota*—was local produce. The fertile lower slopes of the Sierra Nevada, lying to the south-east of the town, produced hundreds of tons of grass a year. Nowadays it is thousands of tons. Fiercely hot, plentifully watered, full of hidden cul-de-sac valleys, and mostly impassable to any vehicle larger than a mule, the *macizo* is ideal marijuana territory. Colombian grass is considered by many connoisseurs to be the finest in the world, and nine times out of ten this means one of the Sierra Nevada strains—Santa Marta Gold, Blue Sky Blonde, Red Dot, etc. These are pale, tan-coloured grasses, instantly distinguishable from the darker, moister, greenish-black strains—Mango Viche, La Negra—grown in the south of Colombia. A handful of flowering tops of Santa Marta Gold, *muños de oro,* looks like an exotic kind of rough-cut blond tobacco. The general rule is, the paler the gold, the stronger the grass. The palest weed is grown at the lowest range of the optimum growing altitude, around 500 meters above sea level, where the sun is hottest (any lower and the humidity saps the vital resins in the plant). The drug-lore further has it that these lower plantations run a greater risk of being discovered, and that the potency of the *marimba* derives from the daring and panache of the *marimbero,* the marijuana planter. Probably most potent of all is Punto Rojo, or Red Dot, so-called for its tiny splashes of red on the gold buds. The legendary Panama Red is the same strain from a neighbouring country.

In those days the vast marijuana market in the United States was mainly supplied by Mexican grass. It wasn't until the later 1970s, after a massive US herbicide campaign had wiped out many Mexican plantations—and what didn't get destroyed quickly lost its market value as smokers started turning up in casualty wards with Paraquat poisoning—that

Colombian marijuana reigned supreme. The profits were big, but they weren't yet in the mega-buck units they talk in nowadays. And so the resourceful Samario *contrabandista* was becoming increasingly involved in another illicit chemical: cocaine.

Santa Marta's involvement in the cocaine trade is a simple and vital matter of geography. The town stands precisely placed between the major producers and the major consumers of cocaine, between the *cocales* of Peru and Bolivia where the coca plant is intensively cultivated, and the United States where the refined end-product is snorted up by the truckload. There are plenty of side-doors along the way, but the basic route, then and now, is for the drug to be funnelled up north across the mainland as far as it can go, to the Caribbean coast of Colombia, and from there to be shipped or flown to the United States and Europe. In the phrase of a former president of Colombia, Santa Marta is "a victim of its privileged geographic position."

These were still the early days of the great cocaine boom. In America and Europe coke was the chic new chemical toy, the rock star's tipple, Ziggy's Stardust. Down in Colombia the big smuggling syndicates were just beginning to emerge and the two main *contrabandista* syndicates in Santa Marta—the Cárdenas and Valdeblanquez clans—were already battling for control of this hugely lucrative new market. But there was still plenty of room for independent operations, for the local cowboys and the gringo casuals and the small-time dealers. The Colombian press carried regular reports of some gringo caught at customs with a false heel full of flake. For every one who got pulled there were nine who got through.

So, what with the dope and the coke, this part of the Colombian coast, and three towns in particular—the industrial port city of Barranquilla to the west, Santa Marta in the middle, and Riohacha out on the Guajira peninsula—were fast becoming one of the world centres for drug smuggling. In Santa Marta everyone one met, whether gringo, Samario or drifting prospector, seemed to have a finger in the pie, some form of rake-off from some form of drug deal. There was even a missionary who discovered that the sacks of maize flour that the *campesino* farmers gave him to truck down to town were actually stuffed full of Punto Rojo grass. He came to an amicable agreement, whereby a portion of the profits was donated to the mission. In Santa Marta even God gets cut in on the deal.

The town had the feel of a tropical smugglers' den. It was a rakish, seedy, avaricious little place, but somehow exhilarating in the way it lived according to its own laws. The whole thing felt like a game. It was hard to imagine Santa Marta as the world centre for anything. But often at night, lying in my hammock, I would hear the sound of freight trucks backfiring, and I would hold my breath because sometimes there followed a kind of shock-wave, a pattern of silence and shouts, that meant it was gunfire.

A few of the gringos who stayed at the Fruit Palace were putting together small deals of some sort. The coolest of these was Nancy. She was a swan-necked girl from Toronto, who always wore sunglasses. She had me fooled all the way. She was supposedly on the coast to buy and export some pre-Columbian gold pieces. She spent a lot of time with a big man called Luis, who seemed to have a bottomless supply of golden figurines and pendants, no doubt illegally looted from Tairona burial sites in the Sierra. This is another of Santa Marta's stocks-in-trade.

Nancy came and went a lot, but she kept the room paid up even when she wasn't there. Julio was transfixed by her. This exquisite *gringita*, paying twenty-eight days in advance, was like a holy vision to him. One day Nancy said she was going to Cartagena on business, would I perhaps like to meet up with her there in a week or so? My mouth dropped open with delight. She was a beautiful girl, and Cartagena was a beautiful town. Of course I'd like to meet up with her.

A few days later a telegram arrived for me at the Fruit Palace. It was from Nancy. Through a veil of misprints the message read, "PLEASE FIND OUT PRICE AND CONDITION OF LUIS'S GOLD FROGS DISCREETLY LET ME KNOW WHEN YOU COME ROOM 32." I dutifully sought out Luis. "Tell her I've got ten frogs, ready to go," he said. He named a price per frog.

"Is that in pesos or dollars?"

"She'll know."

I took the bus to Cartagena, tingling with hopes of romance in the old white city. When I got there she seemed more interested in Luis's figures than in me, and to my disappointment she left the hotel early that evening and didn't return. The next I saw of her was two weeks later at the Fruit Palace. It was only then that she told me. I never learned the details, but I learned that the gold "frogs" had really been kilos of Santa Marta Gold, and that I had unwittingly couriered information for a drug-run out of Cartagena, now successfully completed.

I was aghast. How could she use me like that? Why had she used me like that? She shrugged. "Timing. Security. I often use guys like you, places like this. It's like they say— innocence is the best cover."

Thanks a bunch, Nancy. Her name wasn't really Nancy, either. She had another name in a hotel down on the seafront, and probably a third name in Cartagena. I don't think I ever did see her without her sunglasses on.

I still have the telegram she sent me, a souvenir of something, I don't quite know what. You would think I might have learned my lesson, but just a few weeks later I found myself mixed up in yet another drug move. It was cocaine this time, where the stakes are higher, the people crazier, and the comebacks nastier. From this night of folly I have no souvenirs, except the occasional flashback when my nerves are bad.

2

A NIGHT WITH
CAPTAIN COCAINE

It was a Saturday night. I had no particular company. The
back room had been empty since Nancy left. There were few
tourists in town. It was April, the hot, slack month before
the brief rainy season. Soon after dark I left the Fruit Palace
and made for the sea-front, thinking to get a beer or two at
the Pan-American, where they usually had a band playing on
Saturday nights. A fat orange moon, two days past the full,
squatted over the low hills inland.

As I crossed the Parque Bolívar I could hear the music
already, but by a habit swiftly acquired in this small, predatory town, I crossed over the main beach-drag and walked
under the tall palms of the promenade. Thus separated from
the sea-front cafés, one could observe who was drinking
where and select one's watering-hole accordingly.

The Pan-American was Santa Marta's smartest café. It had
white tables laid out under a blue awning, and the legend
"Aire condicionado" emblazoned in scrolly red neon. Featur-
ing that night on the little stage in the corner was a Barranquilla trio, Bruno y su Jazz. Bruno was a squat, check-shirted
costeño with an old Gibson electric guitar. He played fast,
upper-register licks somewhat in the manner of Carlos San-
tana. His combo consisted of a ferrety bass-man in beret and
sunglasses, and an energetic black drummer in a sleeveless
blue singlet already soaked in sweat. Slightly off to one side,

self-invited, an old black in a hat was playing the wooden rhythm stick called a *guacharaca*. The waiters wanted to get rid of him, but he stood just inside the charmed circle of the music and they couldn't touch him.

Sitting alone at one of the tables was a gringo I didn't recognize—a "pure" gringo from the United States, I guessed, as opposed to the hybrid European variety. He was smartly dressed in lightweight gear, mustachioed, bulky, balding, age indeterminate. He was sitting over a beer with his back to the music. He glanced fitfully over the magazine in front of him—doubtless *Time* or *Newsweek*—but it was obvious he was waiting for someone. I took a seat at the next table, and when the song finished we got talking. He was from New York City, I learned. No, he'd never been in Colombia before, in fact he'd never been further south than Phoenix, Arizona, before yesterday. Yes, he was just here on vacation. He wore beige slacks and canvas beach shoes. They looked bought the day before yesterday. He had spilt something on one of them, and now he was spilling a bit of beer as he drank, and wiping the drips off his walrus moustache. He had a high-pitched voice, aggressive in the New York way, and rather catarrhal. He seemed to want to talk, but was anxious to keep a lookout for whoever he was waiting for. Quite a crowd had gathered for the music, and he craned nervously for a view of the sidewalk.

"You're waiting for someone?" I asked.

"Goddamn right I am," he replied, with another irritated check at his watch. "And it looks like he ain't going to show. He said he'd be here at 6. Lahs says. That's 6 o'clock, right?"

I agreed that it was. His watch said nearly 8. "At a guess," I bantered, "you're waiting for a Colombian. They're not the best time-keepers in the world."

"*Mañana*, huh?"

He drummed his fingers on the table, drained his beer, said "Aw, shit!" and dismissed with a wave the sidewalk and the person who wasn't hoving into view along it. I ordered two more beers. We formalized our meeting with a hand-

shake. His palm was cold and damp. His name was Harvey.
He had been in Santa Marta twenty-four hours, he said, and
the whole goddamn place seemed crazy.

We drank and smoked, discussed Colombia, and eyed the
costeñas, the stunning local girls, in their Saturday best. I was
showing off rather, full of tips and lore and knowing the
ropes. I would get my comeuppance soon enough. Harvey
ordered more beers, in English. One of the things he didn't
like about Colombia, he implied, was the Spanish language.
Just a minor hassle, like the bad water, but someone back
home should have warned him about it. He was getting a bit
drunk now. He had been through three bottles of Aguila
beer before I arrived. An unhealthy dew of sweat lay on his
forehead. He looked pale and egg-headed among these laughing Samarios.

Bruno brought a long guitar solo to a climax of high, gull-
like notes, then a dramatic pause before the final bar. This
was spoilt somewhat by the old man with the *guacharaca*,
who kept on hammering the stick on the neck of his rum
bottle, dancing away with his eyes tight shut and a huge,
oblivious grin on his face.

It was in the lull after this number that Harvey leaned
conspiratorially across the table. He was glad he had met me,
he said, because he had this problem.

This did not entirely surprise me. In Santa Marta two and
two do not infallibly make four, but a nervous, catarrhal
gringo fresh into town almost certainly spells "cocaine." Sure
enough. "I'm not really here on vacation," he explained.
"I've come down for a bit of business. You know"—he
touched the side of his nose with his finger—"Cousin
Charlie."

I nodded understandingly, but said nothing.

"Just a quick in and out job," he added sharply. His look
suggested that the way out was not at this moment quite
clear.

"So there's a problem?" I said. He nodded, looked around,
and leant still closer. In anticipation of a long and delicate

story I said, "Why don't we pay, and go for a walk along the beach?"

The story Harvey told me as we walked along the beach was simple enough. For a couple of years now, since arriving in New York from some backwood in Wisconsin, he had been doing a bit of small-time cocaine dealing. He loved the stuff dearly, and the dealing was mainly to keep himself in "candy" and make back the money his habit was costing him. He was living up in Queens, which has a large population of Colombian immigrants. Connections were easy. He would buy an ounce at a time, step on it a little with mannite, and knock it out in grams among his friends. He was vaguely connected with the music business, so selling it was no problem.

"For a time it was great," he said wistfully. "Plenty of candy, plenty of bread. Then you start getting greedy. You're doing two, three grams a night, seven nights a week. When you start getting greedy, it's trouble time. You can't walk away from it any more. That's when you're going to take a fall."

Harvey indeed took a fall. He started selling larger quantities, and one day a Lexington Avenue street dealer "pulled out a piece and spat in my eye"—robbed him, in other words, at gunpoint. Net result: half a kilo of cocaine, as yet unpaid for, "down the john." Fortunately for Harvey, the owner of the cocaine did not exact any violent retribution— "like they drop you in the river twice and pull you out once." Instead he offered Harvey an arrangement. He needed someone to take care of a shipment from the Colombian end. If Harvey would look after it for him, he would forget about this unpleasant business of the missing half-kilo.

"I was fifteen adrift, man," Harvey whined. Fifteen thousand dollars was what a half-kilo was worth in New York in the early seventies. "I had no way of paying up. The man could cut me up into any shape he liked. He offers me a deal. No way I could refuse.

"It all seemed pretty tight. He gives me Air Florida tick-

ets, New York—Miami—Barranquilla—Santa Marta. He tells
me where to go and who to deal with. He gives me a false-
bottom valise with a stack of hundreds in it, plenty of spending money, and an ounce of free candy over the top when I
get home. All I got to do is deliver the money, check the
gear for quantity and quality, and see it on to the boat. Then
I fly home, clean as a bone."

We reached one end of the town beach. In the sand near
the water's edge were black drifts of mica. Specks of pyrites,
fool's gold, glinted in the diffuse, mauvish light of the town.
A station-wagon lurched noisily off the beach-drag into 22nd
Street. It stopped outside a lit doorway where a knot of people were lounging. Two men got out and lifted a third,
wrapped in a blanket, out of the back of the car. Another
patient was being admitted to the emergency ward of the
town's hospital.

Harvey asked what was going on. When I told him he
said, "Christ Jesus!" softly, and rubbed his hands up and
down his white arms as if he were cold. We set off back up
the beach.

Everything had gone fine, he said, till he got to "this
shityard Santa Marta" yesterday afternoon. He was supposed
to meet his contact in the bar of his hotel in Rodadero—
Santa Marta's tourist complex, a couple of miles out of
town—at 6 o'clock. The contact, he had been assured,
would have everything arranged, and he spoke perfect English. Harvey waited, but no one came. Then the barman
brought him the phone—"a call for you, *señor*"—and someone was jabbering at him in Spanish. The caller eventually
got the gist of the message across. Harvey's contact was no
longer in on the deal; Harvey was to take a taxi into town
the next morning; he was to go to the Hotel Venezuela and
ask for someone called Manolo.

The following morning, the morning of this Saturday,
Harvey did as he had been instructed. He met Manolo, "a
little jerk in shades," at the Venezuela. (I later looked over
this establishment from the outside: a poky little clip-joint
with barred windows up near the *mercado popular*.) Manolo

told him the coke would be ready that night, and wanted to see the money. Harvey said the money was back at his hotel in Rodadero. Manolo said to bring all his stuff over from Rodadero, there was a room for him here at the Venezuela, the *portero* would look after him, and so on. Harvey did not like this arrangement, "a back-to-the-wall set-up." Manolo, on the other hand, refused to bring the *coco* over to Rodadero. Communication was difficult. They made a truce arrangement, to meet at the Pan-American at six. Already fearing a rip-off, Harvey sped back to Rodadero. His money-bag was still there. He sat guard over it all day, smoking cigarettes and listening to the clatter of the air-conditioner.

Harvey's second 6 o'clock in Colombia came and went like the first, waiting for a "friend" who did not come, and so it was that a couple of hours later I had seen this balding gringo, casting a worried eye up and down the sidewalk outside the Pan-American.

This, broadly, was Harvey's account of the business so far. From what I knew about the cocaine racket, it sounded like the usual cloak-and-dagger stuff. So why was he telling me? And what exactly was the "problem" he had mentioned, the problem that I—I suspected—was in some way supposed to solve? I asked him.

"The problem?" he snapped. "The goddamn problem is that I got to *do* it!"

"I'm sorry, I don't understand."

"Look, Charlie. Everything about this score smells wrong. First my connection vanishes and I'm dealing with this little hood Manolo instead. Now *he* doesn't show. I've been sitting here scratching since yesterday afternoon and I haven't even had a taste yet. It all smells wrong. OK, ninety-nine times out of a hundred you walk away. No score, no nothing. Don't need a weatherman to know which way the wind blows, right? But this one's different. Number one hundred. I owe it to the man. I'm plumbed right into it."

I murmured sympathy. We were sitting with our backs to a beach hut. The lighthouse on Morro Island was lit: they must have mended it, I thought. Harvey was looking at me thoughtfully. "So what's your next move?" I asked.

"It's all a question of how we handle Manolo . . ."

"Just a minute, Harvey, we aren't . . ."

"I can read that guy like a clock, man! He's just aching to finger the money. What I got to do is make sure I get the candy in return. If he can't take the money and run, he'll come up with the gear. I'm sure of it. What I need is muscle."

"Well, don't look at me, chum," I said firmly. I am not what you would call "muscle." Surely Harvey could see that.

"I don't mean strong-arm stuff, man. I mean negotiating muscle." He gripped my arm. The cards, at last, were landing on the table. "I need two things, Charlie, and you can supply them both. First thing, I need space. I'm not doing any deal at the Venezuela. That's Manolo's patch. This place of yours, this Fruit Castle, sounds just about right. There'll be you, me and that guy of yours, Julio, all nice and cosy, and little Manolo with *his* back to the wall. We'll put the flake on the table, the money on the table, five-o five-o and no monkey business.

"The second thing I need is someone who can speak the lingo. Shit, man. Manolo and me were just talking like babies at each other back there. You can't do this sort of business when you're talking like babies. I need an interpreter, Charlie, someone to whisper sweet nothings in that little cock-sucker's ear. What you say, man?"

Harvey was glinting and glistening at me. Whether or not he had convinced me, he had certainly convinced himself. He was riding high on his own hip talk. He was Harvey the streetwise superfly, the veteran of a hundred daring deals. I could see the fantasy gleam in his bulbous eye. All right, I thought: he wants to play Captain Cocaine, but do I want to play his bloody batman? Sitting here years later, with the benefit of hindsight, it is easy to say I should have told Harvey politely but firmly to go and find someone else to talk him through his cocaine deal. But the night was hot, and these things have a logic of their own. There were risks, of course, but there were undeniable attractions. First, the carrot: $250 on the nail for me, the same for Julio. Second, the story: I was supposed to be some kind of journalist, wasn't I? Third, the general scenario: suitcases stuffed with banknotes, lashings of someone else's cocaine. In short, greed battled with fear, and greed won. "Why not?" I said, and thus with a handshake I became the smallest of small-time accomplices in the cocaine trade.

From that point on everything clicked ominously into place. We headed back for the Pan-American. I skulked on the beach while Harvey scanned the tables from the promenade. He loped back clumsily through the sand. "He's there, man!" he hissed, "we're in business." The next step was for me to consult with Julio. Harvey would meanwhile "keep the little creep happy" at the Pan-American. Back at the Fruit Palace Julio listened patiently. He then said he didn't like *coco*, he didn't like Manolo, he didn't want trouble with the Mafia or the F-2, and consequently he couldn't let his place be used for a trifling 250. He wanted 500.

Back I toiled to the Pan-American. Manolo rose suavely to shake hands, a little man with a thin smile and gold in his teeth. His slicked-back hair shone like wet coal. I was relieved to see he was unaccompanied and, judging from the trim fit of his clothes, unarmed. I told Harvey of Julio's price. He grumbled but, as Julio had doubtless divined, he was in no position to refuse.

"OK, OK," he said. "Now, Charlie, I want you to explain it all to our friend here, nice and gentle. You tell him he does the deal our way or not at all. We meet at the Fruit Palace at"—he checked his watch—"at midnight. He comes alone, with the gear. Five kilos, as arranged. Any monkey business and the deal's off. OK?"

Manolo listened blandly to my polite schoolboy Spanish. It's all right, I thought. He'll simply say "No" and the whole business will be over. But it was a night for wrong decisions, and what he finally said, with a last lingering look at both of us and a light shrug, was: "OK, I'll be there."

The arrangements confirmed, Manolo slipped away through the crowd like a lizard. Harvey let out a long sigh of relief and ran his hand up through his hair. Bruno launched into an up-tempo samba shuffle, and my heart raced along in time to it.

Midnight found the four of us—Julio, Harvey, Manolo and myself—sitting round the "private table" at the Fruit Palace. The air was hot and sweet. A single light shone down on the table: coffee cups, ashtrays, a half-empty bottle of Medellín rum. The street door was shut and bolted. A passer-by might have seen the light under the door, but he would have kept on walking, because at midnight on 10th Street the rule was always to keep on walking.

Harvey had arrived by taxi an hour before, stumbling in with two suitcases, one of them containing $50,000. While we waited Julio tried to sell him some emeralds, but Harvey's mind was elsewhere and his palms were sweating, and he kept on dropping the stones. Now Manolo had just turned up—without the 5 kilos, but with a small *muestra*, a sample, instead.

Harvey did not like this. "Where's the deal, man?" he whinged. "I want to see the deal."

I translated, nervously formal. *"Harvey quiere ver toda la mercancia."*

"I can get it. No problem. Half an hour." Manolo spoke smoothly, with flashes of gold from his teeth. "Doesn't Señor Harvey trust me?"

Harvey said, "Shit, man. I can't afford to trust anyone. He knows that. I don't even trust myself."

"Harvey is a little nervous," I relayed reassuringly.

"Why doesn't he try the *muestra*? It's real good stuff. Ninety-eight per cent pure."

Harvey caught the last phrase, *"pureza de noventa y ocho por ciento,"* and snorted tetchily. "I've heard *that* up in Spanish Harlem. I didn't believe it then and I don't believe it now."

I told him to cool down and try the sample. Manolo

pushed the small, rectangular fold of paper over to him. It was cheap lined paper from a letter pad. Harvey took it. Grumpily, but with gentle care, he opened it up and inspected the small, flattened heap of cream-coloured cocaine inside. He nodded abstractedly. It seemed to please him. He dabbed a bit on to the end of his forefinger and tasted it. Again he nodded. Now he wet his finger and took another dab, and watched while the powder dissolved. He held the finger out to me. There was a trace of grey, fluffy dust on it. "The cut," he murmured. This is a fallible test, I'm told— many "cuts," or adulterants, are quite as soluble as the coke itself—but right then it seemed impressive enough. Harvey looked every inch the professional. He was on home ground at last.

Julio, slightly out of the arc of light, rocked back on the thin-legged café chair. He looked poised and philosophical, as always, but his brown eyes didn't miss a trick. Hardly moving a muscle, he called out for coffee. *"Hay tinto, Miriam?"* A sulky, droned *"Sí"* came out of the bedroom, and Miriam plodded kitchenwards, scraping her flip-flop sandals on the floor. She did not look at us as she passed. She did not approve of *narcotráfico*.

"Looks OK to me," said Harvey. He took out a small Stanley knife with a retractable blade, and began to dice up some of the cocaine on the table. He cursed when grains of crystal jumped away from the blade. I saw that his hands were trembling. He fashioned a small pile of coke into thin lines. Manolo unhooked a coke-spoon from a silver neck-chain under his shirt, but Harvey shook his head—"Uh-uh"—and took out a crisp $100 bill. He rolled it neatly into a thin pipe. "I take it Wonder Warthog style," he chuckled. The imminent pleasure of the cocaine-hit was sweeping aside all his grumbles and paranoias, clearing his mind like a runway for take-off. He hunched over the table and hoovered up a line through the bill with a single deep snort. He winced a little and jerked his head back. His nose stuck up like a shark's fin. He emitted a long, slow hiss of pleasure, as if the cocaine had gone in like a spike and let out all the stale air

in him. He opened his eyes but kept staring up at the ceiling.
"Nice," he sighed, "nice," then "Hmmmm," and an odd,
girlish giggle. He bent back down to repeat the procedure via
the other nostril, then pressed some leftover dust off the
melamine table-top, and massaged it into his gums.

He handed me the little pipe. I took a hit, rather smaller
than Harvey's. I felt my nostril scorch, my mouth freeze, my
veins hum all the way down to my feet. I had tasted coke
before, but this felt lethal. Simple case of motor stimulation,
I reminded myself. Heart racing, adrenal secretions, everything hastening to some unknown crescendo. Purely pharmaceutical, of course. Not *really* on a big dipper at all. Not
falling, not flying, not swooping through the room like a
white owl over a dark field.

My hand was waving the rolled-up bill at Julio. He shook
his head. "I'm thinking of getting some sleep tonight." Manolo also declined it. Instead he stuck his coke-spoon straight
into the *muestra*, and sniffed up two level spoonfuls with a
practised, haughty movement, like a coffee-house fop taking
snuff. Harvey lit a cigarette with trembling hands. The
smoke eddied under the light. His face had a sheen, a chilly
polish. He looked like he had a gum-shield in his mouth.

"Pheeee-ew!" he went. "White line fever!" I felt the first
bitter tang of mucus coming down the back of my throat,
and Miriam came in with a trayful of *tintos*.

It must have been about three in the morning when Manolo
at last came back with "the deal." It was a big cardboard box
tied up with packing-string. Harvey's eyes were out on stalks
by now. He was chain-smoking and jiggling his knees up and
down under the table. He had seen off the rest of the *muestra*
more or less single-handed, with rum and coffee on the side.
He had talked till he was hoarse and now he was apparently
trying to grind all the enamel off his teeth. I had urged cau-
tion, but Manolo's *coco* was the first nice thing that had happened to him in Colombia and, deal or no deal, he was going
to savour it.

The box was on the table, Manolo's jewelled fingers resting on it. "So this is it, huh?" said Harvey, with a pitiful, lockjawed attempt at a smile. "Let's take a look." He moved to take the box, but Manolo's pressure on it hardened.

"La plata?" he said politely.

Harvey sat back. "The silver?" he said, with a baffled, half-focused stare at Manolo. He knew the word because he had bought a silver ring from a hawker at the Pan-American.

"He means the money, Harvey," I hissed. "He wants to see the colour of your money."

The money—a good touch—was in the smaller, flimsier suitcase, the tartan zip-up rather than the stouter Revelation piece. Harvey fumbled up the top section—shirts, socks, sponge-bag—and there they were. Ten neat wads, so fresh you could almost smell the ink, each one containing fifty $100 bills.

"There she blows, man! Fifty grand. Five kilos at nine apiece makes forty-five, and five over for the boat."

I stored these figures away and later worked on them. Harvey's man would sell on his merchandise pretty quickly, but he would almost certainly "step on" it a little before he did so. Even if he only put a light hit on it—turned 5 kilos of pure into 7 or 8 of adulterated—he still stood to clear, I reckoned, something approaching $200,000. Not a bad margin from one fairly modest run, with someone else doing all the sweating.

The stakes are high, but it is all or nothing, and right now his investment was on a fulcrum between the two. Harvey held open the tartan money-bag, Manolo nursed the box of cocaine. Like swapping captured agents on a frontier, neither party wanted to be the first to surrender its bargaining piece.

The money had straightened Harvey up. "I want to check the stuff he's brought," he said.

"Quiere verlo."

Manolo shrugged and smiled. He took a thin, black-handled switch-blade from his back pocket, held it thoughtfully in his delicate fingers. The blade sprang out like a snake's tongue. He cut the string around the carton and sliced down the adhesive tape along the top flaps. Inside were folds of sacking, and under them the kilo bags, polythene, each about the size of a small pillow. "Which one?" he asked. Harvey shrugged. Manolo tossed one of the bags on to the table and nicked a slit in it to expose the cocaine inside. Harvey took some on to his knife and, as before, he poked and sifted, tasted and tested, and finally snorted some of the specimen, frowning all the while with concentration. He said nothing.

We waited in the silence, the smoke, the hot, stale air of the small hours cloying with the rank smell of fruit. Manolo inspected his fingernails, wrinkled his brow, a study in quiet confidence. I wished fervently I was somewhere else, not in this stuffy little room with two knives sitting on the table.

Harvey had digested his hit. He said softly, "You goddam little creep!" Manolo, still attending to his manicure, raised an inquiring eyebrow at me. I felt Julio stiffen beside me.

Harvey's voice was low and fierce. "Tell him, Charlie. Tell him this shit's been stepped on so hard it's flat as a fucking Frisbee."

"God, Harvey, are you sure?"

"Sure I'm sure. Looks different, tastes different. It's the oldest trick in the book, the beginner's rip-off. They hit you with a sample of heavy and sell you a crock of shit while you're flying. You tell him, man."

I told Manolo, as if he didn't know, that Harvey did not like the *coco*. He stiffened into an exaggerated air of surprise and regret, shoulders up in a shrug, eyebrows up towards the brilliantined hair-line, can this be true señor? He actually said nothing.

"Tell him it's crap, Charlie."

"No, no," said Manolo. "It's real good *perica*, very pure."

"Ask him if it's the same stuff as before."

Manolo chose his words with care. "No. It is not the same. It is better!" I groaned inwardly. He can go on lying all night, I thought. I hardly had the heart to tell Harvey of this latest pitch. "The very best," Manolo urged. "Fresh in from Bucaramanga tonight."

Harvey was looking very bad now. His face was white as

paper and wet with sweat. His cigarette, one of Julio's un-
tipped Pielrojas, was falling apart as he smoked it. He began
to rock up and down, spitting flakes of tobacco off his lips
and saying, "Oh no! Oh no!" He turned straight to Manolo
and said two of his few words of Spanish: *"No quiero."* I do
not want it.

"*Sí*," said Manolo steelily. "It is all agreed." They glared
at one another across the table.

It was at this moment of impasse that things began to get
seriously out of control. Out of the silence, with just a faint
rustle of warning, came a sudden loud knock at the street
door. Harvey leapt up, a gargle of fear in his throat. "It's the
cops!" he shouted. "Its a fucking burn!" Julio and Manolo
were both up too. Julio shot a questioning look at Manolo,
Manolo shook his head. Briskly they began clearing away the
cocaine. There was more knocking and a muffled shout. "No
way, man!" cried Harvey. He grabbed the tartan case and,
holding it under his arm, blundered past me into the backyard. I called after him, but he raced down to the end, pushing aside my hammock, looking for a way out. Seeing none,
he made a flying leap on to the hen-house and began to scale
the end wall. The hen-house promptly collapsed, with much
indignant squawking from within. "Oh Jesus, God, please,"
Harvey wailed. He now started scrambling up the side wall
by the kitchen door, but the guard dog on the neighbour's
roof came snarling and snapping at him from the other side
of the parapet. I had heard it many times but never seen it
before—it was a sleek black alsatian, and this was the first
piece of action it had seen in months. Harvey let go with a
yelp and crashed back down, splintering wood and scattering
feathers. He lurched across to the other wall. He jumped to
grab the top of it and screamed in pain as his hands closed
over a serried line of broken glass, put there for some such
occasion as this. He crumpled back into the hen-house and
lay still, whimpering faintly, clutching his money-bag to him
like a teddy bear.

"Tell him to shut up," said Julio. They had stowed the
drugs in Julio's bedroom. The Fruit Palace was just a room

full of smoke and rum glasses: a quiet evening among friends. He went to the door and called, "Who is it?" A voice answered from the other side. Julio swore softly, and called back to us to relax. He unbolted the door and a very drunken negro swayed in. It was the old *guacharacero* who had been playing down at the Pan-American.

"What the hell do you want, Jo-jo?"

"Breakfast," said the old-timer, and tacked across to a table.

Soon there came a sudden dawn, and then it was Sunday morning in Santa Marta, another hot day on the way. Julio told Manolo to push off, and in accordance with some imperceptible Samario pecking-order, Manolo meekly left with his carton of low-grade *coco*. Miriam washed the chicken shit off Harvey's face and shirt, cleaned up his bleeding hands and bandaged them with strips of cloth. Jo-jo fell asleep at a table, his head on his forearms, his hat still on. There were two *papagallo* feathers in his hat-band, one blue, one orange.

Julio mixed us a morning-after *jugo*—papaya, lemon-water and crushed ice. It was always a pleasure to watch him at work. Even after this night of fiasco he attended to it with the same casual, tender care, choosing just the right fruit from the glass-fronted case, chopping and shredding, assiduously observing as he blended it up in the antique Kenwood with Art Deco fluting round the base. In a trance-like calm Harvey paid us our fees. Struck with pity and remorse I made to refuse, but Julio swiftly reminded me of monies owed for food and board.

The last I saw of Harvey was when I put him in a taxi on the beach-drag. He was going to the airport, going home. His immediate task, unenviable and unprofitable, was carrying $50,000 *back* into the United States—not actually illegal, but prone to awkward questions. Then there was the music to face in New York. But as he sank back into the taxi, I could see that just being in a car, even in a jalopy like this, was making him feel better already. Whatever the music back in New York, it would be better than Colombia's crazy syncopations. We made to shake hands, but he winced and drew back his bandaged hand.

"Sorry it didn't work out, Harvey."

"That's showbiz," said Captain Cocaine. The taxi moved off, and I walked on down to the French Corner for some breakfast.

3

THE ASSIGNMENT

Twelve years later I was back in Colombia, on what I laughably called an "assignment." I stood blinking in the raw mountain light outside Eldorado airport, Bogotá. A short, burly, oriental-looking policeman in a short-sleeved grey-green uniform was arguing with a peasant woman. She carried a basket of doughnuts in the crook of her arm, half-covered with a cloth. The policeman wore his white gun-belt at a slant, cowboy-style. He was treating the *campesina* like a child, laughing down into her wrinkled face, joking off sideways with a couple of airport-workers, but all the time his cupped hand was fidgeting round the handle of his gun, just in case.

I smelt again that gut-tightening, high-octane Bogotá smell. A pall of fumes, diesel and human, hangs over the shallow dish of mountains in which the city stands. At getting on for 9,000 feet up the oxygen is scarce and the hydrocarbons never seem to burn up. It is said of Mexico City: "Fifteen million people, and it smells like they all farted at once." Bogotá is half the size, and doesn't smell so bad, but there is the same feeling of a vast, corrupt energy sending up a feverish steam into the chill mountain air.

I took a *colectivo* taxi into town, jammed up against a plump, smiling woman with great tufts of black hair at her armpits. There were four of us in the back, plus a child on a lap, and two more in front. The skinny driver drove fast, and shouted at the other drivers. He took our fares as he drove.

Mist rose in the early sun. The huge silver-grey eucalyptus stood sadly amid the mean haphazard developments, the half-finished buildings and fenced-off lots, the flat dull spaces round every airport where the traveller's hopes disperse.

At first glance Bogotá hadn't changed much in twelve years. The style of the place seemed still to be locked in a vague composite of old Hollywood movies. The driver's slicked-back black hair was pure James Dean. The marvellous old chrome-flashed cars, Chevies and Plymouths and Mercuries, came straight out of *The Big Sleep.* I saw flower stalls, and huge laden buses with people hanging out at the doors. Cows grazed on brilliant emerald grass in vacant lots. The taxi ploughed through ruts and pot-holes filled with black scummy water. The water came up through the floor, and the fat lady lifted up her feet, crying *"Ay! Mis zapatos!"* There was some general banter about the state of the car. The driver said that if he could afford a decent car he wouldn't be carting the likes of us around in it. Half-elated, half-exhausted, I listened vaguely as they argued. Jesus of the Sacred Heart stared down at us from a little laminated card strung from the rear-view mirror.

We swung into 10th Avenue, the downtown sky-scrapers—Hilton, Tequendama, Colseguros—picked out against the dark, sheer hills behind. A hoarding proclaimed the municipal motto of the day: *"Sí usted quiere Bogotá puede."* Loosely rendered, "If you've got an itch Bogotá will scratch it."

After a few outroads and inroads I took a room in a cheap *residencias* in La Candelaria, the old colonial quarter running up from the Plaza Bolívar to the skirts of the Monserrate mountain. It was a big, dusty room with bare floorboards and an iron bed, and a fine view east over the red-tiled roofs to Monserrate. Everything seemed to smell of the porter's hair cream. A thin, mournful woman put fresh sheets on my bed, and told me the window would break if I opened it, but after she left I opened it anyway. The trucks jockeyed in the narrow street below, Paloma Street. At the corner a man in a trilby sat on a piece of sacking, tying up chick-pea plants into bunches. From the little shoe-shop opposite came the sound of hammering. Music drifted up from a radio. I closed my eyes and listened, and the first *vallenato*, the swirling accordions and plangent harmonies of Colombian Rhythm and Blues, burst over me.

For the first twenty-four hours I took things gently. The altitude is fairly modest by Andean standards, but to the unaccustomed lowlander it can be devastating. The first time I had arrived in Bogotá I had ignored all the rules and crashed badly. On the plane from Panama City I had met a Colombian journalist, Jorge, and he invited me back to the family house in the working-class suburbs in the south. There I was plied with aguardiente, fried eggs, guava jelly and the rest. I spent the next two days sweating on Jorge's floor, racked with poison headaches, and evacuating out of every orifice into the new flush toilet of which the family was so proud. What I had was Acute Mountain Sickness (AMS), known in the Andes as *soroche*. It was entirely self-inflicted. Any strong drink when you are unused to the altitude is a recipe for disaster, and aguardiente—Colombia's national hootch, an anise-flavoured liquor that tastes like a mixture of paraffin and gob-stoppers—is the worst of the lot.

This time round I stuck to the straight and narrow, and had nothing worse than a few breathless flutters. The worst of these was not *soroche* at all. Mooching around the bookstalls on 19th Street, I joined the edges of a small crowd. The midday edition of *El Bogotano* had just come out, and they were looking at the front page. There was a full colour picture of a young man lying dead in the dirt, shirt rucked up to his shoulders to reveal a mess of blood and bullet-holes. The headline read, "MATADO OTRO TRAFICANTE DE COCAINA."

I sat on my hotel bed, wondering how to get this ball rolling, and where the hell it was going to roll to if I did. It had all looked different a few weeks ago, when the publisher—youngish, ginger-haired, upwardly-mobile Malcolm Goodman—had telephoned to say he was looking for a book on

Colombia. I fondly imagined he was talking about a travel book. I saw it in my mind's eye—plucky expeditions, picturesque locals, a few photos, a nice black and white map at the beginning with different kinds of dotted lines showing routes taken.

Over lunch the next day the truth dawned. The truth was that Malcolm had discovered cocaine. He pushed aside his platter of *fruits de mer*, and drew forth a wad of cuttings and colour supplements from his briefcase. "There's been a tremendous amount of publicity," he said. There were articles about the huge popularity—"epidemic proportions"—of cocaine in Europe and the US; grisly accounts of cocaine-related gang warfare in Miami; a tabloid piece headed "DIARY OF A COKE SMUGGLER." I saw passages lined and asterisked with Malcolm's busy felt-tip. Colombian connection. Colombian mafia.

"It all comes out of Colombia, you know."

"Yes, I know."

"And you're an old Colombian hand, as you yourself said."

"Well, yes."

Once he was on to his hobby-horse there was no stopping Malcolm. He was a man perennially in quest of that grail among publishers, the fabled Right Book at the Right Time. Eyes glinting behind his large, fashionable tortoise-shells, he spoke of the fan-*tas*-tic scope here, how *the* book about the drug trade had yet to be written. He conjured up pictures of Fleet Street editors queuing cap in hand. He spoke of serial rights, screen treatments, networking. He mentioned sums of money that made me weak at the knees.

I had absolutely no choice. It is the hack's first principle to rush towards every conceivable assignment crying like Molly Bloom, "Yes I will Yes." You may have a hundred misgivings, a hundred reasons for saying "No," but you silence them all. A publisher wants the moon, of course you'll get it. Time enough later to talk him down to the bit of green cheese you come back with. "Inside the Cocaine Underworld," as Malcolm was calling it, sounded nasty, dangerous and downright improbable, but there was no way I could refuse. He ordered another bottle of cheap Frascati. We clinked glasses as if to celebrate. A vision flashed through my head, as clear as day—Harvey sobbing in a broken hen-house, daubed with blood, shit and feathers.

The plan of action, if I can call it that, was to spend a week or two in Bogotá, gathering background material about the cocaine racket, and then to repair up to the coast, to the smuggling centres like Santa Marta and Riohacha. There I would address myself to the main task. "A hard-nosed, on-the-spot report. The who, the how and the why of Colombian cocaine smuggling. That's what we're after!" Malcolm seemed strangely indifferent as to exactly how I was to achieve this. He thought up the ideas, provided the cash, and fashioned the package. The rest was up to me, the old Colombian hand.

We said a last goodbye in the rain, outside his office near Park Lane. A black cab burbled beside us, ready to whisk him off to some meeting. "And for goodness' sake," he said as we shook hands. "If you're in any kind of trouble, give us a call."

So here I sat, the intrepid reporter on the trail of the Great Cocaine Story. I felt more like a new boy on his first day at school. I gazed blankly at what was—with the exception of the wedge of dollars in my wallet—Malcolm's sole contribution to the logistics of the operation. The Letter of Introduction. "A Quien Se Interese," it boomed, beneath the publisher's tasteful green letter-heading. It announced me as a British author, gathering material for a book "on the country and people of Colombia," and pledged undying gratitude to any who helped me complete my "assignment." It was signed, "Muy atentamente, Malcolm Goodman, Senior Commissioning Editor." It even had its own little plastic folder. "Rather crafty, don't you think?" Malcolm had beamed. "Completely non-committal. Could be pretty useful cover, I think." Apart from this absurd document, my kit comprised an out-of-date press pass, a few old business cards describing me as a "consultant researcher," an Alwych All-Weather Cover notebook, a standard SLR camera, a compass and a

Swiss Army knife. It made a small pile on the woollen bed-spread.

The light faded from the broken roofs. Too late, among the jitters and the jet-lag, a truth dawned. The whole thing's a set-up. I'm a burnt offering on the altar of Malcolm's autumn list. This is the kind of bright idea that gets bright young publishers noticed: all you need is some poor sap to go out there and *do* it.

And then came the waves of guilt and disgust. Had I really come all this way to write a story about cocaine? Not the plight of the Indians, the politics of underdevelopment, the ruination of the forests, or a dozen other worthy topics, but cocaine. Greed and folly in a handful of snow. A cheap, one-eyed glimpse up the skirts of South America. *That's* what we're after, Malcolm.

Malcolm said he wanted to know "the who, the how and the why" of the cocaine racket. I could tell him the "why" without going to Colombia at all. The "why" is money.

It is important to remember that buying cocaine, down at the end user's market, is a mug's game. Prices fluctuate according to supply, but as cheap thrills go coke is always pretty expensive. In US and European cities, a gram of cocaine, Standard Street Toot, is liable to cost you anything between $70 and $100. That gram—one twenty-eighth of an ounce, one basic spoonful of medicine, one long night of fun for four—is not, of course, a gram of pure cocaine. It will have been cut, or "stepped on," probably by different people at different stages of the pipeline. You will be lucky if it is even half cocaine. Much of it will consist of an inert cut, simply there as a make-weight. This might be lactose, mannite, baking soda, talc, borax—anything so long as it looks something like cocaine and has no immediately noticeable side-effects. To make up some of the potency lost by adulteration, most street coke also contains an "active" cut. There are two types of active cut—speed and freeze—and your gram may well have a little of both: a lacing of powdered amphetamine (methedrine, sulphate, etc.) to give it an energy kick; and some synthetic, cocaine-related anaesthetic like Novocaine or Benzocaine (the dentist's injection) to simulate the mouth-numbing effects of genuine cocaine. Together these cuts, far cheaper and easier to acquire than the coke itself, give a crude approximation of the true cocaine high.

If you have a really good friend in the smuggling business you may be lucky enough to sample nearly pure coke, off-the-boat quality, and then your nerve-ends will feel like they've been bathed in champagne and you will know what all the fuss is about. If you score in a doorway off Dealer Street, you will probably end up with a cocktail of cuts and no cocaine at all. Anywhere in between, it's pot luck. The customs officers' rule of thumb is that retail coke, your average gram, is unlikely to be more than 30 per cent pure. Some coke-fanciers are so habituated to the cut that they are to all intents and purposes speed-freaks, paying way over the odds for a bit of crank because it smells sweeter by the name of "coke." Speed kills, but coke is hip, the achievers' drug.

Why is it so phenomenally expensive? There are two obvious answers. First, because it is illegal. It is not the coke that costs, but the high risks of supplying it: the buyer pays the dealers' wages, all down the line. For the actual cocaine in your gram of toot you are paying about thirty times as much as it costs someone to buy it, in bulk, in Colombia. The second answer is the old economic adage: it costs that much because people will pay that much. The market will stand it, even up to $100 for 0.33 gm. In a sense people like it expensive. The price is all part of its ritzy mystique. On the grace and money circuits, a phial of white snuff is visible kudos. It used to be chopped up with razor blades, but now it's all credit cards.

People will also tell you that the price of the stuff has its comforts, that there is a kind of security in knowing that all the dangers of chronic cocaine abuse—deviated septum, digestive disorders, progression on to the needle, a whole range of psychological disruptions culminating in the paranoid delusions known as "cocaine psychosis"—are simply way out of their price bracket. "A cocaine *problem*? I should be so lucky!"

Every year, there are more and more people buying more and more cocaine. According to the US drug agency surveys, 20 million Americans have "tried" it, 5 million are "regular" users (at least once a month), and about half a million are "profoundly dependent" on it. The figures are round and possibly high, but one gets the general picture. Taking cocaine is not confined to some lunatic fringe of degenerate no-hope junkies. It is what millions of affluent young Westerners want to spend their money on. In the United States alone about $35 billion a year is being spent on it.

The States is *the* cocaine market, but Europe is doing her bit too. In Britain, seizures of coke rose from less than half a kilo in 1968 to over 70 kilos in 1983. It is reckoned that the customs and police net catches only about 5 per cent of the coke coming into the country. If so, British consumption is running at about 1½ tons a year—wholesale value some £50 million, street value, after all the dilutions and mark-ups, about £250 million. Seizures in France, Italy and Spain—the latter a popular staging post between South America and the rest of Europe—are all higher than in Britain. Cocaine is, in short, one of the great growth industries of the 1980s.

4

THE FLYING SCOTSMAN

My first move in this game without rules was to drum up some connections from twelve years ago. I pondered my list of old names and addresses. Some of the faces were hazy, some had dropped off the register completely, but I could never forget Augustus McGregor.

Gus was a half-crazed Scottish newspaper-man—I call him Scottish, and he called himself Scottish, but in fact he had been brought up somewhere in the Kentish London suburbs, and his proud assertions of Highland blood were couched in unmistakable South London accents. He had come out to Brazil in the sixties, studying at São Paulo University and working as a stringer for a news agency. Gus was one of those people who disappeared into South America, lost all notion of where he had come from and where he was going. They call this the continent of fugitives, the place where a man can lose his own shadow, and it is not just the Nazi war criminals and the Lucky Lucans who disappear from view in its nooks and crannies. He had worked for a while for the *Brazilian Herald*. He was a good journalist, but too long in South America and too many bad drugs had turned him into a compulsive fantasist. By his own account, as I remember, he had wandered the length and breadth of the subcontinent, left a wife in São Paulo and another in Paraguay, narrowly escaped the death-squads in Chile, and located the fabled Brotherhood of the Seven Rays in some hidden valley south of Cuzco.

All this was behind him, if anywhere, when I knew him in Bogotá. We worked together for a while on the *Andean Echo*, an English language weekly aimed mainly at the North American commercial and diplomatic community. The *Echo* paid miserable penny-a-line rates, but together with a bit of English teaching he just about scratched a living. He was a tall, gangling, whey-faced man, with long, straggly ginger hair, somewhat like one imagines the Pardoner in *The Canterbury Tales*. He was a great favourite with the caretaker at the *Echo*'s offices, who called him "El Rojo" on account of his red hair, and was always feeding him up on fried rabbit and creole potatoes in his little hut behind the office block.

Most of Gus's money went on cocaine—"peach," as he called it. By a fine reverse argument, he blamed this on his alleged Calvinist upbringing. "We're all doomed to the bonfire anyway, so we might as well have some fun on the way." I remember the nights we went up into La Perseverancia to score a gram, which in those days cost around $10. There's a saying about Perseverancia—"*Se sube a pie y se baja en ambulancia*": go in walking and come out in an ambulance—but everyone knew Gus and we never had any trouble. We would score in a little lamp-lit room, two steps straight down off the dark street. I can see Gus now in his grey *ruana*—the Colombian woollen poncho—funnelling up a sample off the corner of his Brazilian press-card. "The finest peach in town at Alfonso's!" he would say, grinning his grey-toothed, alley-cat grin. At other times we would go up to the University campus, where he had friends among the revolutionary "Movimiento 19" cadres, and where the shoe-shine boys could be relied on for competitively priced coke. From them you could buy really tiny amounts, a couple of lines for a few pesos, just as the cigarette boys will always sell you a single cigarette.

It was *aut Gus, aut nullus*. If Gus couldn't furnish me with a few leads on the Great Cocaine Story, no one could. I got on the phone in the hotel lobby and dialled Gus's old number—not actually his own place, he never really had one, but the apartment of a benevolent Italian painter, which he used as a message-drop and lodging-house. I rang three times, but all I got was an asthmatic sighing in my ear. I tried the number of the *Echo*. A woman curtly told me the paper didn't exist any more. I was not surprised. These expat papers have a limited life. Down at the Telecom, the Bogotá directory had no news of McGregors, or of the *Echo*'s editor, a bespectacled American named Carson Askew. For one reason and another, I wasn't that keen on renewing my acquaintance with Askew anyway.

I couldn't remember the name of Gus's mentor, the Italian painter, but I had his address. Perhaps he was still there, under a new phone number. Perhaps there would be news of Gus there. Outside the Avianca building on 7th Avenue, on my way to catch a *buseta* north, I saw a small brown dog lying in the morning sun. Its tail twitched a little as it dozed, and I thought how splendid this was, to slumber in the sun amid the downtown jostle of commuters and hawkers. When I got closer I saw that the dog was dead. It was only the breeze stirring the fine sandy hairs of its tail.

The painter's apartment was on the first floor of a dilapidated red-brick block off 22nd Avenue, in the mid-town residential district of San Luis. The Venetian blinds were shut on the windows. I pressed the door bell. It made no discernible sound. I knocked twice: nothing. I was about to be on my way, when I heard faint sounds within, shuffling steps down the stairs, a child crying, and then a woman's voice, shrill and aged, saying, "Who is it?" behind the door.

"Good morning, *señora*." There was silence. "I am looking for Señor McGregor."

"Maggegar?"

"Señor McGregor," I enunciated. "The Scotsman. He used to live here."

"Scotsman? I do not know him. He is not here."

I pressed closer to the door, trying to gauge where the old crone's head should be. "He was a friend of the painter, the Italian gentleman. Perhaps *he* is here?"

"No, *señor*. We have no foreigners here." She sounded annoyed. I started to say something else, but her reedy voice

cut in. "You must go now. My son will be home soon." She
receded, muttering. In a moment of pique I slapped my hand
against the floor and hissed an English obscenity after her.
Unflattening myself from the door, I turned back towards the
street and saw a small, rotund policeman staring at me. I felt
an obscure pang of guilt.

"You are looking for Señor Bruno?" asked the policeman.

"No, I'm—I mean, yes, yes, of course, Señor Bruno."
That was the name of the painter. Alessandro Bruno, the
bearded modernist from Bologna.

"He does not live here any more. He moved nine, ten
months ago. I knew him very well. This is my patch."

This was encouraging. Did he perhaps know where Bruno
lived now? He pursed his lips and waggled his head, as if to
shake the answer loose. *"Mas allá,"* he said with an airy gesture. Over that way. "Up north. Unicentro. El Chicó." His
truncheon bobbed gently against his thigh as he gestured. It
was obvious he didn't really know, but the answer was not
quite random. The areas he mentioned were upmarket. In
place of information he was humouring me with an oblique
compliment. These small courtly transactions count for a lot
in Colombia. I shook the little policeman's hand, and
thanked him.

At the Telecom on 22nd Avenue I found Bruno's name in
the directory, and dialled his new number. He answered in
his Italian-accented Spanish, which sounds too sing-song and
airy for the sombre, throaty stresses of Spanish. Yes, with a
little prompting, he remembered me. No, he had not seen
Gus for a while, but as far as he knew he was still in town.
We talked for a bit. Then he said, "Listen, Charlie, I'll tell
you because I know you're Gus's friend. I think he's in some
kind of trouble. I haven't seen him for weeks. Someone came
for his things, a Colombian boy. He had a note from Gus,
but all it said was not to worry. Well, I gave up worrying
about Gus a long time ago, but this isn't like him."

Other than this all Bruno could give me was a few names.
There was a girl Gus knocked around with, Anita. Where
might I find her? Try the streets of Las Nieves—the red-light

quarter, a warren of cat-houses on the edge of the business district. Then there were some bars and eating-houses Gus frequented: he gave me three names and addresses. We were just about to ring off when he remembered one more name, a street-dealer called Julio Cesar. "Gus mentioned him a few times. I think he bought his *perica* off him. He used to say that Julius Caesar conquered the English 2,000 years ago, and now he's selling drugs to the Scots."

By the time I entered the Paso Doble, the third of the three bars Bruno had mentioned, I was getting seriously disgruntled. The first two had turned up blank. Sure, they knew Gus—one knew him as "El Rojo," the other as "El Escocés," the Scotsman—but no one had seen him around recently. The names of Anita and Julio Cesar meant nothing to them. It was now about 4 o'clock. I had been tramping to and fro all day, had got soaked in a thunderstorm, and was about ready to give up.

The Paso Doble was a small, murky café-bar off Caracas Avenue. It was one of a row of tumbledown, single-storey houses under a tangle of overhead cables. A bus lurched up the dirt street, listing like an overladen boat. This was a bad part of town. Bogotá is laid out on a grid system. As in New York, danger can be mathematically computed, and this was well south of 12th Street, which is one of the demarcation lines. The café was quiet. Three dusty workmen sharing a half of aguardiente, an old woman in black nursing a bowl of milky coffee, a pair of corner boys lounging at the doorway, and the inevitable children running in and out, the dark-eyed grubby children that play round the edge of every scene. Everyone appraised the stranger, with no great interest.

I bought a beer. The barman was stocky and simian, with tight curls of white hair fizzing up out of the neck of his shirt. After a few pleasantries, I trotted out my weary formula. I am looking for Gus, Señor McGregor, El Rojo, El Escocés, the Flying Bloody Scotsman . . .

"You mean Gustavo," said the barman. "No, I do not know where he is."

"I am his friend. I think he might be in trouble. I have come to help him."

The barman gazed at me. "You are Scottish, no?"

"Of course I am," I lied.

The barman nodded sagely. I seemed to be winning through. We Scots stick together, I told him. He called out over his shoulder, "*Oiga!* Julio Cesar!" and with an almost comic, Punch and Judy promptitude a face poked out from a curtained-off doorway behind the bar. The barman jerked his head at me, and turned away with the air of one washing his hands of the whole business.

Julio Cesar advanced, plausible, false and wary. He looked about eighteen, had a pencil-thin moustache, light brown hair and a black jacket with a diamond pattern picked out in gold. "*Ola, hombre,*" he said, with a firm handshake. We went over to a corner table.

"You want *perica, basuko,* real good grass?" he asked pleasantly.

"No, not really, I—"

"Emeralds?"

"No, I—"

"My father works in the mines."

"I am looking for Gustavo the Scotsman. I'm told you know where to find him."

His patter hiccoughed briefly. "Gus? Ah yes, Señor Gus. Yes, I know him. It is very difficult . . ."

"But you do know where he lives?"

Julio Cesar shrugged, long and slow, hands juggling the possibilities. The classic Colombian gesture: yes and no, *señor*, take your pick. In this case: yes, I know where he lives; no, I'm not going to tell you.

It took two beers, a crisp 100 peso bill and a lot of guff about how Gus was like a brother to me—"my teacher, my *compadre*"—before Julio Cesar admitted that he knew how to get in touch with Gus. Another 100 pesos and he agreed to take him a message from me. I scribbled a note. It was folded away neatly in the sequinned top pocket, along with the two bills. He told me to come back the following evening.

"Don't worry, my friend," he said as we parted. "Señor Gus trusts no one, *no one*, but Julio Cesar."

It was dark now. A thin rain was falling. Caracas Avenue shone, and the air was thick with smoke from the *fritanga* stalls. At the bus stations on 13th Street a man was shouting, "Fucker! Fucker! Fucker! Directo Fucker!" The night bus for Facavita was about to leave. I felt exhausted. It had been a long, circuitous day—the old crone behind the door, the policeman and the painter, three bars, and at last Julius Caesar, the street-corner *conquistador*. As I cut up east towards the dark hulk of Monserrate, the white church at the top lit up like a mirage, I pondered the day's final poser. What in God's name had Gus been up to?

I returned to the Paso Doble the following night, as arranged. It was a Friday night. The sleepy, dusty bar I had been sitting in yesterday had changed unrecognizably. It was full of people. The tables had been pushed to the side, coloured bulbs flashed above the bar, and the air was filled with smoke and laughter. A pair of antiquated speakers were bashing out *música trópical* at a tooth-rattling volume. "Every night's fiesta night," they sang, amid a swirl of trumpets and distorted percussion.

I could see no sign of Gus or Julio Cesar. I pushed through to the bar. A drunken black woman with dyed hair like a lion's mane grabbed my arm—"Hey, gringo!"—but someone else pulled her away again. The barman greeted me like an old friend, and poured me a straight shot of aguardiente. It seemed to be the only thing he was serving. "It's my birthday," he explained. I sipped at my drink gingerly, remembering the heightened potency of liquor at high altitude. "No, *hombre*," he cried. "Like this." He drained his glass with a flourish. With an inward shrug of resignation I did likewise. I was still struggling with the spasms when he refilled the glasses. These too were despatched in unison. He wiped his hand across his mouth and laughed. He called over to a woman serving at the other end of the bar. She came over, a large, slow-moving lady, who regarded all the revelry with an imperious air. She seemed, as Colombian *señoras* often do, to be the boss. The barman put his arm around her waist, looking like a little white-haired monkey beside her bulk. "Look, *querida*," he said. "It's the friend of Gustavo I was telling you about. The Scotsman." He filled my glass yet again. She surveyed me through half-closed eyes. She made little tutting sounds, as if what she saw somehow exasperated her.

"So you are Scottish too?" she asked. I nodded brightly: it was too late to turn back on this one. She narrowed her eyes still further. "Is it true what Gustavo says, that the men all wear skirts?"

"Yes," I said uncertainly, "well, some of them do." I did not feel I wanted the idea broadcast around the bar at this moment. "We call them kilts," I added.

She tried the word out, but discarded it as unpronounceable. "They are very strong," she continued. "They throw tree-trunks." It took me a moment to work out that she probably meant cabers. She gazed at me sceptically. She found it hard, perhaps, to imagine me tossing trees around. I was already beginning to feel very drunk. I wanted to get away from this mountainous woman, to slip away and quietly slough off my newfound Scottishness. God knew what other Scottish nonsense Gus had been spinning. But the crowd hemmed me in tight at the bar. The barman came back, poured me more aguardiente. Not to be outdone on the matter of Highland lore, he said, "You like very much the *cornamusa*, no?" This completely stumped me. Seeing my confusion, he had one of those drunken bright ideas. "Wait, I have some here." He fumbled under the bar for a bit, and came up holding a tape-cassette. "It's Gustavo's," he said. "It makes him cry." I guessed then that the *cornamusa* was bagpipes, but it was too late. The *música trópical* was silenced in mid-flow. The new cassette was put in, and my heart sank as a familiar skirling dirge ground out at top volume. It was Andy Stewart singing "A Scottish Soldier." Heads turned in surprise, and some in frank displeasure. I was quickly located as chief suspect in the matter, indeed the barman was cheerily shouting, "*Música escocés* for our friend here," and

holding his hand out to me like a nightclub compère, hoping
perhaps that I would leap on to the bar and dance a Dashing
White Sergeant or two. All eyes were upon me. I blushed to
the core, nodded and grinned like an idiot, and when the
refrain came the barman wrapped his arm round my shoulder,
and I was forced into a dreadful duet, he crooning wordlessly
along with the tune, me thinking less of the green hills of
home than of how I was going to wring Gus's neck when I
found him. I have never known a song last so long. Another
began—"Speed, Bonny Boat," I think—but mercifully there
were shouts of protest, and the tape was ejected. The *música
trópical* returned, and I lurched away from the bar.

I found a seat and tried to regain some anonymity. I was
sweating aguardiente like a squeezed sponge. The crowd
seemed to have thinned a bit: perhaps the bagpipes had
driven them away. Looking round I saw, as I had already
dimly realized, that virtually all the women were tarts. Some
lolled at the bar, some had joined up with groups at the
tables, and a gaggle of half a dozen of them sat huddled together at the corner table, all eye-shadow and shiny black
boots. One of them was staring at me. She said something to
the others. They looked round at me and cawed with laughter. I hauled a newspaper out of my jacket: the print swam
before my eyes. I looked at the ceiling: the cobwebbed rafters
seemed to pulsate to the music. Still the girl was giving me
the sultry eye, a plump little *chulita* in a tight red dress. My
eyes kept sidling back to her. She winked and pouted,
crossed and uncrossed her legs. She wore stockings that
ended just above her knee, her nut-coloured flesh plumping
over the elastic, the underside wobbling a little as she crossed
her legs. I lit a cigarette, tried to concentrate on the paper.
My heart was pumping too fast. Now she was getting up,
bringing her chair with her, leaning her hands on my table,
black hair falling over her face, black eyes heavy with mas-
cara. She looked older and more brittle than she had a few
yards away through the smoke. She had a black patent-
leather handbag slung crosswise. The leather had peeled off
the strap where it ran down between her breasts. "*Buenas*

noches, churro," she said. She took some lottery tickets out of
her handbag and asked to look at my newspaper: "I think it's
my lucky night tonight!" Someone pushing past the table
knocked her, and she fell forward, much further than she
needed. Her hand gripped my thigh and her face was a few
inches from mine, and she was laughing cheap scent, tobacco
and liquor in my face. Then she gave a little squawk of surprise. Someone had grabbed her round the waist: a gold-
sequinned arm. It was Julio Cesar. He sat down on her seat,
pulled her on to his lap, and held her there like a recalcitrant
kitten.

Out of his jacket pocket came a crumpled piece of paper.
He handed it to me. "There you are, my friend." It was the
note I had written yesterday. On the back, in a rickety sloping hand, an address was written. It was a high numbered
street, somewhere out in the south, in the sprawling, non-
descript *barrios* off towards Soacha. "That's Señor Gus's
place," said Julio Cesar. "There's a taxi waiting for you now,
at the corner of Caracas. He'll take you to the corner of
Gus's street. After that you walk. Ten minutes, no problem.
Just keep straight on till you find No. 99. Don't talk to anyone on the way."

We went to the bar. I paid for my drinks and bought a
bottle of rum to take to Gus. Julio Cesar slipped off behind
the curtained door. He came back and slid a little package
into my hand. "For Gus," he whispered, closing my hand
round it. The barman shook my hand warmly and told me to
come back soon. The fat *señora* inclined her head like a
duchess at me and made some comment, probably about me
wearing skirts, to someone at the bar.

As I left I looked around for the *chulita* in the red dress,
but she was already at another table, with a man in a cowboy
hat. She was snuggling up to him and putting her tongue in
his ear as I stumbled out into the cold night air.

5

WELCOME TO THE CROW'S NEST

It was drizzling again when I paid off the taxi. I had to hope he knew where we were, because there were no street signs, just a wide, featureless road with most of the streetlights broken, and a dark little side-road leading off. This, I hoped, harboured Gus at No. 99. I had tried to take some bearings on the way, but the taxi-driver was taciturn, and I felt sick and drunk, and I mostly just sat back in a torpor, grateful for the cold air on my face.

With a squeal of rubber the taxi hung a U-turn and roared off back towards town. I set off in silence down the side-street. There were no lights, and most of the low-built houses seemed derelict. Empty windows stared like sockets in a skull. Spiky vegetation curled out of doorways. Behind me a car turned into the street. As it lurched over the ruts its lights raked up and down like searchlights. I hid in a doorway till it passed. I was getting jumpy. It was cold and late, and this felt like no-man's-land. Crossing a small intersection, the character of the street changed. On either side were junk yards, smelling of oil and rust and old tyres. Rickety workshops loomed out of the mist. In one I saw the blue crackle of an arc-welder. Someone was here at least. But where was No. 99? Just keep straight on, Julio Cesar had said. None of the buildings had any numbers that I could see.

A curve in the road ahead was lit with an odd glow, and coming round it I found myself in a stretch of muddy waste-ground. Away to my right a huge fire blazed. I saw figures around it, and dogs and children, even a small pig or two. I froze into the shadows. *Gamines? Gitanos?* Street *bandidos* with knives under their rag-blankets? The road ran on, a muddy track, through the rubbish and dismembered cars. It would take a minute, perhaps less, to get to the buildings on the other side. Steeling myself, I began to walk. I was half-way across when the dogs caught my scent. They loped bark-ing towards me, rangy sand-coloured curs of the kind you see all over Bogotá. A drunken voice called to me from the fire-side, *"Venga, hombre, venga!"* I waved vaguely back and quickened my pace. I had just reached the buildings, where the track became a recognizable street again, when a small boy suddenly appeared in front of me. I stopped. One of the dogs came snarling up, but the boy ran at it with a shout, and rapped it across the snout, and it yelped off back towards the fire. I made to walk on, but the boy nipped round in front of me again. He stuck his hand out and asked for pesos. First he used the word *regalo*, asking for a present, but then he added another word, *peaje*, which means "toll," implying that I had better pay up if I wanted to carry on down the road. He was about ten, I guessed. He chewed a splinter of wood. His hair was crew-cut, his eyes little cold pools in the darkness. He looked like he could get a knife between my ribs before I could say "Juancho Robinson." I dug into my pocket for change. He took it silently and backed off into the shadows. In the corner of the building I now saw a rough shelter of polythene and old rafter-wood. An old woman was sitting on a box at its entrance. The boy pushed past her into the shelter. She too held out her hand, and I went over and gave her some money.

It really was as if I had paid a toll and crossed a border, for now the street took on a more inhabited air, poor but lived in. In a half-lit room I saw a crucifix on the wall, the flicker of a black and white TV. And at last I saw a number: 87, 89. I was just five doors away from Gus's bolt-hole.

No. 99 was an old two-storey house with political posters peeling off the frontage. It had tall windows, many broken, behind iron grilles, and the legend "CUIDADO CON EL PERRO" roughly painted beside the door. I knocked but there was no sound. The *perro* was apparently not barking tonight. I pulled open the door by a piece of rope that served for a handle, and came into a dark, evil-smelling passage. This gave on to a courtyard, unexpectedly large, with a rickety balcony all round it. What looked like sacks of cement were piled everywhere, but here and there you could see the old cobblestones of a once-fine colonial patio. A line of washing was strung between the balconies. Pushing through the sheets on the line came an old woman, wiping her hands on her apron.

"*Señor?*"

"Good evening, *señora*. This is Number 99?" She nodded. She was one of those small, doll-like *campesinas*, wrinkled and wiry, with her hair combed up into a tight bun. "I have come to see Señor McGregor," I said. "He is expecting me."

She shook her head and began to disclaim all knowledge. I was half-expecting this, and had the scrap of paper ready, with Gus's own scrawl on it. I thrust it at her. She didn't even bother to look at it, perhaps because she couldn't read. She again shook her head. Then suddenly a voice hissed out from somewhere above us. "*Oiga, señora, tranquilo!*" And then a moment later, in the same stage whisper but now in English, "Up here, mate!"

We both turned. I couldn't see anyone. The old lady gave a stiff little bow of apology, and gestured me towards the corner-stairs that led up to the balcony. "*Siga, señor,*" she said, "*siga, no mas.*" There were doors and shuttered windows all round the upper storey, but I could see no lights, and where the doors were open the rooms looked empty and derelict. Halfway up the steps, trying to locate where his voice had come from, I saw a thin, pale hand fluttering in the gloom like a trapped insect. Nothing else, just the hand, apparently coming straight out of the wall. As I walked along the balcony towards it, the hand disappeared. Stooping down

I saw a slit in the wall where a brick had been removed, just beneath a shuttered window. I peered into it, as if looking through the letter-box in a door. A pair of eyes stared back.

"Gus?"

"Welcome to the crow's nest, mate. Glad you could make it."

The eyes disappeared from the peep-hole. A key turned in the door. "Door's open!" he called.

The room was narrow and dimly lit. There was a faint reek of damp stone, old food, stale body. Gus was fitting the brick back into his peep-hole. He looked ghastly. He had lost most of his hair on the top since I had last seen him. The rest, shorter than before, hung round his ears like docked rats' tails. He had scabs down one side of his face, as if he had been scraped along a road. His left leg was bandaged, none too freshly, from the ankle to the knee. "Close the door, for Christ's sake," he said. I pushed it, but it didn't close properly. He hobbled past me and slammed it. A thin shower of plaster floated down. The ceiling was mostly gone, rough cane-stem lath showing through, and wires leading to a single 20-watt bulb. The pitted walls shone cold and moist. There was a hole in the outside wall, stuffed with grimy polythene and newspaper.

Gus lowered himself into an armchair, the only chair. It was positioned next to the wall, so that the peep-hole was at eye-level when he sat. He could see anyone coming into the courtyard. The shutters on the window facing the courtyard were barred and nailed, with rag wadding stuffed into the gaps. The door too had strips of cloth around the edges. I had seen no chinks of light when I was out on the balcony. It was the perfect bolt-hole. Wincing with pain, Gus eased his bandaged leg on to a box of old clothes that served as a footstool.

"There," he said, settling with a sigh. He waved in vague apology at the room. "It's not the eighteenth floor at the Tequendama, but . . . under the circumstances . . ."

I refrained from asking what exactly the circumstances

were. Judging from the dust on his scattered belongings, he had been here for some time. There were boxes of papers, tumbled-out suitcases, a tin can brimming with butt-ends. On a makeshift table in the corner I saw, suddenly remembering it, Gus's proudest possession—his typewriter, an old black high-standing Underwood, *circa* 1940, a vintage three-fingers-of-Jack-Daniels-and-hold-the-front-page model.

He surveyed me from his chair, like a gouty old judge about to pass sentence. I proffered the bottle of rum. "Good boy," he said. "Fetch a couple of cups over, and we'll murder some." He poured out two large slugs. We raised our cups. "Up your crack," he said, and drained his in one. He poured a second.

"So what's the story, Gus?" I asked.

"Yes, well, sorry about all the jiggery-pokery, mate. Got to choose my visitors carefully these days. Keeping a bit of a low profile for a while."

"What happened to your leg?"

"That? Oh, nothing much. Machete accident. Tell you about it later."

"It's OK, isn't it? You shouldn't be seeing someone about it?"

"Well, I've got these pills." He rattled a tin that had once contained Nestlé's Condensed Milk. "The old biddy changes the bandages from time to time. She's Julio Cesar's mother, you see. I pay her for the room and one meal a day. J.C. keeps me in the style to which I'm accustomed—you know, booze and drugs and so on. I'm not *seeing* anyone. That's the whole bloody point of the operation."

"That reminds me," I said, fishing out the little package from my top pocket. "Julio Cesar asked me to give you this."

Gus sat up with a start and a wince. "For Christ's sake, mate," he said, very affronted. "First things first. Give it here."

Inside a fold of newspaper was the familiar toy-town package. But as Gus gingerly opened it, I saw that it was not cocaine. It was a rough powder, peachy-brown, like pancake make-up. This was basuko, dried cocaine base. Basuko is essentially a by-product, a halfway stage between the raw stuff of the coca leaf and the end product of cocaine. A few basic laboratory operations could have converted this gram of basuko into a slightly smaller volume of coke: good base yields up to 90 per cent. It is seldom, if ever, found outside South America—anything less than pure snow is dead weight to a smuggler. But in Colombia itself it is becoming more and more the drug of choice, a rougher, milder, and— above all—far cheaper version of coke. Not that it is really an alternative to coke. It is smoked rather than snorted, for one thing. You might feel giddy, benevolent, chattery, vigilant after a *sucito*—a joint of basuko. But you are soothed rather than fired up. It has none of the Ice Nine crystalline quality, the cool fever of the true cocaine high.

Gus sprinkled a few grains into a pile of tobacco, and rolled it up in a bit of paper torn from an old *Time* magazine. Cigarette papers are something of a luxury in Colombia. He lit up and drew deeply. There were beads of sweat above his lips. The smoke had a sweet, woody tang, faintly sickly but very agreeable. He handed me the joint and I took my first hit of basuko. Into the arms of *la morenita*, the brown-haired girl, sweet little step-daughter to *la blanca*, the white lady.

Shivering a little as the smoke spread through him, Gus gazed at me, palpably mellowed. "So," he said, as if our meeting was at last properly beginning. "It's been a long time, Charlie. What brings you back to Bogotá?" He jokily mispronounced it, *à la gringo*, with the first syllable as in "bogey."

I explained, in so many words, about the Great Cocaine Story. He laughed and said, "Pull the other one, mate. It's got bandages on."

"I'm serious, Gus. It's a *bona fide* commission. Inside the cocaine underworld, hard-nosed stuff."

His eyes narrowed. "You mean someone's paying you?"

"Yes. Well, they've stumped up with a bit. You know publishers."

"Yeah. They always find they've left their wallet behind."

He started laughing again. "By the Lord Harry!" He shook his head in disbelief.

"Actually," I continued, "I was hoping you might be able to give me a few leads. You know—"

He puffed in derision. "Leads? Oh yeah, leads! Doggie needs a walk, does he? Look, I'll lend you a bulletproof suit, if you like. That's what you'll need. 'Course, if they come after you with the old coconut-cleavers, you'll need a whole bloody suit of armour." He hissed out the last bit of basuko smoke, and stubbed out the butt with tense, stabbing movements. "Forget about the leads, mate. You don't know where they've been."

"Hell, Gus. I'm as big a coward as the next man. I don't want anything heavy. Just a few stories, a bit of local detail. You know the recipe."

He leaned forward a few inches. His face was shiny and serious. "Listen, cock," he said quietly. "Why do you imagine I'm sitting here on my jack while my fucking leg rots off? Well, I'll tell you why. It's because the cocaine underworld, as you call it, doesn't like reporters one little bit. They like to keep everything, you know, off the record. Reasonable enough, really."

"Christ, Gus. Do you mean someone's after you for poking your nose in?"

He closed his eyes. "Look down there." He waved wearily towards the table with the old typewriter on it. "See that box? It's all in there, the whole sorry story. But take it from me, mate. It just isn't worth it."

I saw a carton stuffed with dog-eared papers, cheap folders held together with rubber bands. "Can I take a look?" I asked.

"No, you bloody well can't."

"Well, what's in it?"

"Everything anyone needs to know about your bloody Cocaine Underworld, that's what. Names, dates, kitchens, boats. I call it my Who's Who. Every damn hood worth his salt gets a mention in it somewhere. I've traced all the pipelines, mate. I know all the moves. That's why I'm not exactly flavour of the month in certain circles."

"How much have you done?" I asked. "Is it ready to run?"

"You're joking. That's it, there in the box. There's twelve years with my ear to the ground in there. I wouldn't start writing anything until I was a good few thousand miles away from Colombia. You know, the shit and the fan. Like I said, these people don't like publicity."

All those years of street wisdom in one box. With all the diligent field-work in the world, I couldn't accumulate a tenth of it. For now I decided to leave the matter alone. I could see he was getting touchy on the subject. Besides, something else was worrying me.

"Do you really mean, Gus, that someone did *that* to you?" I pointed to his leg.

He nodded. "Two weeks ago. Couple of Charlies up in Perseverancia. Look—I was lucky. It wasn't my bloody leg they were after."

Since I had first come in and smelt the fusty old man's smell in the room, I had sensed there was something more to it than damp walls and dirty linen. There was a low, crap-ulent odour I couldn't quite trace. I thought perhaps it was bad food—there were a couple of plates with the congealed remains of chicken and rice on them. Now I was beginning to be sure it was something worse. I went over to him and looked at the leg.

"Is it bad, Gus? You don't smell too good, you know."

He muttered something about "personal remarks," but then he nodded. "It's not great," he admitted.

"Should I take a look?"

He feigned impatience, but he set to unwrapping the ban-dages willingly enough. I was right about the smell. Gingerly he drew away the lint to reveal a vertical gash, 10 inches long, up his left calf. A machete had carved away part of his leg like a prime slice of chicken-breast. The wound was about the shape and size of a large piece of banana peel. It was the colour of an Andean sunset, scarlet, yellow and

black. At the edges it oozed a malevolent pus. I am no doctor, but it was clear that Gus was in a bad way.

He peered at it with just a hint of pride. "It's getting better," he said unconvincingly. "Hurts like a bitch, but it's
definitely on the mend. The old dear puts something on it
when she changes the bandages. *Polvo de la Madre Celestina*,
she calls it. Some mumbo-jumbo herbal stuff, I don't know."

"You really ought to see a doctor, Gus. I mean, you get
gangrene, you lose your leg, that sort of thing."

He gave a wheezy laugh. "Long John Silver, eh?" Then
more angrily, "Look, I've told you. I'm a nowhere man just
now. The walls have eyes round here, and bloody ears. If
someone saw me out and about it wouldn't take ten minutes.
OK, the leg's not great, I know. But it's a whole lot better
than what'll happen if they catch up with me again. There'll
be no second chance, mate. I'll be dog's meat."

"Who exactly are they, Gus?"

He ignored the question, bandaging himself up. I let it go.
We had more rum, another *sucito*, talked of old times. I
didn't mention the leg or the men from the mafia again. It
seemed like bad taste to bring him back round to the harsh
realities of his situation. The drink and the drugs took their
toll on his wasted frame. He began to doze. I stood up,
thinking about leaving. He jerked awake, eyes wide. "Don't
go, mate." For a moment it was a plea, but then he covered
it. "You'll never get a taxi at this time of night. Streets are
bad. You can sleep on the bed."

I shrugged and sat down on the bed. Soon Gus was snoring
gently, head tipped forward, ginger hair dangling monkishly
from the balding pate. I went and covered him with a
blanket. I lay on the grey rumpled bed in a basuko haze. I
wondered if the whole thing was a giant paranoid fantasy of
Gus's own making. He always needed a drama to feed on.
Too many years on the jag in Bogotá could doubtless send a
man crazy. But the machete wound? That was real enough. I
could smell it suppurating a few feet away in the darkness.

Somewhere outside—or perhaps it was only in my head—I

heard a dog howl, and as I drifted down the tunnel of a fitful sleep, I seemed to see Gus hobbling along through the lunar streets outside. The hounds were on his trail, just around the corner, and the whores in the doorways were all wearing kilts.

When I woke the room was still dark, but there were chinks of light in the shutters on the outside window. I had a chill in my bones, catarrh in my head. The previous evening's intakes vied biliously in my stomach. Gus was still asleep, sprawled in the armchair, head lolling, mouth wide. He must have been awake at some point, for the blanket was on the floor and the brick had been removed from the wall. A thin slat of sunlight angled in through the peep-hole, with dust dancing in it.

It was a soft tap at the door that had woken me. Now there came another, sharper, and a woman's voice calling tentatively, *"Buenos dias, señores."* Gus woke with a start. His eyes ranged round in a moment of plain fear. Then he remembered who he was, who I was, and whose the voice at the door was, and he called back a greeting in reply. He motioned me to the door. I unlocked it, the big key making me think of an English church door, and there stood the old lady with two cups of *tinto*. She asked if I would like some breakfast. Of course I would, Gus answered on my behalf. He hobbled to the door and stood there scratching at his ribs and breathing in the morning air. It was early still. Above the wavering gables of the old house the sky was pinkish-grey. In a corner of the courtyard below, beneath a half-dead almond tree, a man in a vest was shaving.

The *tinto* worked fast. Directed by Gus, I sped down the steps to the bathroom. The man looked up from his shaving and nodded at me as casually as if he'd seen me every day for the last ten years. Sunlight caught the blade of his cut-throat razor. His mirror hung from a nail in the tree-trunk. The bathroom was dark and smelly, but newspaper was provided. The lavatory didn't flush. The old lady appeared with a pail of water. We conversed briefly over the top of the wooden door. She said to pour half the water down the pan to flush it. The other half I could use for my *abluciones*. Outside the bathroom, on an oil-drum, was a beaten tin dish and a neatly folded cloth for a towel. This simple, graceful hospitality is Colombia's greatest gift to the traveller. From the kitchen came a clatter of pans, and the smell of woodsmoke and cooking oil. All I could hear of Bogotá was a distant sigh of traffic and the occasional rasp of a buzz-saw nearer by. Scratch the surface of Bogotá, it is said, and you find a *ciudad de campesinos*, a city of peasants. That's what I felt here. The morning sun gilded the dilapidated old courtyard. I liked Gus's bolt-hole a lot better by daylight.

A boy carrying a machete and some fruit boxes came into the courtyard from the street. He waved at me perfunctorily, and started slicing the boxes for kindling. As I washed I could see him looking at me, and as I headed back to the stairs he strolled over to cut me off. "You with Señor Gus?" he asked in English. I said I was. "Gus my friend," he said, then added in Spanish, tapping his temple, "he's crazy but he's our friend." He held out his hand, said his name was Alvarito. I guessed he was Julio Cesar's brother—same mousy, wavy hair, same lean, stubborn face. In a couple of years' time—he was about thirteen—he'd probably be sporting the same dandy thin moustache.

Back upstairs the stale air of Gus's room hit me in the gut. He had opened the shutters on the outside window. This was fitted with a metal frame and frosted glass, like a suburban bathroom, but the window was too small for the tall colonial jamb, and makeshift slats of cardboard had been put in above it. One of these had been removed, showing a patch of sky. When the door was shut, this and the peep-hole in the opposite wall were the room's only ventilation. For now it was apparently all right to have the door open. The morning was "safe time," Gus said. *They* wouldn't come now. The edginess of the previous night returned to me like a twinge of toothache.

Gus lumbered off to the *baño*. Out of curiosity, I stood on the bed and stretched up to look out of the open square of window. It looked on to a scrap-yard. A couple of men were lazily talking, perhaps arguing, in the sun. A small brown dog was licking its rump. Something about this trio made me remember it was Saturday morning. Over a corrugated fence were the roofs of another street, parallel to the one I had walked up last night. Directly below me I saw a pile of rotting old mattresses. I realized that it would be possible, by tearing back the cardboard slats, to lever yourself straight out of the window, and jump the 15 feet or so on to the mattresses. Difficult, especially with a septic machete wound in your leg, but possible.

So Gus had his back way out, if ever "they" came up the stairs. The manic ingenuity of it all made me nervous.

Breakfast arrived, two enormous oval platters of eggs, plantains, yucca and rice, with bowls of sweet milky coffee. The *señora* hovered for a moment. "Pay the lady, will you, mate?" said Gus pleasantly. "200 pees should do it." I paid her. His eyes furtively appraised my wad of notes.

He set upon his breakfast, shovelling the food into his mouth. He ate like a dog, hasty and mistrustful. I was still halfway through when he pushed his plate aside scraped clean. He gave a loud belch, rolled up a *sucito*, poured out a slug of rum and leaned back in his moth-eaten throne.

"So you want to write a story about the cocaine trade," he said reflectively. "'Course you do. It's the only story in this place. Any other story, you follow it hard enough, it comes back round to *nosola*. They've got snow in their blood here."

Outside in the street a truck backfired. I saw Gus stiffen and listen. I thought of those nights at the Fruit Palace. It was all just a game then.

He settled back. "Debt and deadly sin, who is not subject to, mate?" he said unexpectedly. "I can handle the deadly sin, but the debt really gets me down. These people have been very good to me, you know, and I just can't pay them. And then there's the nights, when the candyman don't come no more."

For a moment I missed his drift. He was staring at me through the brown-tinged smoke of his *sucito*. It seemed like a look of expectancy, but it was hard to gauge what emotions were playing across that pale, wasted dial. "Come on, cock," he said. "It's obvious, isn't it? Look. I need a bit of cash, you need a bit of information. Normally, of course, I'd be glad to give freely, but . . ."

This wasn't quite what I'd had in mind when I set out to look Gus up, but under the circumstances it seemed sensible. We made a deal of sorts. Years of living rough in South America had severely limited his financial horizons. All he wanted, to begin with anyway, was "a few blue ones"—a few thousand pesos—and plenty of basuko. I didn't even have to bring the basuko: Julio Cesar would bring it over from the Paso Doble, or Alvarito would fetch it, for a small consideration. All I had to do was keep him supplied with pesos. In return he would open up his box of delights, his Who's Who of the Colombian cocaine trade. It was another of those offers I couldn't refuse.

6

WHO'S WHO

The next day, after dark, I set off once more for Gus's crow's nest. I didn't have to brave the hobo-jungle on the way this time. Gus had explained a quicker and easier way to get on to his street. "We brought you round the back way first time. Little bit of disorientation, just in case. Sorry about that."

I brought him money, rum, a bagful of bread and fruit and canned food, and some medicaments and bandages. I even offered to change his dressing, but he refused. His hand closed over the fresh 1,000-peso notes. "Cheap at the price, mate. It pays to know what you're up against in this game, believe you me." Alvarito came in with some basuko, and I paid for that, and then deep into the night I sat at Gus's feet while he discoursed like a guru on the nature and philosophy of the cocaine mafia.

Gus's Who's Who was a vast pile of jottings, cuttings, photographs and scrawled, arcane organigrams. He had amassed it, haphazardly but doggedly, over the years. It was in part a by-product of his own cocaine habit. He had almost become part of the furniture among the lower echelons of the Bogotá cocaine circuit: Gus in his dirty *ruana*, scoring another little bundle on credit. He traded gossip with the razor-boys, listened in on the Perseverancia street telegraph, drifted through long snowbound raps with other users—and the next morning down it all went in the Who's Who. It was also the product of his journalistic skills, or what was left of them. He had chased up all the leads and cross-checks.

There were company brochures, government statistics, survey maps in the box. He'd done everything except write it.

Gus also had the newshound's knack of being at the right place at the right time. One Saturday in July 1977, for instance, he was lunching lazily at a café on 59th Street, when he heard the noise of machine-gun fire. A block away, outside El Grill Canecao, a man lay dead on the sidewalk. That day Gus got a scoop, and a by-line in the evening edition of *El Bogotano*, because the dead man was one of Bogotá's biggest cocaine *capos*, Mario Gil Ramirez. Gus remembered all the details—the blood on the snazzy white suit, the dreadful grin of a man whose mouth has been shot away, the distraught wife, name of Bersey, who had only escaped because she had left the restaurant by another door to bring the car round. Now the recollection of it prompted a series of forays into the Who's Who. Guided by an invisible cross-referencing system, crouched over the carton like some scabrous old ferret casing a burrow, he hauled out the names and dates of the long vendetta, of which the killing of Gil was a part, between the Gil-Espinosa and the Vargas-Rivera gangs. This in turn brought out a sheaf of dog-eared cuttings about Veronica Rivera, the "Cocaine Queen." Other women have borne that title—he named Martha Cardona, and Marlene Orjuela—but Veronica Rivera was probably the biggest of the lot, *la reina auténtica*. He had seen her once, short and dark, like a dumpy Colombian housewife, but somehow you could smell the money and the death all around her.

"You'd be surprised at the number of women involved in this business," he said. "The cocaine queens, the money-laundresses, the molls, the mules. Above all the mules. It's a well-known fact that women make the best mules. There's a girl in town I know, Spanish girl, who's carried enough snow through the customs to start up a ski-resort. She's retired now, I believe. You ought to pay her a visit, mate. Julio Cesar will tell you where to find her. Tell him you want to see Rosalita. He'll fix you up."

On a new page of my notebook I wrote: Rosalita the Mule.

"And of course the biggest Queen Bitch of them all," Gus was saying, "is cocaine itself."

Gus had said he wanted to warn me about what I was "up against," and the gist of his message was that there had been a lot of changes since I was last in Colombia in the early 1970s. Those were "the good old bad old days." It was a free-for-all. There was big money up for grabs, and anyone with a bit of *chispa* and plenty of luck could get a piece of it. That deal I had got briefly tangled up in at the Fruit Palace was pretty typical. Someone with money in New York, someone with cocaine in Colombia, and someone—poor old Harvey—to act as go-between. In those days Colombia was only one of many countries supplying cocaine. A lot of it came straight out of the coca-growing countries, Bolivia and Peru, while some went south, to be refined in Chile and northern Argentina, before being shipped out from the Pacific ports. Up in the States, too, the Colombians had only a small share of the action. Apart from the independent operators there were only two main syndicates: Cuban exile groups in Florida, and the traditional *cosa nostra* mafia.

Even later, as the Colombian slice got bigger, partly because of the country's "privileged geographic position," and partly because of the innate Colombian genius for *contrabando*, it was still a simple, old-fashioned operation. Take the case of Paco. For about three years in the mid-1970s, Miguel "Paco" Sepulveda was one of the most successful Colombian *capos*, running over a million dollars' worth of cocaine into the States every month. But it was still, said Gus, the old piecemeal smuggling. He brought it in in fives and tens. He used a lot of "mules," carrying it through airport customs, different stop-overs every time: Puerto Rico, Bahamas, Costa Rica, and so on. And he used merchant seamen a lot, Flota Mercante Grancolombiana. His favourite move was on the Barranquilla to Houston line. He'd have a man on the boat, with the gear in a couple of *mochila* bags. The ship docked at Houston at night. Everyone had to stay on the boat till morning, when the customs rummage-squads would come aboard to give the tub the once-over. The trick was to make the drop that night. The seaman threw the *mochilas* overboard, and there'd be a diver come out to pick it up. It was so sweet, so simple. Paco paid out $3,000 a time, half for the seaman, half for the diver. His buyers were getting the stuff in Colombia at give away prices—$6,000, $7,000 a kilo. The moment he landed it, it went up to $30,000 or $35,000.

But now, Gus said, now it's all different. "They're not gangs any more, they're bloody corporations." Now it's all what the economists call "vertical integration," controlling every phase of the operation from raw material to end-user, eliminating the middle-man, or at least putting him on the pay-roll and enveloping all his profits. There are still thousands of Colombians involved in the drug trade, but the whole business is ultimately controlled by a score of giant, mafia-style syndicates. They've got huge production plants down in the south of Colombia, mainly in the empty departments of the south-east, where the grasslands of the *llanos* merge into the jungles of the Amazon basin. There they process the cocaine, either out of raw cocaine paste smuggled up from Peru and Bolivia, or—increasingly—from their own coca plantations. They've got small private armies guarding the plants. A lot of them have formed an unholy alliance with the Colombian guerrilla factions, the Movimiento 19 and the FARC, which are numerous down there. They pay the guerrillas money and arms, in return for protection. The processed coke is ferried northwards in private planes, hundreds of kilos at a time, to the wharves and landing strips of the Caribbean coast, especially the Guajira peninsula. There the planes refuel, or the cargo is switched to another plane or boat, and on towards the States.

Up in Florida, they've got it all sewn up as well. There's been a long feud between the Cubans and the Colombians for control of the wholesaling network, but the Colombians are right on top now. They've got a whole business sector going, fuelled by narco-dollars, with all the latest gear— computer links, electronic surveillance, helipads and the rest. And they've got people in place all down the line: bent police and customs agents, *representantes* in all the major ports and airports, Colombian travel agents to handle their comings and goings, Colombian realtors to handle their offices and apartments. And underpinning the operation is a brutal army of hit-men who are rapidly acquiring a reputation as the meanest sons of bitches in the whole underworld scene. The traditional *mafiosi* might put a .22 bullet through someone's head, and leave a note for his wife saying how much they regretted it, but business is business, *omerta* and all that. The Colombians don't bother with all that. They go in with the "big key"—an axe or sledge-hammer—and blow away the whole family with M-16 machine-guns.

At this top end of the smuggling market, the profits are immense. The statistics are hard to substantiate—no one's publishing end of year accounts—but the guesstimate is that in the early 1980s about 50,000 kilos, 50 tons of pure cocaine, is leaving Colombia every year, mainly destined for the United States. At a conservative reckoning this earns around 2 billion dollars annually, more than the country's major legitimate export, coffee. Add in the healthy marijuana trade, and it is probably true to say that Colombia's entire export earnings, just over 3 billion dollars, are matched dollar for dollar by illicit drug earnings.

But the money is only the beginning. It is what the money does that counts, the power-grip that the drug mafia exerts on Colombia. A lot of drug money never finds its way back into Colombia. It stays in the States, mainly in Florida, where it is said of the Colombian drug mafia that they don't rob banks, they buy them. Or it is salted away in off-shore accounts in Nassau, Curaçao, the Caymans, Panama, etc. But as much as a third, say a billion dollars a year, does flow back into the country. There it not only supports the fantastical opulence of the drug *capos*. It also buys off police, judiciary and administration, flows into all sorts of legitimate business fronts, becomes a major source of low-interest credit, vastly increases the growth of the country's money supply, and jacks up the inflation rate, currently running at about 30 per cent. These are only the direct economic effects of the drug trade. There other spin-off effects. There is the government money diverted, under US pressure, to finance anti-trafficking operations. There is the increasing bill for food imports, as marijuana and coca plantations swallow up agricultural land. There is the loss of tourist earnings, as Colombia's gangland reputation scares off the holiday-makers.

These narco-dollars are only a part, though now much the biggest part, of Colombia's whole subterranean economy, the black market and contraband interests so widespread they are simply known as *la otra economia*, the other economy. Huge quantities of green coffee, sugar, cattle and cement are creamed off for illegal shipment and sale. These "clandestine" exports are said to net about $500 million a year. And then there are emeralds. Official exports of gem emeralds, bought from the Banco de la República or from recognized franchises, are worth $50 million a year, but at least as much again goes out by the back door, smuggled out by Colombians or bought by gringos from the thousands of small-time merchants like Julio at the Fruit Palace. The other side of the "other economy" is the profusion of contraband goods coming *into* the country—cars, cigarettes, whiskey, electrical appliances, any consumer item that high import tariffs make pricey in the shops. These are stolen from the ports, or smuggled across the Venezuelan border around Maicao and Cucuta, or brought up the Amazon from Brazil to Leticia. Colombia is a smuggler's paradise. Drug traffic is the big one, but most of the drug *capos* have their fingers in the other pies, and make full use of the ingrained profiteering networks of *la otra economía.*

The influx of blue money into the national economy is deleterious in much the same way as pumping a body full of anabolic steroids. It is a short-term fortifier which in the long term weakens, and one of the most pervasive ways in which it weakens is through the corruption and bribery of officialdom. When I was first in Colombia it was a well-rehearsed rumour that *the* Mr. Big of the cocaine racket (and had been since the whole thing started to move in about 1970) was none other than the Supreme Commander of the DAS, General Ordoñez Valderrama. The DAS—Departamento Administrativo de Seguridad—is essentially the government's secret police. It was originally set up with a specific antisubversive brief: infiltrating leftist movements, gathering intelligence on guerrilla groupings, rubbing out the odd troublesome trade unionist, etc. With the blossoming of the cocaine trade, the brief was extended to cover narcotics, and the profiteering began in earnest. Stories began to circulate about mysterious disappearances of seized cocaine from DAS stocks, and about embarrassing shoot-outs when customs officials found their adversaries were not smugglers but DAS agents. In May 1973, the DAS chief in Leticia—Colombia's port on the upper Amazon, and the main smuggling point for cocaine paste from Peru and Bolivia—was arrested at Bogotá airport with 19 kilos of cocaine in his suitcase. Official inquiries eventually unearthed a whole can of worms, orchestrated at the highest levels of the department. In effect the whole DAS network had been turned round, and was functioning as a giant drug racket, reaping vast profits from the resale of seized cocaine, and from protection money paid by favoured *traficantes*.

Ordoñez was arrested in 1974 and receded into the comfortable twilight of disgrace, but the profiteering doubtless continues on a more discreet level. And what was happening in the DAS was repeated in all the other agencies involved in the "fight against drugs"—most notably the F-2 (the plainclothes Special Branch of the Policia Nacional), the customs service, the armed forces and the judiciary. The involvement of army planes, Colombian flagships and national airlines in actual trafficking is well documented, and the use of the Colombian diplomatic bag in this respect is part of basic smuggling lore.

The corruption percolates through to every level of Colombian political life. In the mid-1970s the finger of suspicion pointed up to ministerial level. *Los tres reyes*, they were called, the Three Wise Men: Minister of Defence Abraham

Varon, Minister of Labour Oscar Montoya, and Minister of Foreign Affairs Indalacio Liévano. Nothing was ever proved, of course. The peak was reached in 1978, with the election of José Turbay Ayala as President. Turbay's inauguration at the Nariño Palace was somewhat overshadowed by a barrage of accusations—some of them originating from leaked CIA documents—about his hand-in-glove relationship with certain *costeño* smuggling syndicates. At the other end of the political spectrum local governors, mayors, judges, police chiefs are obvious targets for payola and intimidation. In the key drug areas—the departments of Meta, Caquetá and Cauca in the south, where the processing and packaging is done, and the northern coastal departments of Guajira, Magdalena and Atlántico—whole administrations are on the pay-roll. In Barranquilla, the largest city on the Caribbean coast, exposures of official profiteering are so commonplace that throughout the 1970s only one *alcalde* (mayor) completed his full tenure of a year. They call the city *un crematorio de dirigentes*, a graveyard of officials.

In theory, of course, the Colombian government is pledged to fight the drug mafia. The president since 1982, Belisario Betancur—"B.B." to the press and the people—is very vocal on this, despite the implication of his brother Juvenal in money-laundering scams, and the assassination of his Justice Minister, Rodrigo Lara Bonilla, by a cocaine hit-squad. The machinery is in place. There is state-of-siege legislation empowering police to shoot suspected traffickers on sight. There are new extradition treaties with the US, specifically aimed at the drug barons. There are US-trained SANU squads (Special Anti-Narcotic Units of the Policia Nacional) and a network of North American "U-cs"—undercover narcotics agents—in place. The army makes periodic seize-and-burn forays into the drug badlands. During the famous Operación Fulminante, aimed at the Guajira peninsula, 3,000 tons of marijuana, eighty-five aeroplanes, and seventy-six boats were seized, and some 1,500 people arrested. More recently, a single raid on a production plant in Caquetá netted 12 tons of cocaine, worth over half a billion dollars at US wholesale prices.

The arithmetic seems dizzying, but it is always only a fraction. In reality, the whole Colombian power-base is so deeply implicated, through bribes and kick-backs and drug-related political funds, that any concerted action against the drug racket has a built-in softness, one hand waving a cudgel while the other pockets a share of the proceeds. The big busts are good propaganda, but it is always the small fry who get caught, while *los peces gordos*, the "fat fish," swim on happily in their fortified haciendas and Miami-baroque mansions. The biggest *capos* are well-known, high-profile figures—men like Carlos Lehder, probably the biggest of the lot, who owns his own newspaper, the *Quindío Libre*; his own neo-Nazi political party, the MCLN; and his own island in the Bahamas, Norman's Cay. Everyone knows about Carlitos, "Joe Leather," who worships John Lennon and Adolf Hitler, just as everyone knows about the other billionaire barons like Pablo Escobar, the Botero brothers, Benjamin "Papa Negro" Herrera, Gonzalo "El Mejicano" Rodriguez, and the big *costeño* clans, Ochoa, Valdeblanquez and Cárdenas. These people don't need anonymity. For all Betancur's threats and pledges, they reckon they are untouchable. The removal of mafia capital from the country's banks and businesses would cause economic chaos, the full naming of names on the pay-roll would tear the entire administration apart, and, as the bottom line, the cocaine mafia has enough arms, aeroplanes, manpower and high-placed military friends to start another civil war of the kind which dots the country's recent history. This is an extreme scenario, but with the stakes that high it will take a brave politician to call their bluff.

7

SNOW WHITE

This, in broad outline, was Gus's view of today's modern cocaine trade. It wasn't a startlingly original view, but on a chill Bogotá night, with the light flickering from bad connections and a blanket of basuko smoke on the air, it struck home. The moral was clear. Forget the Fruit Palace, forget the droll capers of yesteryear. Above all, forget the Great Cocaine Story. The utter naked absurdity of my assignment loomed before me. The echoes of Malcolm's boyish blurbs mocked me. Inside the Cocaine Underworld! Gus had an answer for that one. "The only way you're going to get inside the cocaine underworld, mate, is after it's chewed you up and swallowed you."

It was very disheartening. But I turned up again the next night, as I had said I would. I found him in good spirits. His leg was freshly bandaged. We talked aimlessly for a while. Then I asked him if he had any particular stories on the boil at the moment. I want something I can get my teeth into, Gus. And—I might have added—I want my money's worth off you.

He looked at me for a long time, and then he said, "Yes. Yes, I have. One *very* particular story, as a matter of fact." Even as he said it he glanced nervously at the door, and slipped the brick out of the peep-hole for a quick scan of the courtyard, and I knew that at last I was going to learn why he was holed up here in the back-streets like an animal on the run.

Gus's story concerned a new syndicate that was elbowing its way into the Bogotá cocaine market. "It's very big, very streamlined, and very secretive," he said. "It took me three months of buggering about to get what little I've got on it."

The first thing anyone noticed was the sudden, unexpected appearance of some very good cocaine on the circuit. Casual purchases of coke in Bogotá tend to be as disappointingly dilute as they are in London. "This was stronger and purer than anything we'd seen for years. Mean peach, mate. Everyone sat up and wanted some, but no one seemed quite sure where it came from." All drug-dealing networks are very compartmentalized, a series of dealers ranged in descending order of size between the wholesaler and the consumer. Each guards his own secrets. Your gram-dealer doesn't ask questions of the ounce-dealer he buys off, your ounce-dealer doesn't ask questions of the pound-merchant, and so on. Gus asked around but no one knew, not even Julio Cesar, who was a fount of drug-gossip. Or if they knew, they weren't saying.

There were other hints and traces: new whispers of rivalry, small seismic disturbances from the underworld. To the trained ear like Gus's, the regular fare of gangland killings, kidnappings, rip-offs and run-outs assumes a kind of pattern. "You know who's treading on whose toes. And when you *don't* know, you start to wonder. A gets knocked off his perch, but you know it wasn't B or C. So you turn a new page and you write at the top: 'D.' A new *banda* in town, carving out a patch for itself."

The primo coke and the subterranean rumours continued. Gus persisted with his usual nosiness. And then at last he got something—in fact, the way it sometimes goes, he suddenly got two quite independent leads in as many days. The first was a name. "It was pure luck. I got it from someone who had no right to know anything. He was just a regular, low grade corner-boy on Caracas. I'd never even seen him before. I was drinking with some friends in this bar. He comes up and asks, did anyone want to score *perica*? It was that kind of bar. As a matter of fact I did want to: J.C. had let me down,

I remember. We went out back and he gave me a *muestra*. No doubt about it. It was that same primo peach again." Gus played it rather crafty at that point. He said to the boy, *"No sirve, no es pura."* This coke's no use. The boy protested—he knew it was good. Gus again feigned distaste. Then the boy said: "*Sí, hermano. Esa es la perica de Snow White.*" He used the English words, Snow White. This is Snow White cocaine.

"I didn't know what the hell he meant, of course. But he was very clear about it. This was cocaine from a source—a gang, a hood, a dealer, someone or something—called Snow White."

Gus tried to get more out of him. Who or what was Snow White? But the boy was wiser than his years. The last thing he wanted was to get cut out of any deals. All he would say was, "You want more Snow White stuff I'll get it for you." But at least Gus had a name of sorts, and names are hard to come by in this business.

The very next night he was with an American called Kreitman, who ran a gold and precious stone shop in the Chapinero district. Kreitman was a recent addition to Gus's list of eligible gringos, good for an occasional cadge of dinner, drugs and a night on the sofa. Gus worked a rota system, so as not to spread his entertaining chat too thin. The favoured ones like the Italian painter, Bruno, had him for weeks on end, but for most Gus was someone who turned up suddenly one evening and disappeared from view the next morning. Anyway, this night Kreitman laid some *perica* on Gus, and it was once again this *premier cru* peach, which Gus now knew to be Snow White cocaine. Kreitman thought he was the bee's knees, having such high quality blow. He was boasting about his contacts, his savoir-faire, his reflected glory from laying such fine stuff on an old street veteran like Gus. "So I came straight out, put my card on the table. I said: 'This is Snow White stuff, right?' No reaction. It didn't mean anything to him. So much for his contacts."

But Gus did learn something from Kreitman. "Do you know what the beauty of this stuff is?" said Kreitman. No,

Gus didn't. "I'll tell you. The beauty of it is, it's never going to run out. I have it on *very* good authority, from the man who sells it to me, in fact. These people are bringing 100 kilos a week into Bogotá. Regular as clockwork. A *hundred* a week."

Gus broke off suddenly. Something clattered down below the outside window, down where the scrap-yard was. He had forgotten his fears while he was talking: they came back now, like electricity switched on. Then came a louder noise, and a scattering waul of cats. Gus breathed out heavily. "Fucking mogs at the bins again," he said. His hand was shaking as he reached out for the rum bottle. After a pause he said, "Well, that's just about it, really."

I stared at him in disappointment. "You mean that's all you've got? You've got a name—a nickname really—and you've a figure for how much they're dealing in. It's not a lot to go on, is it, Gus?"

He looked at me sourly. "Yeah, well, the inquiry got discontinued, didn't it?"

"You mean your . . . accident?"

"Right. Come-back from little Snow White, just as quick as if I'd punched a button. It was my own bloody fault, no doubt about that. Saturday night, bar in Perseverancia. This was just a couple of days after I'd seen Kreitman. There was this guy I knew, small-time hood. I was really hot on this Snow White story, and I was sure, can't quite remember why, that he knew something about it. I started asking a lot of damn fool questions, very indiscreet, broke all the rules. I'd had a skinful. There were dozens of people in there who could have heard me.

"So when I leave the bar, they're waiting for me. Two of them, across the street, in the shadows. I didn't really take them in at first: there were other people on the street. But a couple of blocks later, all quiet, I knew they were after me. I started to run. Any minute now they're going to put a bullet in my back. Concentrates the mind wonderfully. I went like a bloody gazelle. I got myself off the street, down an alley, a lane. You know Perseverancia: it's just like a village. Little houses, yards out back. There's nowhere to hide. So of course the alley's a dead end, but there's a door with light behind it. I hammered on the door. Then the apes caught up with me. They got me away from the door into a dark bit with dustbins. One of them had a machete—no, it was more like a butcher's knife, anyway it was long and sharp, and he was a big bugger, and he was going to do my throat with it. That was my finest moment, mate. I got him a beautiful kick right in the nuts. He must have sliced my leg then. I didn't feel a thing till afterwards. Then this geezer opens the door—about bloody time—and he's standing there in his nightshirt with a Winchester 18-bore rifle in his hands. The double-act pissed off, and that was that. Blood all over the shop, and at least eight of my nine lives used up."

So there it was. Ace McGregor's last story. Our man down a dead-end street in Perseverancia. I didn't know what to believe. It was getting on for 3 in the morning, and I felt completely dried-up. There were no yardsticks anymore. "So what's your plan, Gus?" I asked. "You can't stay here forever."

"Right now I haven't got a lot of choice. You know—no money, one leg, a lot of people with bad attitudes on the look-out for me. Makes travel a little difficult. It's not safe here, but it's as safe as I can get. Julio Cesar isn't known up in Perseverancia. He's a Caracas Avenue boy. That's his patch. If I can stick it out long enough, and if they don't somehow get to J.C., they'll probably reckon they've put the frighteners on me and I've scarpered for good." He jutted his ginger-stubbled chin out, and added, "The long-term plan, of course, is to get back in there and nail them."

"Nail them?"

"Sure. Get the story, name the names. Tell the world about Snow White and the Hundred Kilos. A little Colombian fairy tale."

"And how the hell are you going to do that?"

"Same way as I always do, mate. Look for the weak spots. I've been thinking. Got bugger all else to do all day. I've been putting Snow White into context, you might say."

The Bogotá market isn't what it used to be, Gus explained. It's big still, but it's lost a lot of the export trade. There's a big internal market: a lot of coke and basuko used by the street-boys, and the middle-class Bogotanos, and of course the gringos. And then there's the provincial trade, the ounce-dealers from Girardot, Melgar, Tunja, all the middling towns round about, who come into Bogotá every now and then to replenish supplies. But there's only the remnants now of the big wholesale market that used to thrive in Bogotá ten, fifteen years ago. Then there were a lot of American dealers in town: at the Tequendama hotel it was like a permanent convention. And a lot of high-volume purchases were actually physically made in Bogotá. Now the volume tends to go straight up-country, by air, from the processing plants in the south to the export points in the north. There's no need for it to come into Bogotá at all.

"So why the hell is Snow White bringing 100 kilos of the stuff in every week? That's way too much for the domestic market. It's coming in *and* it's going out again, or a lot of it is, anyway. So. Question number one. Where and how do they bring the gear in? Nothing much to go on there, probably on four wheels, rather than by air. Question number two. Where and how is the stuff going out? Answer, almost certainly by air. There's no point in bringing it into town just to take it out again overland. So you've got a big volume going out, regular as clockwork, from one of the airports. The volume's too big for mules to carry through customs. It's probably too big for a diplomatic bag job. It's going out either dressed up as cargo, or possibly through some scam using airforce or army planes. My money's on cargo. Question number three. Where's it going to? I'll tell you my thinking on that one, mate. It's going to Europe. I just don't see it coming into Bogotá if it's going Stateside. They've got so many supply-lines going up from the northern seaboard. Of course smuggling is like water: it's always finding new channels. So maybe they've got a good new scam and they're flying it straight into the major cities from Bogotá. But my hunch is Europe. Europe's an itsy bitsy market for the Colombians. They haven't got the obvious geographical connections like they have with the States, and they haven't got an organization on the ground over there either. A lot of European coke comes over from the States, a lot comes direct from Peru and Bolivia. If I was a smart *capo*, looking for elbow room in a very tight market, I might well be looking at Europe."

He fingered the scabs on his face thoughtfully. "I'd love to nail those bloody apes. If I can just work out the pipeline, how it comes in and how it goes out, I'll put a cracker so far up Snow White's arse he won't know whether to shit or wind his wrist-watch!"

"And how do you propose to do that?" I asked. I couldn't believe he was contemplating a second go at them.

"Obvious," he said. "I go back to Kreitman, and try to find out who he buys his *perica* off. Because whoever it is seems to know a few details about Snow White." He looked at me. Thoughtfully he said, "Trouble is, of course, I can't do anything right now. But *you* can, mate. No one knows *your* face. Most natural thing in the world for you to breeze into Kreitman's shop. You're looking for a few expensive souvenirs, he's a very pleasant chap, you'll get talking, he'll lay a line or two on you, and Bob's your uncle."

Alternatively, I thought, Bob's your gorilla up a dark alley with a machete. No thanks, Gus. No kamikaze journalism for me. "I'll think about it," I said.

"Think about it! Christ! I'm offering you the story, cock, mint-fresh. A big new syndicate, pouring hundreds of kilos of snow into Europe. This is your Cocaine Underworld, mate. These stories don't grow on trees round here, you know."

When I left that morning, I had Kreitman's business card in my pocket—Galería Pecadillo: Daniel y Claudia Kreitman: Oro y Cerámica Precolombino—and I kept on thinking: No one's forcing you, you don't *have* to do it.

I decided to let Snow White lie for a while, but the least I could do was look up Rosalita the mule. I presented myself once more at the Paso Doble. The fat *señora* sat splay-legged on a chair, "Ah!" she sneered. "El Meester Escocés!" It was a quiet evening. No birthdays, no music, no *chulitas* in tight red dresses.

Julio Cesar took me over to the corner-table. "You see Señor Gus?"

"Yes, I saw him. He's in a bit of a bad way, isn't he?"

"The leg. The leg is not good, but . . ." He trailed off into a shrug.

I told him I would like to meet Rosalita. He darted a quick look over his shoulder. The bandying of names is not encouraged in these circles. "You another damn journalist?" he asked.

It was my turn to shrug. "I've heard she's got some interesting stories to tell."

It was difficult, he said—just as it had been difficult to get in touch with Gus. It was 500 pesos' worth of difficulty this time. He went into the back room to make a phone call. "You're in luck," he said when he came back, flashing a grin. "She says she's lonely tonight."

We took a taxi down Caracas. First we were going to score some *perica* for me to take to Rosalita, then he would take me there. "What's she like?" I asked. "You'll see," he said.

On the way we talked about Gus. Julio Cesar said Gus had been very good to him and his family. "A few years ago, when times were hard, when my papa died, Gus lent us money. He put a lot of contacts my way when I started selling the drugs. Gus is special to me. That's why I always get him good stuff for up here"—tapping his head—"and that's why we're helping him now."

"If you really want to help him, you ought to get him to a doctor. He needs to get that leg properly patched up."

Another shrug, another quavering of the pencil moustache. "It's not easy," he said vaguely.

"But surely he could get to a doctor without anyone knowing. Taxi there and back. I mean, is he really in that much danger?"

He looked at me thoughtfully. Chilly, street-wise eyes. Arm resting loosely on the back of the seat, behind my head.

He seemed to be sizing me up for something. "Look," he said. "Gus tells you what he wants to tell you. That's OK by me. I don't want to say anything against Señor Gus. But the truth . . . well, in Colombia we say, *la verdad es una puta y hay que pagar*. Truth is a whore and you must pay for her."

I couldn't quite see what he was grappling at. His breath had a sweet, sickly tang: he'd been drinking a *gaseosa*. "Do you mean that Gus isn't really in danger after all?"

"Bogotá is dangerous. Look——" He bent down and flicked up his trouser leg. In his sock, held by a thick rubber band, was a pearl-handled flick-knife. "You take good care in Bogotá. You carry a friend. OK, Gus asks too many damn questions. He pokes his nose in. But I don't think anyone's wasting much time looking for him."

The taxi suddenly slowed down. There had been an accident. A *buseta* had left the road, and was lying on its side on the central reservation. There was a lot of broken glass and wood, at least three bodies lying in the litter. Two young soldiers were trying to calm a small but volatile crowd. There were no policemen that I could see. The driver leaned out, had a shouted conference with other drivers leaning out, and brought back the news that the *buseta* had killed a man with an ice-cream cart, with two others injured, one of them the driver. "*Carajo!*" said the taxi-driver, and spat onto the road. For the next few minutes, not having spoken a word till then, he regaled us with a bitter harangue against *busetas* and their drivers, their speed, their carelessness, their clannishness, and, of course, the way they took custom from good honest cabbies like himself. This in turn shaded into a moving apostrophe on behalf of the dead ice-cream vendor. The driver's own brother, it transpired, was a *heladero*, and a fine upstanding trade it was, these hot mornings of January with the city dust in your throat. He finally lapsed into silence, but it was still preying on his mind when we stopped at a red light a minute or two later, and he said to himself, with a little grunt of laughter, "*Helado con sabor de sangre*." Blood-flavoured ice-cream. "*Carajo!*"

I was digesting this new angle on Gus, a new pointer to

old suspicions. But the leg? What about the leg? I asked Julio Cesar.

"I don't know," he said. "Gus told you they came after him with a machete, no? He told you he was sniffing around after some big *coqueros* and they sent after him?" I nodded. "Well, I don't know. That's what he told me too. All I know is, one Sunday, I'm down at the Paso Doble watching the football on TV, Millionarios against America de Cali, when my kid brother Alvarito comes running in, saying Señor Gus had arrived at the house, he was bleeding to death, he'd been in a fight, all of this." He waved his arms about in imitation of the dramatic messenger. "He was in a pretty bad way, sure. Well, you've seen him, and it was a lot worse two weeks ago. But I don't know who did it. I mean, machetes, it's not like them. The *coqueros*, they go for guns: hand-guns, shot-guns, M-16 guns. They've got a pride in these things. Charlie. Gus says it happened up in Perseverancia. OK. He's been in fights up there before. He's got this girl, his *putita*, up there. She's a really bad girl—set him up, string him along real bad. You want me to tell you what I think happened? OK. It was Saturday night in Perseverancia, someone picked a bad card, it was Gus. Tomorrow you or me, maybe. *Así es en Bogotá.*"

He was being doggedly logical, enumerating the points on his hands. I had to admit it sounded dreadfully plausible. But the logic itself led me back round to the same question. "So if there *isn't* anyone after him," I said, "why the hell can't he go to a doctor?"

He chafed his thumb and forefinger, the universal sign for money. "*Plata, hombre. Falta la plata.* Doctors cost money: 10,000, maybe 15,000 pesos for the treatment. That's just for starters. Señor Gus got nothing."

"Couldn't someone lend him the money?"

"Who? You wanna lend him? Everyone's lent money to Gus. He don't have no more credit. We've given him back that money he gave us twenty times over. We are poor people, *hombre*. You don't understand about Gus, I think. He's been bad for a year or so now. He don't work, he don't do nothing but bum *perica*. He takes too much *perica*, I buy him basuko. If he don't get basuko he starts to go crazy. I see many, many people like this. They go bad up here. They don't want to do nothing but sniff and smoke. After a time no one wants them around, you know? We stick by him, even if he is a bit *loco*. But he's got to work it out for himself."

He leant forward and told the taxi-driver to hang a U-turn at the next lights. We stopped outside a club called El Gose Pagano. "So what about this Snow White, then?" I asked. He didn't answer. He started to open the door to get out, naturally leaving me to settle up. I grabbed his arm. "What about Snow White?" I repeated.

He looked at my hand on his sequinned forearm, then up into my face. He gently removed my hand and said, "I never heard of Snow White from anyone but Señor Gus." He slid out of the cab, tweaked up the lapels of his jacket, slicked his hair with two quick sidestrokes, and strolled with an easy, rhythmic gait towards the knot of people outside the club.

8

ROSALITA

Perhaps it was the tripping lightness of the syllables, perhaps
it was the Springsteen song—

> Rosalita, jump a little higher,
> *Señorita*, come sit by my fire.

—that made me expect her to be flouncy and bright-eyed
and ready to trip a *bambuco* or two by moonlight. She was
overweight, tired and puff-faced, with a mouth turned down
by the way things had gone. She wore glasses, and slacks that
were too tight at the thighs. Somewhere behind it all you
could see she had been pretty once, and the sharpness still
flashed in her eyes like a zoo animal's memory of the jungle.
Her eyes were sunk in sallow, mauvish shadows. She lived in
a half-finished modern apartment out in Quinta Paredes, towards the airport. It smelt of plaster and oil-paint. The new
doors had warped and wouldn't close properly.

I gave her the *perica*. This seemed to be my act at the
moment: a notebook in one hand, a little package of powder
in the other. I explained that I was writing a book about the
cocaine trade. She said, "Sure." She followed the first stiff
hit of coke with a small chaser, and by the time she was
laying out the third rail the sloth had gone from her face and
hands, and she wasn't slurring her words any more. She
spoke fluent English in a Spanish-Yankee accent. Her voice
was lovely. If you closed your eyes she was beautiful, tough

and titillatingly foreign. She was Rosalita the mule, the best in the business, who had walked cocaine through the US customs forty-three times and never got caught. Then you opened your eyes and you saw a pale faded woman in a woollen cardigan, huddled beside a single-bar electric fire. I suppose in the smuggling business that's what you call good cover.

She was from Oviedo, a small town in the Cantabrian mountains of Northern Spain. Her father was a local lawyer. She had come to the States in the 1960s. A cousin had made it big in San Francisco, importing clothes from Mexico. He came back to Oviedo once a year, trailing the scent of success, bearing huge vulgar toys for the children. It had always been his promise that one day Rosalita would come and work for him in 'Frisco (as he persisted in calling it), and she would see the cable cars and bridges and deep blue bay of *la ciudad mas hermosa en el mundo*. And one day that's what happened. Cousin Bartolomeo wrote to say he could get her papers, she could come and work as an assistant in one of his Mexican boutiques. She landed in San Francisco in 1967, two days short of her seventeenth birthday. This made her in her early thirties now: she looked ten years older.

The cable cars were fine, and the Golden Gate bridge was too, even if it was shit-brown rather than gold, but Cousin Bartolomeo did not come up to expectations. "He was all big talk and shiny suits, but he was real mean. He wanted me because I was cheap. For a year he didn't pay me at all, only room and board. I was just cleaning, and doing odd jobs for him. He called me his *china*. He tried to get me to do other things too, you know, dirty things . . ." She raised an inquiring eye at me. My pen hovered foolishly over the notebook. "I was pretty then," she said, fixing me with a hard look that dared me to mumble that she still was.

She was also sharp, and it soon came to her notice that Cousin Bartolomeo had other interests besides peasant-style Mexican dresses. For one thing he was dealing in "wetbacks"—illegal Mexican immigrants, so-called because the traditional way of crossing the border was by swimming the

Rio Grande. He was selling passage into the US, selling false documentation—that was probably how he'd got papers for Rosalita—and he was setting up cheap illegal labour for his business friends. The other iron, the one which really opened Rosalita's eyes, was pornography: cheap, inventive hard-core material produced in Tijuana, smuggled in along Bartolomeo's supply routes, and sold under the counter down Broadway, San Francisco's sex street. "I've seen some things," said Rosalita, "but this was really filthy." Her voice curled like a tendril round the word "feelthy."

"So one day I went to Bartolomeo. I said, 'I want a job and a salary.' And before he could say no, I said, 'If you don't I tell the family back home about the porno.' He couldn't believe I'd seen through him. It's like he didn't even think I had a brain."

The following Monday morning she was behind the counter in one of Bartolomeo's Mexican clothes shops, the one up in chic Sausalito, across the Golden Gate. She got her own apartment, lived smart. She despised the pot-heads and the acid-freaks, the Haight-Ashbury flower people, the love-ins and be-ins, all the stuff which made San Francisco a by-word in the late sixties. "I kept right away from all that shit. I was so straight. Like they say, straight as a suicide falling."

She was good at her job, and a couple of years later, when Bartolomeo was expanding his legitimate business front, he put her in charge of a new store. This was selling clothes, weavings and upmarket *tipicos* from Guatemala. From now on she travelled regularly to Guatemala City, to buy from the local shops and dealers and from the Indian markets nearby.

Up to now she was 100 per cent legitimate. "OK, I knew the money behind the Guatemala shop was dirty, but I was clean. Everything declared, everything above board, every cent of import tax paid."

Then, in the fall of 1970, she met Chick. Chick was a Colombian boy, a *paisa* from Medellín. His real name was Ernesto—"just like Che"—but his family had always called him Chico, and he had effortlessly Americanized this into Chick. "That was Chick all over," she said. "He could fit like a glove over any scene. That's why he was one hell of a smuggler." Not that Rosalita knew anything about *that* when this young, handsome, dandified boy came in the shop. They got talking. He became very interested when she told him about her trips to Guatemala. He said he had very good contacts in Colombia, who could supply her with the kinds of goods she sold in the shop. The next week he came back with business cards, addresses, lists of arts and crafts shops, the whole bang shoot. He really did seem to have good connections. Rosalita was in love, Cousin Bartolomeo was agreeable, and a couple of months later she made her first trip to Bogotá. The night before she left Chick gave her a beautiful leather travelling case. For good luck, he says, and kisses her sweetly on the cheek.

She flew down to Bogotá, met Chick's contacts, bought an impressive selection of moderately priced *ruanas*, dresses, wall-hangings, etc., and flew back into San Francisco. As usual she carried as much as possible as personal baggage, and the rest she air-freighted back. When she got back Chick plied her with questions. How had it been, getting through customs? Had there been any problems clearing the stuff she'd freighted? And so on. In fact, Rosalita said, there had been rather more questions than there were when she came back from Guatemala. This was late 1970: there was only a trickle of cocaine coming up from Colombia, but there was already a lot of marijuana, and Colombia was undoubtedly on the customs list of suspicious provenances.

But they didn't search you? Chick asked. No, of course not, said innocent Rosalita. As a matter of fact she knew the customs man quite well.

Chick danced around, and kissed her, and said, "You're perfect, baby! You've just made us *millonarios*!" He picked up the travelling case he had given her. The four little rubber studs on the bottom unscrewed, the base came away, and there was a neat little compartment inside. For a moment she thought she'd been set up. But there was nothing in it. Chick said, "You just carried thin air into the States from Colombia. Next time, baby, you carry in $25,000."

"You want me to carry in *money*?"

"*Plata de polvo*," Chick laughed. Powder money.

Rosalita was shocked. She could just about handle dope: some of her upmarket friends smoked. But cocaine. That was on the outer periphery of the drug world, something she vaguely associated with junkies, blacks, jazz musicians. Chick said, "Trust me," and he also said, "Try some." Rosalita did both. Two months later she flew in from Bogotá with 3 lb of Huanaco White cocaine packed in a long thin wedge in the underbelly of her travelling case. It was Rosalita's first run, and it went like a dream. "And, you know, I'm not sure which got me higher. That first hit of *perica* Chick gave me, or that first run through customs."

It was a very tight operation. The supplier in Bogotá was one of the clothing wholesalers Chick had introduced her to. He had a warehouse full of *ruanas* and he had a regular supply of high-grade cocaine. Rosalita wouldn't tell me anything about him: "He's still active, you'd better not know about him." The cocaine was packed by him, at his warehouse, in the course of their legitimate business. No money changed hands then: it was sent by Chick from San Francisco, a perfectly straight-up money draft. As soon as Rosalita brought the cargo in, Chick buffed it lightly with mannite, and laid it off as 4 lb to a wholesaler in San Francisco, another Colombian, who hailed from the southern department of Huila. The "Huila Dealer," as Chick called him, paid $8,000 a pound. Chick was buying it in Bogotá for $4,000—a highish price in those days, but it included the packing and no-hassle facilities. "It was nothing huge," Rosalita said. "We weren't greedy. It was the simple, classic run—buy, carry, sell: minimum people, maximum cover." And it may not have been huge, but over a couple of years Rosalita did that run ten times, clearing about twenty grand each time. Overheads were zero, of course. All the expenses of the trip were picked up unwittingly by Cousin Bartolomeo. He for his part was happy with the profits from his Colombian shop, "Andes," on the first floor above the Guatemala shop in Sausalito.

Sometimes, for luck, she varied the run. "Sometimes I carried in *en el conejo.*" I looked up in surprise. In a rabbit? She laughed and pouted. "*Sí, hombre. El conejo.* I brought the stuff in up inside me." Of course—*conejo* is the South American equivalent of "pussy." She was referring to what the customs boys call "vaginal caches." I refrained from asking her how much she brought in on these occasions. Not, I imagine, 3 lb. She also carried it sewn in ribs into her bra.

These, like the false-bottomed case, were the simplest kind of mule work there is. You just hide the stuff in the last place they'll look. If they bring out the screwdrivers and the torches your number's up, but any lesser degree of searching and questioning you can get away with. This kind of mule work is only worth it with high-density, high-profit merchandise like precious metals, jewels and cocaine. A pound of grass is hardly worth it, and you'd look pretty conspicuous with it stuffed up your bra.

They contemplated broadening their horizons. The other method obviously available to them was to import the cocaine in one of the crates of woollens and weavings which Rosalita air-freighted from Bogotá. The plus of this was that you could bring in much higher volume. The minus was that crates from Colombia were routinely searched before clearing customs, mainly because freight traffic was the main smuggling mode for marijuana. It was just too risky, they decided. Then the *ruana*-man in Bogotá came up with a bright idea. Impregnating the *ruanas* with a solution of cocaine. When the solution dried, the cocaine deposit nestled invisibly in the deep woollen pile of the *ruanas*. At the other end the *ruanas* were soaked once more and the cocaine recovered in solution.

But before they could put this into effect, Rosalita had her first near miss. She had the cocaine in the false-bottomed case, and she got a real going-over at customs. "He had all my stuff out of the case, and he was pushing and prodding. Luckily we'd just put new rubber studs in the bottom, and they were real stiff. They didn't bust me, but they sure scared the shit out of me. You know, running drugs is all up here in your head, it's all good attitude. You convince yourself, you're three-quarters there to convincing the customs man. I was good, there's no doubt. I knew the ropes, I'd brought in legitimate imports for years. I felt right. When I started wearing glasses I felt even better. Not too smart, not too ragged. Just be what I am. That's the secret of smuggling—one big lie with lots of little truths around it.

"But once you see the other side—once you think: They've got my number—then you're into all sorts of problems in your head. It's all a question of what you see when you look in the mirror. Do you see a young business-woman importing goods for a Sausalito boutique, or do you see a cocaine mule pissing in her pants with fright?

"I swore off it right there and then. Chick tried to persuade me. I said, 'It's OK for you.' Chick was always very cool. He spread everything around: different bank accounts, a couple of apartments, different phoney company names when he sent the money drafts down to Bogotá. Always have a back door open, that was Chick's motto. I said, 'That's fine when you're dealing the stuff. But when you're running it,' I said, 'that's when there aren't any back doors. You just got to keep on going forward: one way out, no way back. I've had enough.'"

Chick and Rosalita lay low for a while after that. But smuggling is like a drug itself, it gets in your blood, and after a while they were craving for action. Rosalita didn't want to do the simple Bogotá run any more. "It's just statistics," she said. "No matter how good your cover, you can't keep coming in from Colombia without the customs turning you over once in a while." She'd drawn a rum card on the last run, and got away with it. Next time not so lucky, perhaps. By the mid-seventies the heat was really on for travellers from Colombia. Dope and coke were pouring into the US. Every scam in the book was being tried by smugglers of every shape and size.

Rosalita didn't travel to Colombia any more, but she did still visit Guatemala regularly. Why not get someone else to ferry the merchandise from Bogotá to Guatemala City? she suggested. She could then relay it on from there into the States. A Guatemalan stamp in your passport was perfectly cool. There wasn't much worth smuggling out of Guatemala, nothing you could carry on your person, anyway. This time it was Chick who demurred. It meant cutting someone else in, relying on someone else's cool. "Put another link in the pipeline," he said, "and at the very least you're doubling the risk of a screw-up." It was against their hitherto so successful creed—Small is Beautiful.

Then, in the summer of '75, they found their new move. It answered both their objections: Rosalita didn't have to fly in with Colombian stamps in her passport, but Chick didn't have to lose sleep over the risks of additional mules. This was a scam that wasn't in the book. They called it the Magic Eraser move.

One day Chick brought a stranger back to their Sausalito apartment. He was an Englishman. He had blond hair scraped back and tied in a bunch, and little wire-rim spectacles. He wore an expensive suit. "He was something like a smart hippie, something like a professor. Chick introduces him. 'This is Doctor Richard,' he says. 'Dr. Richard's in plastics.' Jesus, I thought—*plastics*, I'm really excited. But Chick *was*. He was really wired up, on to something new. He said, 'Dr. Richard's got something to show you, Rosalita.'

"So the guy opens up his briefcase. He takes out a piece of paper, a rubber stamp and two aerosol cans. The cans were unmarked: one plain black, one plain white. The way he put the things on the table, it was like a conjuror we used to see in Oviedo at Christmas, and that's what Dr. Richard called himself. A technological conjuror.

"He took a can, the black one, and sprayed something over the paper. It smelt like new car seats. It made a sort of a sheen over the paper, but after a few seconds it dried, and the paper looked just the same as before, except if you picked it up it was stiffer, perhaps heavier. Then he inked his stamp and put a stamp on the paper. It said, 'Downstream Enterprises.' That was Dr. Richard's company: it did all sorts of weird clever things with plastics. Chick kept pacing around and grabbing me, and saying: 'Baby, isn't it beautiful, you ain't seen nothing yet.' Then Dr. Richard took the other can and sprayed that over the paper. A different smell, bleachy. In a moment all the surface of the paper went a white colour, sort of frosted, like a smashed windscreen. He shook the stuff in shreds off the paper, and with a little knife he very carefully scraped the rest. When he had finished, the paper was blank. No stuff on it, and no stamp on it: it looked just like it had before he'd started.

"Dr. Richard explained. It's simply a very thin, transparent film of plastic. It's something called linear low-density polyethylene laminate. He'd been doing research for years. Breaking the micron barrier, he called it. Getting down to really small molecular thicknesses. A lot of technical stuff I didn't understand. He was offering Chick the spray-cans at $5,000 apiece. I hadn't really caught on. Then Chick said, 'Baby, think about it. Think what you could do with that stuff sprayed on your passport!'"

Chick and Rosalita took a long weekend and made a trial run. They motored down to Mexico with the magic eraser sprayed on the pages of their passports. They got stamped at the border, going in and coming back out. The customs also turned them over on the way out, looking for grass or heroin. They were clean, of course. This pleased Chick enormously. Everyone has a few falls waiting for them, and this one hadn't hurt them at all. They were even more pleased when, in a motel outside El Paso, they sprayed the white can of solvent on to their passports. The plastic skin frosted up into view, they scraped it off, and—eureka!—there was absolutely no visible record left of their visit to Mexico.

This was the basic premise of the Magic-Eraser runs. Rosalita was able to move in and out of Colombia without any record remaining in her passport. Passport stamps aren't everything, but a Colombian stamp undoubtedly multiplies the likelihood of getting pulled. She would fly down to Guatemala City, in the course of her legitimate business. There she would buy a round-trip ticket to Bogotá and back. She sprayed on the magic eraser before she left Guatemala City, peeled it off when she got back with the cocaine, supplied as usual by the *ruana* man. There was never any problem getting through customs when coming back into Guatemala. They were really slack. When she flew back into the States there was no evidence she'd been anywhere near Colombia. She had a bigger suitcase now: it carried 10 lb. Chick had a new dealing network. The Huila Dealer had moved off to LA, and now Chick was knocking it straight out to dealers. There was a Chinaman called Jack up in North Beach, others in Berkeley and Oakland. It was more hassle, but the profits were bigger. They were making $50–60,000 a run now.

The magic eraser was cumbersome. For a start Rosalita had to spray all the pages of her passport every time—you can never be quite sure where the immigration people are going to put the stamp. There was also a slight risk because she was filling in immigration and emigration forms every time she moved between Guatemala and Colombia. She had a little side-scam on this, one of the mule's regular tricks. Every time she filled in a landing card or such-like she made two deliberate errors. She put her first name where her family name should be, and vice versa—her family name was Amparo, which is a fairly common female Christian name. She also transposed two of the digits in her passport number. If anyone noticed on the spot, which they never did, it would be easily explained away as a mistake. It was just another bit of insurance, another spanner in the official works. If anyone started running checks, there was a chance that Amparo Rosa, passport number 1234, wouldn't get connected with the real Rosa Amparo, passport number 1324.

The magic eraser worked like a dream for half a dozen runs. But Dr. Richard's invisible laminate had one major flaw: it was susceptible to heat. He had told them to keep the passports clear of any heat source, otherwise the film would crack apart, as it did when the solvent in the white can was applied. One day in Bogotá, staying as always in the Tequendama hotel, Rosalita made one of her rare mistakes. She had to leave her room in a hurry—there'd been a change of rendezvous with the *ruana* man—and she left the passport on a window-sill. It was unseasonably hot, the window faced south, and when she returned, the passport was well and truly baked. The magic plastic film was crinkling off the pages, but not coming off neatly like it did with the solvent. The pages looked like eggs beginning to fry. She hadn't got the solvent with her, to make a proper job of it. It was back in Guatemala—the last thing she wanted to do was to remove her Colombian entry stamp *before* leaving Colombia.

She had to ditch the passport, go to the Spanish embassy—she still travelled under a Spanish passport—and get a temporary replacement. She flew back to San Francisco empty-handed, and they laid the magic eraser move to rest.

Chick went downhill. She said this in a matter-of-fact way, as if everyone naturally did. They drifted apart. She left Cousin Bartolomeo's employ and moved down to Los Angeles. But she didn't stay away from smuggling long. In LA, living in Laurel Canyon, she met two people who between them offered a new mule trail. The first was a Swiss girl called Ilse, who had done some dope-smuggling, and was up for anything. She was wild and bitter. For Ilse, said Rosalita, running stuff through customs was like saying "Fuck you!" to all the men who'd done her wrong. The other person who offered his services was someone with a ready supply of false passports.

Ilse and Rosalita ran the classic two-suitcase move. The great advantage of this is that you can almost *afford* to be discovered. All you need for this move is two identical suitcases and a lot of nerve. Rosalita flew down to Bogotá. Ilse flew on a different flight to some place en route between Bogotá and whichever US city they had chosen to come in at. The return trip was prearranged between them before they left. Rosalita boarded at Bogotá, checked her case stuffed full of coke. Ilse boarded at one of the flight's stopover points: Panama, Costa Rica, wherever. Her case, containing nothing but legitimate female hand baggage, joined Rosalita's somewhere in the hold of the aircraft. They didn't acknowledge each other during the flight, of course. When they got to the States, Rosalita picked up Ilse's case off the baggage carousel, and took it through customs. If her Colombian stamps caused her to get pulled, she was entirely clean. Blouses, skirts, knickers and beauty-kit. The danger was that an officer might notice that her baggage identification tag didn't match the one on her ticket, but this was unlikely. A little while later—as long as possible—Ilse came through, carrying the coke. If all went well, she breezed through: no Colombian stamps, of course. If she did get pulled over, and cocaine under the false bottom was discovered, she went into a screaming fit—"Oh my God, this is a frame-up, I've never seen these things before in my life—Look, look the baggage identification number is different—Look, it's come from Bogotá, and I've only been in San José—this is *someone else's* merchandise." It could be nasty, but in the end they would have nothing to pin on her. Checks would be run on the bag, but all that would come up would be the false name that Rosalita was travelling under.

Another time Rosalita worked for a Colombian called Juancho Leone—Johnny the Lion. Leone claimed to be bringing in 10 million dollars' worth of *perica* a year. He had a very elaborate front: the Santa Teresa Pan-American Bible Mission, headquarters in Fort Lauderdale, Texas, employing scores of people, stocking thousands of bibles in indigenous Indian dialects, and entirely devoted with crusading zeal to the importation of cocaine and marijuana. There were Santa Teresa missions in Colombia, Ecuador, Peru, Bolivia. He had supply lines of all sorts, but he mainly used mules, almost always dressed in nuns' habits or dog-collars. The Colombian mission was near Florencia, in the southern department of Caquetá, convenient for the Amazonian tribes whose souls needed saving, and for the cocaine-processing plants that dot the southern jungle. Rosalita, alias Sister Dominica, carried the cocaine back sewn into long thin pockets inside her voluminous black habit. Sometimes she brought back religious artefacts, naïve crosses carved by the noble savages and hollowed out in the back-rooms of the Florencia mission.

Another of Leone's moves used tropical birds—all properly documented and above board, some of the birds unfortunately dead on arrival in the US. In fact the birds had been dead when they were loaded in Colombia—dead and stuffed with cocaine.

So why no more? Why not make run no. 44 if all the others had worked so well? It was a question of love and the mule again. She had got into smuggling for love of Chick. Now she was married to a Colombian lawyer—"The first straight person I'd met in ten years, and I had to go and marry him." He made her swear off smuggling. They were going to have a child. Then a year ago she discovered—at the same time that Colombian fiscal investigators discovered—he was involved in a big fraud and money-laundering racket centred in Medellín. He was now serving a three-year sentence in Ladera prison. She was through with it all now. "Everyone's living a lie," she said. "You too, no?"

She was tired. The edge was fading from her voice. Her nose was runny from too many lines. She wrapped her cardigan round her and went to fetch a box of Kleenex.

"What happened to Chick, Rosalita?"

Back over her shoulder, so quiet that I wouldn't have heard it if I hadn't half-expected it, she said, "Chick's dead."

I was laying out another line for her on the plate. One last line, one last story. She was standing over me, looking at me from the shadows of her eyes. "You're a friend of Gustavo's, aren't you?" I couldn't deny her my own paltry little secret in return, despite Gus's exhortations that I'd never even heard of him. "I thought so," she said. "You fucking Brits ask too many questions."

The last time she'd seen Chick was in Miami in 1980. He was back where he'd begun, knocking round the lower circuits of the Florida drug mafia. "He'd survived. That was something. You know what they say about Colombians in Miami? Colombians are like Dixie Cups: use them once and throw them away. The mortality rate is very, very high on the lower rungs of the ladder. I never once worked in Miami.

Dadeland County: we call it Deadland County. Well, Chick was still hanging in there. He was doing regular runs, on a false passport, and he was doing small jobs—transportation, minding. But he was in a bad way. He'd gone all the way with *la tia blanca*. He was on the spike, he was snowballing, he was free-basing." These are the three hard-line cocaine habits: intravenous injection, combining cocaine with heroin or morphine, and inhaling volatile vapours from heated cocaine—all of them short cuts to the cemetery.

"On top of this Chick was doing the most damn fool kind of smuggling there is. He was body-packing. When I used to work with him he tried to make me do it. He'd say, 'Baby, it's fool-proof, you carry it in your stomach, it's the one place they can't shine their torches.' I never did it, though. That's what Chick was into. He was carrying in a pound at a time, a hundred *uvas*—"

"Grapes?"

"That's what you call the capsules. Four or five grams of *perica* wrapped up in a rubber johnny, or a bit of surgical glove."

There are two types of danger for the body-packer. First, the *uvas* can be detected by X-ray, and most of the major airports now use X-rays routinely on suspicious-looking Colombians. "If you don't confess," Rosalita said, "they put you on the pot and wait for the evidence." The other danger is mortal. That is when one of the capsules punctures inside you. This can happen at any time after ingesting it, but the most common thing is for a capsule to get lodged in the *caecum*, or blind gut, the first part of the large intestine. If this happens the packer knows he's living on borrowed time. No amount of laxatives or enemas is going to shake that obstruction free. The gastric juices work on, and wham—5 grams of undiluted cocaine instantaneously absorbed through the lining of the gut, hitting the central nervous system like a Force Ten gale. This is called the White Death. Heart on overdrive, temperature like a tropical fever, haemorrhage, pulmonary oedema, convulsions, respiratory arrest. All this to cope with while your brain's gunning up through the gears towards the state known as acute toxic psychosis.

Nine times out of ten a ruptured cocaine package is fatal. If the packer gets himself to a hospital in time, and if he is treated right—oxygen and the maintenance of airways to keep him breathing, heavy shots of short-acting barbiturates to counter convulsions, a course of psychiatric sedatives and blockers—these might just bring him through.

Like many others, Chick never made it to hospital. One day in New York Rosalita heard from a friend that Chick was dead. She checked out the back numbers of the *Miami Herald*, and sure enough, there it was among the small print. She showed me the cutting, with the sombre dignity of a mother showing a photograph of her dead daughter. It was a single paragraph news item:

Nine Mile Island Suicide Was Narcotics Suspect
A man who shot himself in public yesterday has been identified as Ernesto Diaz Marcoletta, a Colombian national. Shoppers scattered as Diaz, 35, appeared in a tenth floor window of a Nine Mile Island apartment block, brandishing a shotgun and screaming. He shot himself in the stomach and fell to his death, witnesses said. According to police, Diaz was suspected of trafficking and other narcotics offences, and had been under surveillance.

So there it was. Chick's epitaph: two column inches for the narcotics suspect. I copied it solemnly into my notebook.

"But don't you see?" said Rosalita. "Even then they couldn't touch him. He blew himself out through the stomach, so they couldn't find the *perica* inside him. That was Chick all over."

When I left she was sitting, turned away towards the single-bar fire, clenching a Kleenex in her fist. I thanked her once more, but she didn't answer. I said, "I'm sorry." She said, "Sure."

9

THE BEST COOK ON
CARACAS AVENUE

Julio Cesar was football crazy. One evening we went together
to a match at El Campín stadium. It was a showpiece
friendly, the Cachacos versus the Costeños. The Cachacos
were made up from Bogotá's two teams, Santa Fé and Millonarios, the Costeños from the Caribbean teams, Junior de
Barranquilla and Unión de Magdalena. There was a concert
before the match. We missed the *vallenato* duet, El Binomio
de Oro, but saw Juan Piña in a black tuxedo singing "Cómo
Quieres que te Olvide" and "La Morena." Julio Cesar had
got us the best seats my money could buy—Occidental Nu-
merada, precisely aligned on the halfway-line. The vendors
threaded, selling bags of *chicharrones*—giant pork-scratchings
—and glasses of fizzy *gaseosa*, piped through a rubber tube
from a tank strapped on the back. The smoke and dust of the
crowd hung in a silvery mist over the floodlit arena. The
grass shone like an emerald.

Just as the two teams ran on to the pitch, the floodlights
flickered and crackled, and the stadium was plunged into
darkness. There was a momentary silence, then an ironic
cheer. A pair of Radio Caracol land-rovers on the touchline
switched on their headlights. Footballers were wandering
confusedly about the pitch. The radio-car in front—orange
and white, "EL PERIODISMO ELECTRONICO"—revved
up, crunched gears, and promptly reversed into the car be-

hind, knocking out its headlights. Another cheer. Eventually the match got underway, florid and scrappy in the way friendlies usually are. The game was filled with the reassuring, global clichés of football. The Costeños won by a single goal, scored early in the second half by Junior's black striker, William Knight. The Cachacos missed a late penalty. Beer cans sailed on to the pitch. The *carabineros* pranced their tall horses and unholstered their guns.

Outside the stadium the *fritanga* stalls and *arepa* grills had sprouted in the darkness like mushrooms. Out of the crowd a man hailed Julio Cesar. He advanced, grinning broadly. "Bloody Costeño," muttered Julio Cesar, who was not well-pleased by the home team's performance. The *costeño* was called Jairo, from Santa Marta, affable and pushy. He had the Arab features of some *costeños*, a legacy of the Moorish traders who came in the wake of the *conquistadores*. He nuzzled conspiratorially up to Julio Cesar and said, "You got anything?" Of course, said Julio Cesar, but not on him. "I've got a motor," said Jairo. They pushed off through the crowd. I tagged along, vaguely hopeful of a few more pickings for the Great Cocaine Story.

We drove to the Gose Pagano, on Caracas and 78th, the same club where Julio Cesar had scored the coke I took to Rosalita. The Gose Pagano—the name roughly means "Pagan Good-times"—is a *salsateca*, a discotheque devoted to *salsa* music. An old town-house was still discernible in the warren of small, dark rooms, some bare, some with tables and chairs and candles stuck in bottles. Downstairs was a bar, upstairs the dance floor. The dance floor was empty. It was about nine-thirty. The place would be jumping in a couple of hours, Julio Cesar said. Undeterred, the black disc jockey was crouched in an alcove, playing records so loud that even the scratches jarred your skull. Salsa is spiky, uptempo Afro-Spanish music, full of complex syncopations and multi-layered percussion tracks, with much Hispanic chanting and whooping over the top. There are Puerto Rican, Cuban and Colombian strains, but the heartland of salsa is in the *chicano* clubs and studios of New York's Spanish Harlem.

We bought high-priced beer, the only form of entrance fee. Julio Cesar processed rapidly through the nooks and crannies of the place, sometimes stopping to shake a hand and pass a few words, sometimes waving a brief forefinger of salutation across a room. Whoever he was looking for wasn't here. He installed Jairo and me at a table and said he would be back *ahorita*. I had the feeling that Julio Cesar regarded Jairo more as business than pleasure. Jairo was a rich boy. He lived with his family up in the exclusive Santa Ana suburb. His father was a chemical engineer with one of the big breweries. Jairo was about to—his sort often seems to be "about to"—study architecture. The natural *alegría* of the Caribbean Colombians had become in him a slightly jumpy, false bonhomie. He smiled like an Arab dealer concluding a deal, and his eyes roved round the room while we talked. Nevertheless, I was glad to talk with him about Santa Marta. He assured me the smuggling and dealing were still very active up there. Most useful of all, he gave me the name of a Santa Marta dealer, Waldino. "He's got a black beard, and he'll fix you up with anything you need," said Jairo. "*Anything!*"

Julio Cesar returned with a *muestra*. We trooped off in turn to the john. Lavatory clogged with newspaper, spots of blood in the wash-basin, a graffito reading "JESUCRISTO NACE—UN PAGANITO MAS," Jesus Christ is born, another little pagan. Two quick scoops on the knife blade, and out again. All night long there would be people coming out of that john, with a motorized zip in their steps, a new sparkle in their eye, and a lopsided leer on their face which they fondly imagined to be a smile.

We had more beers. The floor began to fill up. The music was racked up another decibel, ultra-violet lights went on, eyes and teeth flashed, tail-feathers were shaken. Spanish Johnny was beginning to cook for the night. Then, suddenly and unaccountably, we were leaving. The music was too loud to find out why. Julio Cesar shouted something about going down *el camino viejo*. The old way? What was it and where did it lead? El Camino Viejo turned out to be a restaurant a few blocks away, and we were going there to meet a man called Mario, who was bringing the deal for Jairo. "You'll like Mario," Julio Cesar told me. *"Es un perro viejo"*—he's an old dog. Upstairs in the restaurant a band was playing *vallenatos*, a small black on the squeeze-box running sweat. They were coasting through the Diomedes y Colacho hit, "Diana." None of us wanted to eat, so we ordered a bottle of aguardiente. Already, it appeared, I was the only one with any spending money left. Jairo was saving his wad for the *perica* he was buying, Julio Cesar's pockets opened strictly one way. In a last stab of lucidity, as the second bottle was ordered, I transferred 11 pesos to another pocket—enough for a bus-ride back downtown—and offered up the rest to the gods of the night.

Later there were no diners left in the restaurant, only after-hours drinkers, and the tables had imperceptibly melted into one long straggling party. The musicians were relaxing, arms round available girls. Only the little accordionist, a Guajiro, kept going, coaxing the drunken riffs from his squeeze-box, staring off into a high corner like a blind blues singer. Everyone was talking. People sat down opposite me, beside me, some of them talking a language that made sense. Suddenly one of them was Mario, the man we'd come here to meet.

He was very tall, with a streaked beard, black and grey. He was slow, sombre and precise, and brought a breath of chill night air into the booze-heated room. Put a black topper on him and he would have made a cadaverous Victorian gent. Put a skipper's cap on him and he would have been a dead ringer for Captain Haddock in *Tintin*. His voice was deep and sonorous. He was a Southerner, from Tulua, a small pleasant town set among the cane-fields and bamboo groves of the Cauca valley. I judged he was in his late forties. The wrinkles on his forehead gathered like a force-field round a frown of concentration. His eyes were blue and hard. One knew right away that he was not a man to be trifled with.

He hadn't brought the *perica* that Jairo was buying, but he had brought a couple of *sucitos*—basuko-reefers. Jairo wanted to light up straightaway—he had a nervous greedy look in

his eyes, like a kid worrying about chocolate cake. Mario said
the restaurant had been in trouble with the police over drugs:
Jairo would have to smoke it outside if he wanted some now.
I had almost forgotten that all this druggery is illegal in
Bogotá. One is always being told that the last thing to worry
about in Colombia is the police. They are overstretched and
underpaid, and you have to be very unlucky to find one who
hasn't got a price.

As Jairo left clutching the *sucito*, Julio Cesar said to me,
"You go on. I'll come in a minute." He was talking earnestly
with Mario as we left. He didn't look drunk at all: a touch
dishevelled perhaps, a faint sheen of sweat on the brow, but
otherwise a man in control of his destiny.

He joined us on the sidewalk. The street was quiet. We
smoked the *sucito* in a phone booth, two keeping watch
while the third toked behind the mouth-piece. Two men
came round the corner. "Talk, talk," hissed Julio Cesar. I
gabbled something into the phone as they passed. A thin
dead whistle answered me through the ear-piece. I suddenly
saw, just a few yards away in the recessed doorway of a shop,
a bundled figure asleep on flattened-out cartons. It was quite
motionless, too cold and uncomfortable to move, and anyway indifferent to our giggling charade. You wouldn't have
known it was human but for the feet.

While Jairo smoked, Julio Cesar said to me, "You like
Mario, no?"

"Of course I do."

"He's a very interesting man. Like I say, *un perro viejo*. He
knows a few tricks." The smoke rolled through me, mists of
basuko over seas of aguardiente, a strange inner hush through
which I heard and recognized a distinct tightening in Julio
Cesar's voice. Business was afoot. "He used to be what we
call a *mano verde*, you know?"

"A green hand?"

"*Un cocinero, hombre.* A cook. A cocaine processor. They
get green hands from treating the coca leaf. Look, I've told
him you might be . . . interested. He can tell you the tricks,

how it's done. I promise you, Mario was the best cook in
Colombia!"

I snorted sceptically. Even at this gone stage there were
vestiges of perspective to protect. "OK," he said, with a light
laugh. "He's the best cook on Caracas Avenue tonight. He's
here, and he'll talk with you for 5,000 pesos."

I didn't want to do it. I was in no fit state to do it. But
5,000 was about what I had in my top pocket, and as Gus
had pointed out, these stories don't grow on trees. Summon-
ing reserves of fortitude from my swaying, jellyfish frame I
said, "After we talk, I pay, OK?"

Julio Cesar considered. His pencil moustache disappeared
behind a broad, gold-capped smile. "In that case, Señor
Charlie, you pay me 1,000 now, and Don Mario 4,000
later."

What the hell. It was company money, publisher's pea-
nuts. I spat cocaine mucus on to the sidewalk, hating Malcolm, hating myself, his dishonest broker. Julio Cesar
pocketed the bill like a card-sharp. As we passed the dark
doorway, the hump of rags coughed and mumbled to itself.

There were delays and detours, mainly connected with the
cocaine that the wretched Jairo was trying to buy. There
seemed to be some hitch. Mario had to confer with someone:
it turned out to be a girl behind the counter at a Rapido-
Burger joint on 10th Avenue. Then we had to return to the
Gose Pagano, and wait some more, and drink some more,
Jairo petulant, Julio Cesar slick and reassuring, Mario grimly
courteous, the boss-cat of the group. Julio Cesar slipped off
to make regular phone calls. No one answered and no one
came. We waited, strung out between cup and lip, until finally the place was empty but for us, and the barman threw a
vast lock-chain to his assistant—"Here, take your animal!"—
and told us that even the salsa had to stop sometime, be sure
and come back tomorrow. Painted behind the bar were the
words, "QUIÉN NOS QUITA LO GOZAO?" Who can take
away the good times we've had?

Outside, damp gusts of rain, the moon balanced on a tree

in a vacant lot. A few taxis cruised, always with someone riding shotgun in the passenger seat. We were going to Mario's lodgings a few blocks east of Caracas, to continue the assault course of drink and drugs. At some point I was going to get an interview: the great secrets of cocaine-making. Please God let me not pass out first. We set off up the baleful avenue, Julio Cesar's hand resting lightly between my shoulderblades.

Mario lived in a single, ground-floor room, just large enough for a double bed and a couple of chairs, with a small bathroom off. He didn't seem to own much: a few clothes, a mirror, a couple of books by his bed: Castaneda, García Márquez. The walls shrank in, encrusted with magazine photos. Heavy drapes hung over the window. Another shuttered room in Bogotá, another night in the half-lit burrows of the cocaine world. More aguardiente, a production line of *sucitos*. It was like a treadmill, an aching mechanical task. Mario would brook no refusal: you *had* to smoke and drink. You had to ride all the way.

At some point Mario mentioned something about going to a Turkish bath. This seemed an unlikely idea, but the time for likelihood was past. Julio Cesar put on the radio. All-night *vallenatos*, booming slogans: "Radio Santa Fé—*Siga gosando!*" . . . "Radio Santa Fé—*Radiando la alegría!*" Then Mario emerged from the bathroom. The *baño turco* was ready, he announced. He had a do-it-yourself steamer going, behind the shower curtain in the bathroom. He handed me and Jairo a pair of swimming trunks each. With as much dignity as possible in a cramped smoky room, with a pair of Bogotá street dealers lounging on the bed opposite, I removed my clothes and donned the trunks. They were too big for me, a faded pastel pattern of swirls on them. I took my turn after Jairo. It was impossibly hot inside the cocoon of the shower curtain, but the length of time one endured it seemed to be a point of honour, and Julio Cesar kept forcing me back in for more. A wad of eucalyptus leaves had been placed over the steamer. The raw, minty steam scoured my lungs. The sweat poured out of me. Why was I here?

Later there came a knock at the door, and a soft, busy voice said, "It's Ana." She was a tall girl in tight jeans. She worked as a dancer at the Carousel Club, a winky bar downtown. She sat next to Mario on the bed. He held the *sucito* sacramentally for her to smoke. Jairo simpered at her, and at one point made some remark to her about how basuko made you feel sexy. Mario did not like this. He began to shout at Jairo. "You are my *guest* here, I treat you as a *friend*, but I do *not* give you the *right* to *talk* to her like that!" He lumbered up off the bed, thin and slow, the frown branded between his eyebrows. Jairo sat in his swimming trunks, quivering with fear, saying "Yes" and "No" like a scolded schoolboy. Julio Cesar said, "*Tranquilo!* Don Mario!" Ana studied her fingernails. They had heard it all before. I slipped away for another session in the Turkish bath.

When I came out, a miffed Jairo was just leaving, tucking his shirt in as he fumbled with the door handle. Mario ignored him imperiously. The door closed. A faint puff of fog licked my sweating skin. Mario said to me, "We can talk now." I wrapped a blanket round my shoulders, gathered some scraps of paper from my jacket, and settled down opposite him.

"I learned to cook cocaine in Cali, '68, '69. I learned from a Chilean chemist. The Chileans were the best cooks then. He was selling his secrets. There were others like him coming into Colombia at this time.

"My first kitchen I built myself, up in the hills above the Rio Cauca, near a village called Las Animas—the Spirits. This is in the country of the Gumbianos. These are Indians that chew the coca leaf—well, a lot of them get drunk on *chicha*, but some still use the leaf. There are some *cocales* there, and plenty of coca in the markets. The Gumbianos are good, strong people. Few words, much patience. They prune the coca bush small, about a metre high. They call their bushes *ilyimera*, which in their language means little birds.

"I was the first *blanco* to set up a cocaine kitchen in this area. At first they thought I was crazy. A Gumbiano who chews the leaf perhaps uses half a pound a week. I was going into the markets and buying up 4 *arrobas*—100 lb—of leaves at a time. In those days you could buy an *arroba* of coca for 50 pesos. With good leaves and good chemistry, 100 lb of leaves will give you 1 lb of cocaine.

"Later I made a deal with a grower and bought the leaves fresh from the *cocal*. The bright, undried leaves are the best for cooking."

Mario spoke with slow, gruff precision. The voice was untroubled, but there was always a challenge in his eye. His beard jutted. He sent out jets of smoke through his nostrils like a cartoon bull.

There are, he explained, essentially two stages in the "cooking" of cocaine. "*De coca a pasta, y de pasta a perica.*" From coca leaf to cocaine paste or base, and from cocaine paste to crystalline cocaine. The first is a simple process of extraction, which draws out the all-important vegetable alkaloids from the leaf. "The cocaine is hiding inside the leaf," said Mario. "The *cocinero* must get inside the leaf and fetch out the little bit of cocaine." His thin hands writhed to gesture this process.

There are many alkaloids in the coca leaf, but only one of them is the psycho-active substance known to organic chemists as benzoyl-methyl-ecgonine, and to the world as cocaine. The second, more complex stage of the cooking is designed to separate the cocaine from the other alkaloids, and to crystallize it into a salt. The coca grown in Colombia and Peru, the Trujillo leaf (*Erythroxylum novogranatense*), has a slightly lower proportion of cocaine to other alkaloids than the Bolivian strain, the Huanaco leaf (*Erythroxylum coca*).

"To make the *pasta* out of coca leaves is very simple. You need some petrol: kerosene is best. You need a quantity of sulphuric acid, and you need an alkali. For alkali you can use lime or sodium carbonate. I used the simplest of all: *potasa.*" *Potasa*, or potash, is a crude form of potassium carbonate derived from vegetable ash. "Most of all, you need patience," he added.

"The first part of the operation is what we call *la salada*, the salting. Here you sprinkle and mix the potash into the leaves. If you are treating a big volume of leaves, you can do this in a pit lined with plastic sheeting. Otherwise you do it in an oil drum or plastic bucket. When you have salted the leaves you let them stand for a few hours. The potash makes them sweat. It starts to melt the alkaloids in the leaf.

"The second part is *la mojadura*, the soaking. This is when we pour the kerosene on to the leaves, drown the coca. You can also put in a bit of dilute sulphuric acid to help break the leaves down. After the soaking you must leave everything to steep for at least a day, better for thirty-six hours. While you wait, the potash is drawing out the alkaloids from the leaf. They float free in the kerosene, which holds them.

"By the end of the second day you are ready to begin *la prensa*, the pressing. If you don't have a press, you use your feet, like they do when they make *chicha*." (*Chicha* is maize liquor, a traditional *campesino* hootch now officially outlawed in Colombia.) "The purpose of *la prensa* is to get as much of the kerosene out of the leaves as possible. The kerosene is rich with the alkaloids. The leaves are dead now, black and rotten. You siphon off the kerosene into drums and throw away the leaves.

"The fourth stage is very delicate. This is when we take the alkaloids out of the gasolene and put them in water. This is done by pouring in water and sulphuric acid. Again you leave it, absolutely still, for a day. The acid goes in and takes the alkaloids, and they are dissolved in the water. We call this part of the process *la guaraperia*. At the end you have the kerosene on the top, and the *guarapo* underneath. The *guarapo* is a solution of cocaine and the other alkaloids." (In ordinary circumstances, *guarapo* is the name of a drink, either a juice or a liquor, made from sugar cane.)

"Into the *guarapo* you pour more potash. This makes the alkaloids precipitate. You see the *guarapo* go milky-white. This is the first time the cocaine becomes visible. If you have some ammonia this is the best for precipitation.

"Now you are ready for the last part of the operation: *la secaderia*, the drying. This is filtering out the precipitate—

you can use a sheet—and drying it in the sun or under light-bulbs. You dry it until it is like moist clay. And so you have it: *la pasta de cocaina!*"

So far, so good. You had your cocaine paste, the greenish-grey sludge that is the building block of the whole cocaine racket. This is already a valuable commodity. It can be dried off and sold as basuko. It is chemically stable, and can be transported through any climate without damaging its potency. How much it is worth depends on where you stand on the ladder, who you are selling to, and in what quantity. At today's prices a pound of *pasta* can fetch anything from $500 to $2,000.

But what about the other half of the operation, the turning of *pasta* into pure cocaine, snorter's snow? This is where the real money lies. A good cook can turn that pound of *pasta* into nearly the same weight of cocaine, worth around $5,000 on the Bogotá market. Here, however, I was to be disappointed. Perhaps Mario did not consider me worthy to enter this secret inner sanctum of cocaine chemistry. Perhaps I hadn't paid enough. Perhaps he was getting forgetful himself. It was eight years since he'd done any cooking. He had been nearly killed when a carboy of ether exploded in his outhouse laboratory at Las Animas. He showed me the burns on his back, marbled whorls of tissue. The fire had destroyed his materials and, worse, it had burned up most of the money he had saved. He had given up then. One of the big, Cali-based refining groups that began to emerge in the late 1970s offered to set him up with a backstreet kitchen, but he refused. He had been a cook for the love of it, he said, not the money. He was a *mano verde*, an old-style cocaine alchemist. He spat on the mafia, the faceless *peces gordos*, who ran the business now.

I tried to wheedle the process out of him, but in the scrawled scraps of my notes from that night I find only broken phrases—

Potassium permanganate: knocks out the inessential alkaloids by oxidation . . .

Organic solvents: acetone, ether, benzole, toluol. Toluol best, balsam of *tolú*, derived from Caribbean tree . . .

Gas crystals . . .

Hydrochloric acid bonds with cocaine alkaloid to form a crystalline salt. Snorter's snow is cocaine hydrochloride. Sometimes other acids used: cocaine sulphate, oxalate, hypochlorate . . .

Balance. Too much acid, coke will be *agrio*, sour. Too much carbonate, coke will be *jabonoso*, soapy . . .

To the aspiring drug-chemist these might mean something. They don't mean much to me, as I'm sure Mario knew. His demeanour was getting uglier. He was tired of my questions. He threw the information out impatiently. He ran a hand over his furrowed brow. I decided it was time to give it a rest. I'd had my fifty quid's worth.

The moment I decided this I began to feel ill. A desperate, last-ditch concentration had held me together while Mario was discoursing. But all the while Julio Cesar had been quietly circulating *sucitos*, and shimmering round with the aguardiente like a butler. As I sat back I felt the blood drain from my face, and the low flame of liquor burning up and down my gullet.

Ana was curled up asleep on the bed. Mario woke her and told her to go and make some *tinto*. There was a small primus for this purpose in the bathroom. As she clambered off the bed she brushed against the heavy grey drape that hung over the window. A momentary stab of light passed through the room. My God, I thought, it's daylight out there. It's the real world. I've got to get out of this place now. I got to my feet and began to totter back into my clothes.

It took me ages to extricate myself. First there was a scene about money. I gave Mario the agreed 4,000 for his information. He also wanted money for all the basuko we had ploughed through. I had vaguely imagined this was on the house. But no, the account was totted up, a great reckoning in a little room. He would settle for another 2,000. I had nothing left in my pocket save 11 pesos for a bus-ride back to my hotel. Julio Cesar interposed. "Señor Charlie can give me the money later. Tonight, tomorrow, no problem."

Still Mario wouldn't let me go. He became aggressively solicitous. "You must take another *sucito*. It is not done to refuse. We have more to discuss. You are my honoured guest." His thin, powerful hand gripped my arm. I said how much I would like to stay, how interesting it had all been, but now I was tired and ill, and must go.

"Tired?" he cried. "Tired? I have the thing." His long arm dipped into the cabinet by his bed, and drew out a pill-bottle. He worked out a pill and handed it to me. It was a long, white capsule. My bleared eyes focused on the tiny stamp on it: "LEMMON-714." It was a Quaalude, an extremely potent sedative used by doctors in preference to habit-forming barbiturates, and by pleasure-seekers with a penchant for jellied legs and catatonic trances. "You will sleep like a stone with this," urged Mario. "You will be clean when you wake." He swayed above me like a pine tree in strong wind. I had heard about this from Gus: a little-known aspect of the Colombian drug scene. Methaqualone base, shipped out of Eastern bloc laboratories to the free-port of Hamburg, thence to Barranquilla or Santa Marta, imported under false documentation, elaborated into bootleg Quaalude in special laboratories, stamped with counterfeit presses— Rorer and Lemmon—and then on to the US market for the animal-trank *aficionados*.

Very interesting, but not tonight. Not this morning. The Great Quaalude Story could wait.

"I really *must* be going," I said, absurdly plucking at my sleeve to look at the watch that wasn't there because you don't wear a watch when you're walking around Bogotá. Ana came back in with the jug of coffee. Of course: just to keep the body guessing, you wash your Quaalude down with jet-black *tinto*.

I stumbled out, the day glaring, the unremarkable street getting on with its morning chores. Three men tinkered beneath the bonnet of a pick-up truck. I slunk furtively past them, trailing a reek of butt-ends and guilt. A cat rooted in a trash-can, arse-up, tail high, its big pink eye staring accusingly at me. My head throbbed wildly. I put my hand over my right eye, where the pain was worse. A wall which should have been 3 feet away came and hit me on the shoulder. I reeled back and trod in a dog turd. On Caracas Avenue, the cars moved with a jagged, deadly rhythm. Each of them seemed specially targeted on my brain. I got myself across, and boarded a southbound bus. Almost immediately I knew I was going to be sick. I lurched down the aisle, knocking an old man's newspaper out of his hands, and pushed back through the turnstile. The driver put me down, grumbling about people too lazy to walk 100 metres. I dodged up a side-street, gagging at the smell of frying *chorizos*. The patron saint of losers had put a vacant lot halfway down the street. Rubble, grass, litter. I went to the furthest corner of it and lay down. Now began the purgatorial period: what went down must come up. I vomited, I sweated, I vomited some more. I moaned and cursed. I promised the good Lord I'd give up everything—booze, cigarettes, drugs, damn fool cocaine stories—if only He'd got up these last few dregs of bile from my belly and let me sleep. Finally came the blessed fitful sleep, curled among the litter, knowing at least that I'd nothing for anyone to steal. Only my shirt, and they're welcome to that. A far backdrop of car horns and shouts from the street. A mazy fever dream in which I fell, spiralled, disappeared, like a drowning spider down a plug-hole.

It was late afternoon when I got back to the hotel. I had walked sixty blocks or so, having spent my last coins travelling half a block. The *portero* nipped out from his diminutive office. His hair cream stirred unhappy memories of nausea in my stomach. "A message for you, señor," he cried, flourishing a scrap of paper.

Oh no, I thought. Not Gus, not now. I read the note with difficulty, partly because of the handwriting, partly because my eyes were not properly working yet. It read, *"Lola ha llegado y le pide telefonear."*

10

THE RAPIDERO'S RETURN

Tio Juan drove the family Renault. His big hands rested, almost seeming to doze, on the steering wheel. A few miles out of Bogotá, the Autopista del Norte—the country's main arterial road, and the only overland route between its two largest cities—narrows into a pitted two-lane blacktop, choked with trucks belching up black smoke from their stove-pipe exhausts. Tio Juan settled the car at a comfortable speed, around forty, and held it there against all comers. We overtook the truck convoys at forty. We swerved on to the hard shoulder at forty. Later we would be lurching down the dirt roads into Boyacá at forty, with only an occasional, grudging deceleration for the sharpest and sheerest of the hairpin bends.

Early on Lola told me to stop worrying. "It's all right," she said, "Tio Juan knows every inch of the road. He used to drive a *rápido* between Tensa and Bogotá."

"That explains it," I said, and indeed it did. The Colombian bus driver is the undisputed king of the road, and the fact that Tio Juan was not actually driving his *rápido*—the term is used for any bus or truck service, often anything but rapid—was beside the point. He would have driven in this same dogged, imperious way in a bubble-car.

Flota del Valle de Tensa, his bus service was called, he said. Four hours from Tensa to Bogotá, and four hours back again, landslides and breakdowns permitting. He had driven

News of another world! A friend from London, Lola Aronson, an achingly beautiful Colombian girl married to an American. We had arranged to meet up when she came, with her children, on her annual visit to see her family. I had left the number of my hotel with them when I arrived in Bogotá, and now she was here. Holding my head, fearing like Tchaikovsky that it might actually fall off, I phoned her. "We're going to drive up and see my grandmother tomorrow," she said. "She lives in a little village"—she pronounced it "bee-lidge"—"in Boyacá. You'll love it, Charlie. Come to stay tonight. We set off tomorrow."

Slumped in a taxi I ran a jaundiced eye over the events of the last week. Gus, Julio Cesar, Rosalita, Mario. I had drunk, smoked and snorted myself into a state of near collapse, and for what? An earful of paranoid fantasies, a few old smuggling yarns, some half-baked cocaine recipes, the dull drudgery of the basuko addicts. Was this the Great Cocaine Story in the making?

In a pleasant, modern house in the shrubbed streets of the northern suburbs, I met the Cuadros family. They were courteous, gentle, normal. It was like coming up for air.

"Christ, Charlie, you look terrible," said Lola.

"A touch of fever," I said. "I'll be fine in the morning."

Her mother fussed around me with *manzanilla* tea and aspirins. I was tucked up in bed. In the next room the family sat watching a quiz programme called *Cabeza y Cola*. It was time to take a holiday.

that bus every day, seven days a week, feast days and holy days, for twelve years.

This put Tio Juan in an entirely different light. When I had met him in the Cuadros's living room that morning, he had seemed a listless, melancholy man, with a limp hand-shake, wetted-back hair, and a tawdry white acrylic jumper. Snap judgments are a reflex action when travelling—often wrong, like this one, but more often the only judgment there is time for. Now I saw him anew: a check-shirted maestro of the mountain road, gunning his battle-scarred old *rápido* up through the gears, feeding the wheel through his hands like a helmsman in heavy seas.

Sparing my feelings on this outward journey, he did not tell me until later how and why the Flota del Valle de Tensa was discontinued. One day in Easter week, coming round one of those hairpin bends, the brakes had failed, and the bus, packed with villagers and livestock, had plunged down a gorge into the Muequeta river. "Not a soul was killed, not even a chicken," he said. "It was a miracle!" And he crossed himself lugubriously with an oil-grimed hand. The bus, how-ever, was a write-off, and that was almost like losing a per-son. I had a picture of him standing in the river, looking mournfully on as his beloved old rattle-trap subsided slowly beneath the water. Tio Juan now lived in Bogotá, doing de-liveries and occasional taxi-work, a king in exile. In a few years, he assured us, he would have saved enough to buy another *rápidito*.

There were eight of us in the Renault. Taking Lola as the family reference point, there were her uncle Juan, her mother Ana, and her nephew Andrecito, a dark, quiet boy of eight, in the front. Her niece Nydia, eleven, her son Sam, five, and her eleven-month-old baby Marco were with us in the back. We were off to see Abuelita, Lola's granny, Juan and Ana's mother: eighty-three years old next week, still liv-ing in the village of Tensa where they were born, in the hills of rural Boyacá, *el jardín de Colombia*.

For a while the sprawling, scabby outskirts of Bogotá clung

to the highway, a ribbon of breeze-block shacks and small factories, flower stalls and *fritanga* stalls, a half-finished amusement park. Lola pointed out Altogrande, the president's edge-of-town weekend retreat, a glimpse of white walls and red tiles surrounded by eucalyptus. A single sentry was on guard at the gate. Sam knelt up on the seat to get a better look at his machine-gun: Colombia has its drawbacks for a five-year-old Londoner, but as far as guns went it was a cornucopia. Soon the countryside widened around us. Here the big landowners had their dairy herds, stud farms and *haciendas*. Black and white Holsteins grazed on the brilliant green savannah. On either side of the flat valley floor rose bottle-green, black-ridged mountains. Clouds were banking over the range to our left, but when we came to a fork in the road—left to Zipaquira, right to Tunja—we took the right. Both these towns were once seats of the Chibcha kings, or *zipas*, who ruled these high tablelands before the Spaniards came. The Chibchas were farmers, traders, and sun-worshippers. They traded with lowland and coastal Indians: salt, emeralds and woven blankets in exchange for gold, cotton, parrots and sea-shells. Their *zipas* bore names like Saguanmachica and Nemequene, which meant "Bear's Bone." They were puzzled by the Spaniards' obsession with crosses: to them, two crossed sticks signified the grave of someone who had died from a snake-bite. The typical *campesinos* of this area, small, brown, trilbied and bow-legged, are remnants of the Chibcha. Some still use the old Chibcha name for their country, Cundur-cunca, the land of the condor. The modern name of this department, Cundinamarca, comes from this.

We climbed in brilliant sunshine. The air grew thinner and chiller. This was highland Colombia now. Huge flanks of hillside studded with willow and eucalyptus. Tall *cajicá* grass, black rocks, fast rivers, and the big Andean sky. I would have liked haunting harps and bone-flutes, but Nydia had cassettes by Menudo, a weenybopper Puerto Rican fivesome, and Enrique y Anna, equally winsome. These she played incessantly, studiously singing along with every word, so the grand landscape unrolled to such tunes as "Subete a mi Moto" and "Arriba!"

Down behind us the vast Guatavita reservoir basked in the sunlight. Beneath it lies the drowned village of Guatavita, sacrificed a few years ago in the interests of hydroelectric power. The authorities built a replacement village, Nueva Guatavita, a few miles away, an impressive mix of traditional colonial and modernistic styles, but most of the evacuees from the old village refused to live there, and the place is mostly a show-piece and souvenir-market for weekending Bogotaños. There is also an "old" Guatavita lake, a much smaller body of water a few miles to the east, in a dramatic Andean stronghold. It is reached along unsigned tracks, through maize and potato plots, and lush, high meadows of foxglove and coltsfoot. After a while the track turns to dust, jet black and fine as sand, impassable to cars. You walk the rest, up a steep wooded sandstone ridge, and there it is: the Laguna de Guatavita, also known as the Lago de Amor, a lagoon perhaps half a mile in diameter, set in an almost perfectly circular crater in the mountains, as still and symmetrical as a giant bowl of green-grey milk. In the mythic topography of South America, the Laguna de Guatavita is a nodal point. Beneath the secretive sheen of its waters lies the treasure of Eldorado.

Though the legend of Eldorado sprouted and multiplied, and expeditions hacked through the jungles of Guiana and Peru in search of a fabulous city of gold, the reality behind it lay here in the highlands of Colombia. Eldorado was not originally a place, but a person—el dorado, the gilded man. He was the central figure in a rite performed by the Chibchas here at this sacred lake. It was a kind of coronation ceremony, performed at the appointment of a new cacique, or chieftain, to one of the territories of the Chibcha empire. At the shores of the lagoon he was stripped naked, anointed with sticky resin, and sprayed with gold dust. A raft of reeds was prepared, with braziers of moque incense and piles of gold and jewels on it. The gilded chieftain lay on the raft, and together with four other principal caciques, he floated out to the centre of the lagoon, to the accompaniment of flutes and drums. When the raft reached the centre, the chieftain dived into the lake, washing off the gold, and all the offerings of gold and jewels were thrown into the water. It isn't clear who or what these offerings were for—whether for a sun god or, as a local Chibcha legend has it, for the spirit of an unfaithful *cacica*, who drowned herself and her love-child in the lake, and haunted its depths in the form of a serpent—but whatever its meaning, the rite itself is historical fact, attested by many Spanish *cronistas* who had the details from Chibcha eye-witnesses. A gold *tunjo* recently discovered at Pasca shows a ceremonial raft with figures and offerings on it, and probably depicts the Guatavita ceremony.

As soon as the Spaniards learned of the rites of the gilded man, they reasoned that there must be a fantastic store of gold and precious objects beneath the opaque surface of the lagoon. The first of many attempts to drain the lake was made in about 1545, by Hernán Pérez de Quesada, brother of Jiminez de Quesada, the first Spaniard to make contact with the Chibchas and the co-founder of Bogotá. Using a bucket-chain of Indian labourers with gourd jars, he succeeded in lowering the level of the water by some 10 feet, enough to recover about 3,000 *pesos* of gold. But progress was slow— about 3 feet of water a month—and soon the rains set in to refill the lagoon. Forty years later a more ambitious project was set in motion by a rich Bogotano merchant, Antonio de Sepulveda. With a workforce of 8,000 Indians, he carved a great notch in the rim of the lake to channel the water away: it is still clearly visible today. He got the level down by 60 feet, recovering many golden ornaments and gems, including an emerald "the size of a hen's egg." One day, however, the walls of the cut subsided, killing many workers, and Sepulveda's scheme was abandoned. He tried to get financing for another attempt, but eventually died "poor and tired." He was buried at Guatavita village. His body now lies, ironically, beneath the waters of the new Guatavita lake.

Many other attempts followed, but always with the same teasing result—a few objects recovered, mishap and abandonment, leaving the great mass of the treasure still submerged. In 1825 the value of the unrecovered treasure was put at £1,120,000,000—a figure based on spurious calculations by a French scientist, but big enough to keep the prospectors' appetites whetted. It was not until the early years of this century that the lake was completely drained, but even then the Guatavita jinx struck. In 1899 a British joint-stock company, Contractors Ltd, acquired the rights to exploit the lagoon. Their plan was simple, and to begin with it worked. They drilled a tunnel right under the lake and up into the centre, and the water was sluiced away down this giant plughole, with mercury screens to trap any precious objects. But once exposed, the lake bed itself proved intractable. It was covered with several feet of soft mud and slime, and was impossible to walk on. The following day the sun baked the mud to concrete. Drilling equipment was hauled up from Bogotá, but to no avail. The mud had clogged the sluices and sealed up the tunnel, and slowly but surely the lagoon filled up again with water. Twenty years ago the Colombian government passed laws to protect the lagoon from exploitation. The central area remains untouched to this day, and how much of Eldorado's treasure it contains is anyone's guess.

We came down out of the wind, into the hotter, dustier slopes of western Boyacá. Little pink-washed *fincas* huddled in the lee of the hill, shaded by dark mango, smothered with bright bougainvillea. As the road wound down there was always something just below us, a rooftop, a farmyard, the shiny green canopy of a banana grove. We wound the windows down for the heat, then up again for the dust. A pair of grubby little boys ran out as the car approached. One of them aimed a stone as we passed, but Tio Juan jabbed on the brakes and swung round to fix the boy with such a fierce, bullish stare that he froze in mid-aim.

This is the subtropical *tierra templada*, the fortunate zone of the Andes, halfway between the bleaker highlands of the *tierra fria* and the humid swamps and jungles of the *tierra calida*. Here it is hot, fresh and fertile, near enough to the

equator—Boyacá lies at about 5° North—to keep the air
sweet and warm even up to 7,000 or 8,000 feet. There are
only two seasons, a nine- to ten-month dry season and a two-
to three-month rainy season. In Boyacá the rains come
around May. It was February now, the end of the dry season.
It all looked lush to me, with many fast rivers, but Tio Juan
pronounced that everything was very dry. The upper slopes
were fawn and dusty. Some of the trees in the valley had lost
their leaves, so the woods below us had a greyish look, with
rivers glinting through a haze of tangled scrub, but always
there was some tree in flower, scarlet *ceiba* or the brilliant
yellow, daffodil-like *araguaney*. In these semi-tropical wood-
lands something is always growing while something else is
dying. There is none of the regularity we associate with the
seasons in more northerly regions. The idea of the four seasons of Europe or North America puzzles and inspires people
in the hot countries. One is always being asked about it:
these mysterious springs and autumns when the whole landscape suddenly changes its colour and mood. Sometimes
there is a hint of wistfulness or resentment in the questions.
Seasonal change, and the subtle fluidities of light and landscape that come with it, is something the tropics have been
denied. Here it is brash, lurid and monotonous. God even
gave more weather to the gringos.

We stopped to rest at Guateque. The air was brilliant in
the central square with its wedding-cake church in pink and
white. In a little shop we drank *tintos* and ate slabs of white
Boyacense cheese, not unlike mozzarella, wrapped around
plugs of guava jelly, *bocadillo*, a great Colombian favourite.
Outside in the neat gardens of the square, men in trilbies and
chequered wool *ruanas* strolled among the pollarded trees.
Bogotá fell away, rinsed away in these splashes of light. "This
is the real Colombia," said Lola. Sam sat on a sack of flour
drinking fizzy red *gaseosa*. Tio Juan bought me a bottle of
beer. I tried to pay, but he physically restrained me. "This is
my land," he said. "You're our guest here." I said I would do
the same for him in England, and we laughed because we
knew it would never be so.

Finally we arrived at Tensa, a small, self-contained village, a deep-rooted grid of dusty whitewashed houses and precipitous streets. It was Saturday afternoon, and the streets were full for the weekend market. Abuelita's house was at the lower end of the village, a couple of blocks from the market, a couple of blocks from the square, a couple of blocks from just about everything. She came to the door, raising her hands as if in surprise, though she had been waiting all morning for us. She was short and slightly crooked, but looked very strong. She greeted everyone in a slow motion of delight, her children, grandchildren and great-grandchildren, shaking Marco's sleepy fingers with her big, spatulate hands. She had a thick growth of slate-grey hair tied back in a bunch, a brown dress with a brooch at the bosom, gold ear-rings and a flash of gold in her smile. She would be eighty-three next week: *"nacida con el siglo,"* born with the century.

The sun bounced off the pale streets. Three men stood outside the *tienda* at the corner, drinking beer from the bottle. Three saddled horses were parked in a row beside them. We went in through her front door, dark green paint bleached and flaked by the sun, and down a shady passageway into a small sloping patio filled with pots of busy lizzie and morning glory. A stone walkway ran round the patio. At the upper end it was about 3 feet up off the yard, so designed for provendering your horse there, having ridden it in through the passageway, which used to be higher to allow for this. There was a bench on this high part, looking down over the yard and the roofs below, over the papaya and orange trees in the neighbour's garden, out across to the broad tawny slopes on the other side of the valley. "It is very primitive," said Lola's mama, not unkindly, simply stating the fact, and Abuelita laughed, smiling round at her brood. *"Sí, aquí ya estamos como siempre,"* she said. We're the same as always here.

Over the next hour I seemed to meet that half of Tensa village which was actually related to Abuelita, and several other, unrelated villagers who just happened to be dropping by anyway. Someone brought in a crate of beer, which Tio Juan dispensed. Mama introduced me to her plump, jolly sister, Tia Cecilia; to cousins Miguel and Maurizio, both in jeans; to Señora Fadul, whoever exactly she was. "Ay! Rosalbita! Mi chiquitica!" cried Mama, sweeping a little girl in pigtails into her arms. I shook hard hands and soft hands and little hands that bobbed and curtseyed. The sun beat down, the beer flowed, and this was Uncle Moises, a sharp-faced man with a limp, con mucho gusto señor, this is Charlie, the Englishman, the friend but not the husband of Lola, and I saw the deep country prejudices shift for a moment, in view of the general well-being, to accommodate this grinning figure who travelled around with other men's wives.

Later the crowd thinned, and cooking smells came from the kitchen. A woman came out bearing plates. I had been introduced to her as Clara, but didn't realize till later that she was a live-in servant rather than a relative. Clara was a single mother in her early thirties. She came from a neighbouring village and was quite ostensibly in Tensa prospecting for a husband. Single mothers are common enough, and not really frowned upon in these rural communities. It was not probably her fault, but the man's, and not probably his fault, but the devil's. If she married, her son would become an entenado, a step-son of the family, but would always bear his mother's maiden name. Her son was a seven-year-old scamp called Henry. This name is curiously popular in Colombia, in its English form, even though there is a perfectly good Castilian version, Enrique. I wondered if there was one particular Henry who had inspired this, but the only one I could think of was the pirate Henry Morgan, whose exploits along the Caribbean gold coast in the seventeenth century still have a folkloric currency in Colombia. I suggested this to Clara. She had not heard of Henry Morgan, but was pleased with the idea that her Henry had been named after un famoso filibustero inglés.

The men and boys ate first, the table being only big enough for four: chicken with ají—a piquant sauce of chili and coriander—and potatoes. Tio Juan ate with gusto and concentration, elbows resting on the table as he demolished the chicken. He pushed his plate back and left the table, with due formalities and wishes of *buen provecho*. Already, just a few hours back in Tensa, he looked somehow different. The sun and the beer had brought a leathery brown twinkle to his cheeks. A familiar dust had settled over his trousers. He sat in his vest on the bench at the top of the patio, reflectively picking his teeth, surveying the comings and goings of the courtyard with a slow, taciturn, cordial eye. What had seemed like tiredness in a suburban sitting-room in Bogotá had now turned into a strong, big-boned stillness. The good old Boyacense boy was back home from the city, with his size 12s firmly planted on the flagstones.

11

TENSA VALLEY

In the afternoon Lola and I strolled round the market. She gaily bargained over pomegranates, mangoes, honey-berries. All the delights of the tropical orchard were there, in a hubbub of stalls under a high, echoing tin roof. I was amazed by the variety of potatoes—*papas de primera, tocanas, tuquerreñas*, a whole range from giant boulder-shaped tubers down to the tiny sweetish potatoes, as yellow as a yolk inside, called *papas criollas*. We jostled through, trailing kids and clobber, laden with more and more fruit. At the meat section, strings of gut, skinned guinea pigs, vile smells getting viler as the afternoon wore on, and we hurried on to the balm of the spice and herb stalls. Outside, the stalls straggled on around a small dusty arena, the village bull-ring. *Fritangas* were being served at low trestles: sausages, pork scratchings, black pudding. Fires hissed under haunches of beef. Amid the smoke and noise and general milling there were little islands of stillness—a brightly dressed Indian *campesina* sitting motionless beside a tall rickety tower of baskets, a baby asleep on her mother's back, a bored parrot hunched on its perch at the bird-catcher's stall. Though the place was still busy, all the important transactions, the big sales of wheat and potatoes, had been done in the early morning. There was still some business going on, out where the slatted flatbed trucks were being loaded. A farmer and a wholesaler were arguing loudly about the weight of some sacks of barley.

The *romanador* was called for, the official weighmaster of the municipality. He was dressed much like the other *campesinos*, but after he had set up his ancient scales, he donned a pair of wire-rimmed spectacles as a kind of badge of office. The bushels were weighed and pronounced a fair weight, and they all repaired for *tronches*, the traditional exchange of drinks to finalize a deal. Judging by the crowds in the *tiendas* and hootch-stalls, the afternoon was rapidly sliding into one long *tronche*.

Later we took the kids down to the river for a swim. A long, steep, cobbled pathway ran down from the village to the river, canopied by an avenue of high *palo verde* trees. From the other side of the valley it looked like a long green tail hanging from the body of the village. It had rough stone steps, with a wider dirt-track beside it for horses and mules, which dislike paving on slopes, especially when going downhill. At the bottom were small well-to-do summer houses, with the feathered straw thatch of the region hanging over the gables like a sheep-dog's shaggy fringe. An orange path threaded through the greenery to a cove, where a pair of big rocks formed a pool. Three girls were washing there. There were squawks and giggles and hasty buttonings as I hove into view. Fortunately I had my trunks on already, as the cove was intimate and even just taking down my trousers brought more hushed giggles. The girls were shampooing their hair, like teenagers across the civilized world, ready for Saturday night. I said I hoped I wasn't disturbing them, *"Espero que no les moleste,"* and there was more laughter and some cheeky by-play on the word *molestar*. One of the girls was unbelievably pretty. She was squeezing the suds out of her hair. I headed swiftly into the deepest and coolest reach of the pool, and there was Lola glistening like a river goddess, laughing that wide, breathless, swimmer's laugh. Later we basked up on one of the rocks. The three nymphs had gone, draped in towels. Sam was organizing a game of pirates on a half-submerged tree trunk, with Andrecito and Rosalbita playing along in a confused way. I found myself leaning on an elbow, looking down into Lola's face. She must have seen the danger signals. She had seen it a thousand times: men with that hopeful, hopeless, hangdog glint in their eye. She gave a sweet smile, rolled away onto her tummy, and said how much she wished Luke was here—her husband—he did so love river-swimming.

That evening there was a power cut. I was with Tio Juan buying more beer at the *tienda* owned by Tio Moises, his brother-in-law, the husband of Tia Cecilia. The dim lights suddenly went dimmer and then blacked out completely. Hurricane lamps were lit, and candles placed on the bar. We walked back through the moonlit street, all the doorways open, shadows moving, lanterns glowing. At Abuelita's yet another of her sons, Tio Agustín, had arrived. He had spent the day on the hillside, sawing *estantillos*, the wooden columns that form the frame for the adobe houses. He smelt of sun, sweat and raw, pungent eucalyptus oil. There was music. First it was Tio Juan, revealing yet more *campesino* depths. Lola had bought a *capador* for Sam, a pan-pipe flute, six cane-stem pipes of different lengths bound together. We couldn't get much sound out of it, so Tio Juan showed us. Stretching his mouth into a curious, elongated pout, with his little moustache balanced on top, he blew powerfully at an angle across the top of the pipes. He played a few trills, deep and stately, and then a simple little mountain-tune. Everyone clapped in delight. He gave a short bow and handed the *capador* back to Sam, who was getting to like Colombia more and more each hour.

Tio Agustín, taking his brother's go on the pipes to be his warm-up act, called for the guitar. It was duly brought, and the *coplas* began. *Coplas*, the musical staple of any kind of party in Boyacá, are short ditties, sung or yelled or chanted, four lines with a rising "Oh!" at the end in preparation for the next singer's *copla*. There are hundreds of them, snatches as familiar to these people as nursery rhymes, though the best *copla* singers improvise round them. The proper traditional way to sing *coplas* is while dancing a particular form of the *bambuco* known as *el trés*. Lola tried to organize a dance on the tiny sloping patio, but there was no room. One of her cousins, seventeen-year-old Margarita, was soon to be married, and Tío Agustín sang her a bitter-sweet *copla* which ended with the advice,

> *Cómprate la mantequilla*
> *Que harto cuero te han de dar*

—go buy yourself some butter, to soothe the whippings you're going to get. For the children, wild-eyed with tiredness and adrenaline, he played a haunting song called "À la Limon."

Later the wind got up, the hurricane lamps swayed on their hooks under the eaves, a sudden collective tiredness fell over us all, and Abuelita herself sang the traditional end of the party *copla*, which says, "The little tree is dead where the peacock used to sleep. Now he must sleep on the floor like all the other animals."

Sunday morning in Tensa valley. Bells tolling for matins in the village square. Strange, yearning chants from the high barred window of a convent. Standing at the bottom of the village I could see tiny figures moving down the trail on the other side of the valley, past the roadside shrines, across the green-braided water courses that thread down the hill. They were mostly in groups, a few people, a few horses and packmules, a powder of dust around them. Other groups had already reached the river, hooves clattering on the wooden bridge, and were making their way up the stone stairway under the *palo verde* trees. The whole thing had the gentleness and assurance of a procession. On holy days there are actual processions down this same trail. A month ago, on Twelfth Night, *los tres reyes*, the Three Wise Men, came this way, and made the same arduous, dusty ascent.

In the square, the villagers streamed along in their Sunday

best. The men wore their *ruanas* neatly folded over one shoulder. They doffed their hats before entering through the double doors of the high, domed church, painted in fading yellow and white like an ice-cream sherbet, vibrating with a big bass echo of murmured voices and music. The three cousins came along, Miguel, Maurizio and Margarita, all in their best jeans. And there was Tio Juan in a baggy old blue serge suit. His transformation was complete, sartorial quintessence of *campesino*: shirt-collar flattened over his lapels, sagging panier-sized pockets, a brown leather belt round his paunch, and huge rumpled turn-ups.

When the square was empty and the church doors shut, I sat and smoked in the sun. The square was dominated by a *ceiba* tree, a straight trunk as smooth and grey as an organic steel tube, going up 50 or 60 feet to a shallow crown of dark leaves and brilliant scarlet japonica-like flowers. A few goldfish swam in a stagnant pool. There had once been two small alligators—*caimanes*—kept in the pool, but one night they vanished. It was still something of a local mystery, mulled over in bars and parlours. Who stole the village caymans, and for what purpose?

Everyone was soon back in their workaday clothes. Some of the shops and other services were shut, but otherwise Sunday was much like any other day. There was a market on, there were jobs to be done, and there was lunch to be prepared. Tia Cecilia appeared at Abuelita's carrying a large white rooster. He, she announced, was Sunday lunch, to which we were all invited at her house. She carried him upside down like a shopping bag, held by a string tied round his legs, but despite this disadvantageous situation he continued to jerk his head around officiously, and fixed us all with a baleful, red-eyed gaze.

Tio Moises and Tia Cecilia, with their teenage children, the three cousins "M," lived in a larger house, a block down from Abuelita's, more or less on the edge of the village. Tio Moises' father had been a local bishop, and the house had something of the air of a tropical vicarage, rambling, covert and slightly sinister. You came in off the bright whitewashed street into a shadowy, cool passageway, painted blue. This led into a small chapel. On the altar were two candlesticks, some dead flowers and a box of matches. Above it hung a cheap devotional print, Jesus of the Sacred Heart, with rouged lips and soap-opera eyes. Elsewhere on the walls were faded prints: the cadaverous features of Simon Bolívar, *el Libertador*; an ecumenical meeting at the Vatican; St. Peter. A dim amber light came through the stained glass windows. The squeaky floor, the leather chairs lined along the walls, the smell of furniture polish, made it feel like some funereal waiting-room. The Lord will see you now . . .

A door led out on to a long, rickety verandah, running the length of the upper storey of the house. Flowering plants tangled out of old cooking-oil drums. Tio Moises sat here on a wooden settle draped with brown and white cow-hides, buffing up his trilby hat with a damp brush. I didn't have the feeling he liked me. He had a bad heart and a gammy leg. His face was pinched and ruddy. Miguel, the younger son, fourteen and very affable, showed me round down below. There were store-rooms and disused sheds beneath the house, and a rusting old cane-grinder, and moulds for making the bricks of crude brown sugar called *panela*. An Indian woman was in the wash-house, drubbing some clothes at the sink. She had long, glossy, jet-black hair, like a seventeen-year-old's, but when she turned and came towards us I saw that she was haggish and wrinkled and half-simple. She gave a gaping smile as she passed, nodding away to some inner voice, and went up the steps to the verandah. There were sores on her ankle, loosely bandaged with a strip of yellow cloth. I thought of Gus.

The walled garden rambled down the slope, a quarter of an acre of unkempt fruit-trees, big-leaved avocados and slender guavas with polished, marmoreal, fudge-coloured bark. The bananas were still green, hanging in clusters off what is not so much a branch as a tendril, which droops down like a proboscis from the broad shiny leaves, and terminates in an odd, mauve, heart-shaped glans. Back up on the verandah, Tio Moises was still sitting on the cow-hide bench. He had picked up a "view-master" that one of the kids had dropped, a little plastic projector with eye-pieces and a circular disc of slides, and he was working his way slowly through "A Day at the Circus" or some Spiderman adventure. I strolled into the kitchen, a big, flagged room with a wood-fire range and a grinding stone set into the floor. Abuelita, Tia Cecilia and Margarita were there in a huddle, three generations of Tensa *campesinas*. They did not hear me come in at first. Tiny white feathers floated around them. They were just finishing off plucking the bird. They worked in silence, picking with bloodied fingers, huddled like witches round the pathetic grey corpse of the rooster. And when they did look up, Abuelita shot me an unwelcoming glance and stood half-turned, with her stained hands held out, and I felt I had blundered into some atavistic female preserve. It is not polite, Lola later explained, for the guest to go into the kitchen while the meal is being prepared. The dark secrets of the kitchen must be preserved.

Dinner turned out to be a rather formal, taciturn affair. We were segregated into two groups—Tio Juan, myself, Lola and her children sitting as guests of honour with Tio Moises in the dining room, while the rest of the family sat in a small, crowded and jollier room elsewhere. The chicken was tough and grey—the rooster's revenge—which put Tio Moises into a grump. With it was rice, potatoes, yucca and another tuber, yellow *arracacha*. We drank hot chicken-stock and a shandy made of beer and the pink *gaseosa* known as "Colombiana." The potatoes and the *arracacha* came from Tio Moises' own plot. We hastened to compliment him. *Arracacha* takes two years to grow, he added crossly, as if it did so especially to vex him.

Sam tried to match Tio Juan's manual dexterity with a chicken wing, and snapped it so hard that it shot across the table, leaving a trail of rice and gravy on the white cloth. Lola fussed around with a napkin, Tio Juan bent to his meal with renewed intensity. Sam nibbled contritely. The clock ticked. Various sepia-tinted ancestors stared down on us from dark wood frames. I heard horses' hooves in the street outside, and from somewhere down the passage came the distant sound of women laughing.

The days slid by, bright days and steamy days, picnics beside big rivers, oranges fresh from the tree, morning mists and evening promenades, and even a horse ride or two. There were trips. To Garagoa, where I purchased a black Boyacense trilby in the market. To La Capilla with Tia Cecilia, to get her false tooth fitted: this had taken so long to happen that "Aunt Cecilia's false tooth" had become a family catch-phrase for the slow expectancies of country life. A bus-ride up into the hills, delectably squashed between Lola and Tia Cecilia, a brindled pig squealing in the back, the aisle full of hard-faced, crop-haired *campesinos* smelling of loam, leather, horse-sweat and shed-dust. A day at a cousin's farm the other side of the valley, the sunned village neat below us, roofs and gardens, lanes and squares, and the dusty cemetery off to one side, patiently waiting. At the farm they were cropping the *agave*, stripping the leaves with an ancient petrol-driven machine. The *agave* is the American aloe, also known as *maguey* and *pita*, a bunch of hard, spiky leaves, green bordered with yellow, like a cross between a bush of iris and a cactus, with a single slender shoot growing up to 20 feet or more. The leaves yield a rough, greenish fibre, *fique*, which is soaked and beaten till workable, and used for all kinds of weaving. It is one of those all-round, versatile tropical weeds, like the cane that tangles round the water-courses, its various strains providing sugar, weaving material, and lath for the wattle and daub houses.

Up in Mexico the *agave* is the raw material for that deadly potent liquor called *mescal*. This is not drunk in Colombia. Here the traditional national hootch—now officially banned—is *chicha*. Abuelita, reputed to be a maestra of *chicha*-brewing, told me her recipe. Maize, preferably the type called *maiz blando*, milled in a stone mortar, soaked in dilute cane molasses (*aguamiel*, "honey-water"), fermented in a wooden cask for twelve days, boiled down to a dough-like substance called *masato*, and further fermented in *aguamiel* for another twelve days. The end-product of this was the finest, the *premier cru* of maize moonshine, *chicha flor*. A quicker, simpler recipe produced the everyday liquor called *chicha de mitaca*, and there was always a separate still going to produce the weak maize beer, *runchera*, which is usually taken spiced with herbs like *anicillo*. Every *chicha*-brewer has their own little secret additions. Abuelita used to put in pepper and lime, to hone the thickness of the brew. *Chicha* was officially outlawed in 1948, on the grounds of health and hygiene. Quite apart from the normal dangers of moonshine, and the bizarre ingredients—powdered bone, rat's skull, cow-hide—favoured by some brewers, there are cases when *chicha* is actually poisonous. If the corn decomposes in a certain way during fermentation, the glutens produce a toxic substance call ptomaine. The habit has been hard to break. The *campesinos* of Boyacá still mutter darkly about *Ley Treinta-y-quatro*—Law Thirty-four of 1948, the prohibition law—and Tio Juan gave it as his opinion that the prohibition had less to do with the health of the nation, than with pressure from the big beer breweries.

By night I slept at the Casa de Campesinos on the edge of the village, a hostel administered by the church, 100 pesos a night for an impeccable little white-washed cell, eight by six, one small hard bed, one small table, four pegs on the wall to hang your clothes on, and a cross painted in pale blue on the stucco wall. There were a score of these rooms running round three sides of the courtyard. All the ones I saw into were exactly the same as mine, except that in each the cross was painted in a different way. Mine was in the form of saucers, each made of three concentric circles: five saucers for the horizontal line, seven for the vertical. On the half-wall that screened the kitchens on the fourth side of the courtyard was a lurid mural showing Pope Juan Pablo II dispensing blessings to happy peasants.

One evening, retiring early to my cell, I heard what sounded like gunfire outside my window. Leaning out, I saw it was a game of *tejo* in progress. *Tejo*—also called *turmeque* and *sapo* (toad)—is the Colombian version of bowls. I pulled on my clothes and went to look. Two teams throw metal discs, about the shape and size of a pine cone, aiming at an iron ring at the other end of the pitch. The ring was only about 6 inches in diameter, and they were throwing the discs perhaps 15 yards. It was precision stuff, though there wasn't a sober man among the dozen players. Each game is won by the first team to nine points. If no disc lands inside the ring after a round of throws, the disc nearest it earns a point. A disc inside the ring earns six points: this throw is called an *embocanada*. The best throw of all is a *monona*, which wins the round outright. This is when the disc lands on one of the four little paper bags inside the ring. The bags are filled with gunpowder, and each winning strike is accompanied by a sharp explosion. As the light faded, the reports grew sharper. The tang of cordite mingled with the sweet tropical scents. The village's star player was a lean, grizzled *campesino* called Francisco. When he took the disc, there was a buzz of anticipation from the onlookers, and shouts of "Give us a *monona*, Francisco!" and "Into her mouth, Francisco!" He scored three *mononas* while I watched, curving the disc through the lamplit air with a complex, wristy delivery that would have wreaked havoc on a turning wicket at Lord's.

It had to end. On the morning we were to leave I awoke to the sound of a radio very loud below my window. The music was something marvellous, duelling uptempo guitars under a racing vocal line full of long-held shouts. This wild melody was cowboy music, *música llanera*, up from the great grass plains which cover the east of Colombia. Boyacá is right on the eastern edge of the Eastern Cordillera: it teeters above the *llanos*, a perfect halfway house between the hard uplands and the extravagant prairies.

There were scores of goodbyes. Abuelita graciously assured me that her house would always be my *ranchito*. "You are a Boyacense now," she said, glancing mischievously at my dusty black hat. A titter ran around, broadening into a communal guffaw. The Englishman in the hat had earned his small place in the family mythology.

We arrived in Bogotá late in the afternoon. There was a jam coming off the *autopista*, apoplectic traffic policemen blowing whistles, the dull shimmer of monoxide. Back in Toothgrind City. A week's stubble, a funny black hat and a heartful of cowboy music were all that remained of Tensa valley. Many miles later, on a bootleg music-stall in the town of Neiva, I heard that same song again. It was a band called the Vaqueros, the singer was Rene Devia, and those guitars were not guitars at all but racing rock and roll *harps*.

12

RIKKI SINGS

With deep reluctance I took stock once more of the Great Cocaine Story. According to my original plans I should have been up on the Caribbean coast by now, where the smugglers were: Santa Marta, Cartagena, the hidden coves and airstrips of the Guajira. That, surely, was where the *real* story lay. It was time to forget those bleak, basuko-crazed nights in Bogotá, file them away under the generous heading of "background research."

Here Lola and her family once again came up trumps. Lola's husband Luke would be flying into Colombia in a few days' time, her brother Alberto was in bad need of a holiday. Why didn't we all drive up to the coast together? It was a soft option, a few more days of company and security, and I was all in favour.

In the meantime I had one more lead to chase up in Bogotá. I hadn't seen Gus since the night he had told me about Snow White, and frankly I didn't much want to. He had a way of sucking you into that jagged, malodorous world of his. It was quite likely that Julio Cesar was right—that Gus's story about the Snow White syndicate was just another of his paranoid ravings. But what if it wasn't? A big new syndicate piping cocaine into Europe. That was the kind of hot-shit investigative stuff I was supposed to be after. I owed it to myself—and, yes, to Gus—to check it out. Only this time, I promised myself, I would tread carefully. I would keep my nose clean, my motives ulterior, and learn what I could by stealth. In this world, as Rosalita had observed, everyone is living a lie.

Dan Kreitman—the American who, according to Gus, had a cocaine source connected with Snow White—had his gold and precious stone store, Galeria Pecadillo, up in Chapinero, a pleasant mid-town district full of clothes shops and town houses. Bogotá is an architectural bran tub, and here one picks out an unexpectedly English style: red brick, mullioned windows and mossy roofs. I found the place in a basement off 13th Avenue, unobtrusive to the point of exclusiveness. The door was opened by a small, pretty girl. Inside it was hushed, cool and softly lit, and crammed to the brim with pre-Columbian artefacts and jewellery. A long-nosed American in glasses was inspecting some gold-work which a fat Colombian woman was showing him. "Be with you in a minute," he said. "My assistant will show you round." She showed me golden pendants and pectorals, nose-rings and lip-plugs, strange little stone whistles shaped like birds' heads, priapic figurines—"Es fálico, no?"—and many beautiful necklaces and bracelets of Tairona stone: agate, jasper, jadite, quartz, coral, turquoise. I liked her cool, precise movements, her soft voice. Everything was done in whispers here. She told me she had been in England a year ago. She said something which I thought was "talkie." I foolishly replied in encouragement, "Yes, talkie English?" but actually she spoke English quite well, and was saying that she had stayed in Torquay. She didn't look Colombian at all. She wore a chic blouson, had carefully ruffled mouse-brown hair. Her name was Daniela.

The man in the glasses, who was Dan Kreitman, was writing out a cheque in an enormously large cheque-book. The fat lady watched him intently, hand cupped round her chin, a long red fingernail nervously flicking at the flab under her eye. She was selling reproduction gold—three washes over a copper base—to hang on the Tairona stone necklaces. After she had left I chatted with Kreitman about his jewellery, and about the book I was writing "about Colombia." He was very voluble. He had lived in Colombia for fifteen years and knew every corner of the country. "I've eaten ant-eater stew in Amazonas, iguana stew on the coast, guinea-pig stew in Bucaramanga, and I've lived to tell the tale," he said jovially. He talked out of the side of his mouth, his eyes narrow behind the wire-rim specs, more a knowing glint than a twinkle. The red telephone on his desk rang. He spoke a few words in Spanish—fluently but in a New Jersey accent. Then, in English, "Ambassador? How are you today, sir?"

While he was on the phone the door-buzzer went. Daniela unlocked the bolts and catches that kept Bogotá at bay. A pair of American women came in, one blonde, pale and pregnant, with her sunglasses up on her head, the other sharp, sexy and anorexic. They were diplomats' wives. Colombia is a "hardship placement," they told me—more money, shorter stay, fortified apartments. They browsed among the artefacts with knowing, delicate fingers. The anorexic one tried on a $500 necklace in coral and quartz. "I must bring Bill in here," she murmured, striking poses in the mirror. From somewhere out back a Colombian woman appeared. This was Kreitman's wife Claudia, a tall, raven-haired beauty from Palmira, one of the towns in the Cauca valley where the songs all insist that the *chicas mas bonitas* come from. She had a big, toothy, cocaine user's smile, and great tangles of jewellery round her neck and wrists. The anorexic lady admired her mauve dress, "But I think the colour mauve means you're insecure." Kreitman got among them, very jolly. He held up a sculpted stone foot, the remains of some ceremonial statue. "You might say I paid an arm and a leg for a foot," he joked. The ladies groaned happily and flapped their pretty hands at him.

Kreitman answered the phone again. "Ken? Hold on, I'll take you out back." The Ken in question was Ken Bronkie, son of the late Willis K. Bronkie, and owner of the biggest emerald dealership in Colombia. The anorexic lady said, "I told Bill I was asking Santa Claus for a nice big emerald this Christmas, and he said, 'Don't ask Santa, ask Ken!'"

I sat back, enjoying the plush feel of the armchair, the gentle hush of money all around me. The diplomatic ladies prattled on. One had found a new masseuse, "very reasonable." The water had been cut off for the second time this week. They called the national airline "Avi-nunca" instead of Avianca—*nunca* meaning never. I watched Daniela threading agates onto a wire: red cornelian, orange sard, apple-green chrysoprase. She smiled at me, made a conspiratorial face behind their backs. The pregnant one bought a Tumaco figure, a Valentine present for her husband. He was a Junior Consul, in charge of "jollies"—social activities—at the Embassy. The figure was a stone pot with a humanoid face, halfway between a bullfrog and a Buddha. I wondered if the Junior Consul would find it flattering.

It transpired that I was out of luck as far as Kreitman was concerned. He was busy that day, and the following morning he and his wife were flying to Miami on business. There was no chance at all to wheedle myself into any information about his cocaine source. It was not the sort of question you came straight out with. But I did ask Daniela if she would come for a drink with me. Not this evening, she said, but tomorrow. There was a play she wanted to see at the Teatro Nacional. Perhaps we could go together.

Daniela Duarte—she shared the maiden name of Eva Perón—lived with her family in a smart white apartment block with tinted windows, up the plush end of 15th Avenue, near Unicentro. I was met by a young, mustachioed smoothie—Daniela's brother, Ricardo. "My friends call me Rikki." He wore jeans and an American bowling-shirt, standard issue for the young bourgeois of Bogotá, even down to the pack of Marlboro in the breast pocket. Daniela was still getting ready, he said, flicking his eyes to the ceiling as if to say, "These women!"

We perched uncomfortably on a white sofa. Everything was very polished and just-so, ashtrays too smart for ash, cushions too neat for bottoms. Rikki was soon to leave Bogotá, he told me. He was going to San Andrés, Colombia's island-resort 500 kilometres off the Caribbean coast. He had got a job as regional manager for an American company importing air compressors and conditioners. He would have a house by the sea, lots of sun, money, women. His real ambition was to be a pilot. "All my friends are pilots," he said.

Daniela and I took a bus south, and drank some brandy in a café. The Teatro Nacional was not at all the venerable, neo-Classical institution that the name somehow suggested, but small and modern. It smelt of paint and new wood. The play was *The Hostage* by Brendan Behan, a Colombian production of an Irish play with a red-headed Argentinian actress, Fanny Mikey, giving a spirited performance as Meg. The male actors conveyed their Irishness by walking with a slight limp. In the interval we met a friend of Daniela's, a painter called Garzón, and afterwards we went back to his apartment, met his wife and various friends, and drank a great deal of Chivas Regal whisky, at $50 a bottle something of a status symbol. Garzón was an artist with a capital "A," very melodramatic. His paintings were big, overblown canvases, with grotesque figures in attitudes of pain, madness and beggary. He forgave me for being a gringo because I was a writer, a fellow Artist. He sat very close to me, talking about *los sentimientos duros* and *la nueva sangre* of South America. He put his hand on my knee and said, in English, "I love life, his tragedy, his comedy."

We took a taxi back to Daniela's apartment on 15th. She snuggled up to me in the back seat, whisky on her breath, scented hair. An unmarried twenty-one-year-old, middle-class girl is one of two things in Catholic Colombia—a virgin or a whore. It would be a kiss and a cuddle, and thank you, goodnight. Vaguely hoping otherwise, I accepted her invitation for a cup of coffee. The janitor started up from the folds of his blanket. There was a rifle in the corner of his office. Upstairs Daniela put music on the cassette, very low for fear of waking mama and papa down the hall. David Bowie singing "Back in Suffragette City." We were on the white sofa together when we heard the faint thud of the lift doors in the corridor. A key turned in the lock, and in swayed Rikki.

He looked pretty drunk, and from the way he was grinding

his teeth he had probably been on the snort as well. "How'd the party go?" asked Daniela. Rikki shrugged. He poured himself a large Scotch from a cabinet of cut-glass decanters.

"I didn't go to the party," he said. He sat down on the sofa between us, drained his glass and bounced straight up again. Pouring the second shot clumsily, he chipped the top of the decanter.

"Rikki!" breathed Daniela in a tired, admonitory whisper. She was three years younger and 10 inches shorter, but there was no doubt who was the stronger of the two. "Take it easy," she soothed. "What's up with you?"

He cradled the glass nervously in his hands. "You know," he said evasively.

"Orlando?"

Rikki nodded. "He called tonight, after you'd gone. I went to see him. He needs the money real bad, Dani. He needs it yesterday, he said. He's getting a lot of bad pressure." He checked himself. The facile charm clicked back into place for a moment. "Sorry, Charlie. Money problems. It's the same in England, no?"

I assured him it was. He swayed irresolutely. David Bowie sang *sotto voce*—"Five years! My brain hurts a lot!"

Rikki went off down the corridor to take a pee. I asked Daniela what the problem was. She shook her head ruefully. "It's nothing, really. A bad debt. He wants me to borrow the money off our father. Papa won't give Rikki any more money."

"He told me he'd got a job up in San Andrés. Can't he pay it off then?"

"It's a bad business. You know, drugs. Rikki's been dealing on credit. He was getting stuff from an old friend. Small stuff, but it mounts up. Now his friend's got to collect. I'm worried, Charlie. Rikki . . ."

She trailed off. Rikki was returning. But it was only to say goodnight. "I'll talk to Papa tomorrow," she said to him. "We'll work something out." He plodded back off down the corridor. His door closed softly. Everything was soft in this deep-piled apartment, a sub-aquatic calm.

She stood up. "It's late. Thank you for a lovely evening, and now I must go to bed." She was fussing round with the ashtrays and glasses. I put my coat on. Then I had a sudden thought.

"It's cocaine, is it?"

"What? Oh, Rikki. Yes, he was selling cocaine."

"Did he sell it to Dan Kreitman?"

She gave a half-laugh, a little snort of surprise. She couldn't think why I was asking, but she answered just the same. "Sure. Dan bought coke from Rikki a few times. But . . ."

"It's nothing. Forget it. Yes, it's been a lovely evening. I'll call you." We kissed in the doorway, a lingering teenage kiss. But as the steel doors of the lift puffed shut, it was Rikki, not Daniela, I was thinking of. Was he the Snow White connection?

The following day, around 5 in the afternoon, I called up the Duarte apartment from a phone booth on 15th Avenue. As I had hoped, Rikki answered. "Is Daniela there?" I asked, knowing full well that she didn't knock off at Kreitman's *galería* till 5. "Pity," I said, when he told me she wasn't. "I'm in the area, thought I might . . . do you fancy a drink or something?" "Sure, why not," said Rikki. He asked me where I was. "15th and 102nd," I told him. A couple of blocks north, he said, I would see a cocktail bar called The Place on the left-hand side. He'd meet me there in ten minutes.

The Place was Rikki all over. Chrome-flashed American-style bar, pricey tariff on little laminated cards on the table, table-top computer games in one corner, loud, vapid Californian rock musak. Rikki strolled in, neat and coiffed in denims, and joined me at a corner table. He had the look of a man who had risen late and dressed at leisure. There was a fresh red shaving nick on his dimpled chin.

We drank Jim Bean bourbon. He chatted about his new job up in San Andrés, his plans to learn flying, his many girlfriends. He liked to talk, to image himself: smooth, man

of the world Rikki. I let him talk. The looser the better.
Underneath the patter I could see the worries of the previous
night simmering away. His bitten-nailed fingers fidgeted with
the swizzle-stick, the lacy paper coaster, the ashtray. I ordered more drinks. While he was at the bar buying cigarettes, I tipped most of my drink into his glass. A girl
opposite saw me do this. She was wearing sunglasses, but I
saw her eyebrows raise. We exchanged half-smiles, and she
touched the side of her nose: if I wanted to spike my friend's
drink it was none of *her* business. *Así es en Bogotá*. Her sunglasses and long hair made me think for a moment of Nancy,
back at the Fruit Palace. This time round it was me playing
the false cards. The cheated was now the cheat. Not a lot to
show for twelve years' work.

When I saw the red spots on Rikki's cheekbones, and
heard for the third time his opinion that Brazilian girls were
the hottest in bed, I decided it was time. A convenient lull
came. I said, "Sorted out your money problems, have you?"

His mouth twisted ruefully. "Not really. It's a bitch. I tell
you, Charlie. Never do business with a friend. I'm sorry
about last night—it got on top of me."

"Can't you borrow the money?"

He shook his head. "The only person I can borrow from is
my father, and the bastard won't give me a *centavo*!"

"I might be able to help you."

He was lighting a cigarette. His blue eye, faintly reddened
by bourbon, bulged up at me through the smoke. "Help me?"

"How much do you owe?"

"Two thousand US."

I tried to look like this was a mere bauble, a drop in my
financial ocean. Deep preconceptions ran in my favour: in
Colombia all gringos are assumed to be loaded unless proved
otherwise. "Two thousand," I murmured. I jotted a calcula-
tion on a paper napkin, playing it slow. "That's about £1,400
sterling." He shrugged impatiently: the days are gone when
pounds sterling mean much in South America. He was still
watching me. He was going to start pinching himself soon,
but just for the moment he liked this dream.

I looked him in the face. "And . . . your job. When do you start, did you say?" Next month, he said. "And you could repay me . . . ?"

"Right away," he said, with a magnanimous spread of his palms. "No problem, Charlie. I get three months' salary in advance." I guessed he was lying, but that was the least of my worries. "It's strictly short-term, Charlie. It's just for my friend. He needs the money real bad. Someone is treading on his heels for it. It's for Orlando I want to do it."

What a fine pair of philanthropists we were, I thought sourly. The girl in the sunglasses was leaving: I wasn't quite sure, but I think she winked at me. I said, with a sigh of decision, "I'll lend you the money, Rikki. For a friend. Of course you'll want cash. It'll have to be tomorrow. There's a man I know behind the Tequendama: he'll cash me in dollars. You'll have the bills by midday!"

Rikki closed his eyes, clenched his fist till the knuckles ran white. He gripped my arm, awash into sentiment. "Man," he said. "I can't believe it. You're so . . . Charlie, you're like a brother to me!" His face clouded for a moment. The unanswered question bobbed back into view. "You'll want interest of course?" he said. "What sort of percentage are you . . . ?"

I shook my head, smiling. "I don't need interest, Rikki."

"You don't?"

"No. Like I said, you're a friend. No, all I want is . . . to talk."

"Talk?" He laughed nervously. "Sure, Charlie. We'll talk. We'll have some drinks and we'll talk." He really was beginning to think he'd landed a prize one: a gringo throwing dollars around in exchange for *company*! He put his hand on my shoulder, shaking his head in amiable disbelief. "I *love* to talk," he cried.

The time was now. "Good," I said. "Well, let's begin by talking about Snow White."

His eyes flickered, a wince of unexpected pain. He shook his head, marshalled an effortful, empty smile. "You're shitting me, Charlie. I don't know what you mean. No, *hombre*.

Hey . . ." He trailed off, pale and reproachful. I knew I was right, and Gus was right. Snow White *wasn't* just a figment.

"I think you know exactly what I mean, Rikki."

"No, no."

"Snow White cocaine," I said quietly. "Your friend Orlando works for the syndicate they call Snow White. He's been giving you bits to sell on credit. Now they're calling in the checks. That's about it, isn't it?"

"Shit!" said Rikki, too loud. A couple of waiters looked over from the shiny chrome bar. "*Hijo de puta!* You some fucking narc?" He stood up, tipping his chair to the floor, took a last startled, angry look at me, and began to walk out. I skipped after him. A waiter from the bar and the big man who ruled the cash register moved too, anxious to remind us that we owed for six large bourbons. We all met in a huddle by the door. People were looking up from the tables. I grabbed Rikki's denim shirt. "You want the money, Rikki, or you want to walk out? It's up to you." He jerked his arm away angrily, but the big man was blocking the door and he hadn't anywhere to go. "It's all right, Rikki," I soothed. "Come and sit down. I'll explain."

We trooped back to our table, the big man returned to the till, the waiter brought us two more bourbons, and pointedly slapped the bill down on the table. I lit a cigarette and saw that my hand was trembling.

"I'm not a narc, Rikki," I explained gently. "I'm just an ordinary, nosy journalist. I know something about Snow White, and I want to know more. It's only a story, that's all."

Rikki shook his head. "You'll get us both killed. You don't know *nothing* about this!" He gulped at the bourbon. A little amber rivulet leaked down his clean-shaven chin.

"No one will know," I urged. "Just a few simple questions. Two thousand dollars, Rikki. *Moneda sonante*—cash in your claw!"

He sagged. He was beaten. I felt a surge of remorse. Buying someone's blood and running off without paying: how low could I get? The answer, had I but known it, was plenty lower.

"What do you want to know?" he asked sulkily, stabbing his swizzle-stick into our overflowing ashtray.

"The who, the how and the why," I said. Another of bloody Malcolm's blurb-phrases. Rikki snorted in disgust, and once again called me a son of a whore. Undeterred I said, "Let's start with who, shall we, Rikki? Who the hell is Snow White? Who runs this operation? Who's the Mr Big?"

It was a bad question to begin with, because it was the one he was least likely to be able to answer. He arranged himself into the full-dress Colombian shrug. "*Hombre*. How do I know? Look, you got me wrong. OK, I laid off an ounce here and there for Orlando. It was the best merchandise in town. But who's *running* this show? Look, Charlie, the big people, the *capos*—they don't have names, they don't have faces. And if they do, you forget them pretty damn quick. You remember that, *escritorzuelo!*"

"All right. We'll do an easier one. How do they operate? How does the pipeline work?" He was shaking his head, ready to play his dumb-card again. But I had a better card. "Look, Rikki. You told Dan Kreitman they were bringing 100 kilos a week into Bogotá, regular as clockwork. So I know you know about it."

This knocked Rikki back a bit. I could see his mind clicking: he must be thinking that Kreitman himself had marked my card. "*Carne*," he said in a tired, flat voice.

"Meat? What do you mean, meat?"

"That's the cover, Charlie, all down the line." He lit a cigarette and leaned closer across the table. At last we were getting somewhere. "They've got a big, big cattle ranch. Hacienda Alaska. Thousands of hectares, down in the *llanos*, Meta department. The *pasta* comes in by river-boat somewhere near Leticia. The *pasta* is the very best, made from Bolivian leaves, Huanaco coca from the Yungas. Then it's flown up to Hacienda Alaska. That's where the processing is done. The chief cook is a German, a very brilliant chemist.

Snow White stuff is the best, Charlie. *De primera calidad*: pharmaceutical strength, but natural *perica*. Then they bring it up to Bogotá in cattle trucks. There's cattle coming up from the *llanos* all the time. They've got a fleet of a dozen trucks: thirty, forty head of cattle in each, and a couple of sacks of Snow White cocaine."

There was a break in the musak. Rikki stopped, looked around nervously. A new record was put on: daddy-cool disco music this time.

"So where does it come in?" I asked, anxious to keep him flowing.

"Matadero San Felipe. It's a slaughter-house up in the north of the city. That's the drop."

"Then what happens?"

"It's very neat. The stuff comes in with the cows and it goes out with the meat. Refrigerated trucks, frozen beef, lot of legal snow and ice to hide it in. I don't exactly know how it's done, but that's the general idea."

"So that's how they export it, hidden in with frozen meat?"

"I think so. Look, Charlie. I'm just going on things Orlando told me. Jesus, if he ever knows about this, I'll . . ."

"Don't worry, Rikki. I've told you: no one's going to know anything."

How did they organize the distribution in Bogotá itself, I asked. He shook his head. "*Quién sabe?* I think they've got some meat wholesaling scam. That's just a guess. Christ, Charlie: you need a goddamn crystal ball, you do."

That really was it. I tried to get some names out of him—I knew there must be some kind of company cover: meat transporters, wholesalers, exporters, whatever. But if he knew he wasn't saying. I had scraped the bottom of his barrel. All this lying for a few jottings on a paper napkin . . .

I wouldn't be writing this now if I hadn't had a bit of luck every now and then. That night I was lucky because I wouldn't have learnt a thing about Snow White if I'd waited even ten more minutes before stinging Rikki. We were having a last, consoling drink before parting. I had given Rikki the $100 bill I usually carried, separate from my pesos, for emergencies. I was renewing my empty promises to pay him the rest the next morning. The muffled cries of my conscience, gagged and bound in some cerebral cupboard, grew louder. Then I saw two men out on the sidewalk, now dark, looking in through the plate-glass frontage of the bar. They were cupping their hands against their faces to look in. Their breath misted the glass, but didn't obscure the fact that they were staring straight at Rikki and me.

Rikki followed my gaze. He stumbled to his feet, muttering half to himself, half to the face in the window. "Orlando!" They were coming through the door now. Rikki twisted back at me fiercely. "You keep your fucking mouth shut!" he hissed. And then he was going towards them, hand out, "Orlando, *qué tal, amigo!*" I quickly slipped the paper napkin in my pocket.

Orlando was sleek and smooth. He wore a camel-hair overcoat over his shoulders, an open-neck white shirt gleaming beneath it. He had tight ringlets of black hair, coffee-coloured skin, Gucci shoes and a gold bangle on his wrist. He looked like a million dollars, every one of them blue. Here at last was the cocaine racket in its finery: up to now, I realized, I had seen only the victims, the losers, the small-time crap-flies who buzzed round the back end of the racket. The man with him was more sinister: fat, shiny, slant-eyed, a Guajiro perhaps. He wore a sky-blue linen suit, expensive too, but creased at the crotch and grubbied at the pockets. His black spiky hair was cut short.

On the surface things seemed amicable enough. Rikki introduced me as "a friend of Dani's." Orlando flashed a smooth, casino-night smile as we shook hands. Rikki didn't seem to know the other one, and Orlando didn't introduce us. I made to shake hands, but he just nodded. I felt the hooded inscrutable eyes case me for a moment. He looked like Oddjob, the Oriental heavy in the James Bond story, *Goldfinger*. He looked like he could damage people in quiet, special ways. I thought of Gus up a dead-end alley in Per-

severancia. My mind raced. Could they know? Did it somehow show? Would Rikki tell them? I slid my hand into my
jacket pocket and balled the napkin tight in my fist.

"We'd like a word, Rikki," said Orlando, smiling again.
That smile was like a part of his wardrobe.

"I was just going," I said, getting to my feet too fast, clicking my fingers for the waiter, fumbling for pesos to pay the
bill. Orlando laid a hand lightly on my shoulder: a whiff of
cologne, a thousand-dollar emerald on his ring-finger.

"*Tranquilo, señor.* Finish your drink. Rikki's coming with
us." The smile widened. "We're going to a party. Isn't that
right, Rikki?" Rikki nodded. I glanced at him. It was hard to
gauge his reaction. He looked pretty shell-shocked. Oddjob
looked on silently, with an eye trained to spot trouble before
it starts to get troublesome.

Rikki obediently gathered his cigarettes and prepared to
leave. He said to me—casually, but with a meaningful
glance—"We'll meet here at midday tomorrow, then?" I nodded dumbly. The Confucian eye of Oddjob seemed to know
all my secrets. Goodbyes were said, Orlando's with practised
charm, Rikki's with another warning glance, Oddjob's with
the merest nod, a momentary rearrangement of eyebrows and
chins. I watched them leave, Orlando leading, Oddjob bringing up the rear, bullet head squatting motionless on an expanse of sky-blue shoulder.

I let myself sit absolutely still for a moment, then I paid
the bill and walked to the door. I could see them across the
street, climbing into a white Mercedes. Oddjob eased the car
off the kerb and into the fast-moving southbound traffic.

I was still standing there a couple of minutes later, feeling
the cool air on my face, when Daniela came up. She was
breathless from running. "Charlie!" she said in surprise.
Then: "Is Rikki here with you? The maid said he left to meet
a friend here. I thought it was Orlando." I told her Rikki had
just gone, with Orlando and his ape. "Shit!" said Daniela.

"He's going to be all right, isn't he? I didn't like the look
of Orlando's friend much."

"I hope so. I mean, Orlando's an old friend, but . . .

That's it, you see. I wanted to tell them. I've persuaded Papa—it took some doing. He's going to bail Rikki out one last time. You know, that money business?"

I stared at her. So Rikki the weasel was going to get his money after all. "I'm so happy," I said in relief.

She laughed, her face cocked prettily. "You're a funny guy," she said. "I really didn't think you liked Rikki much last night."

13

ONE *ARROBA* OVER
THE TOP

Gus McGregor was on the mend. His leg was still heavily
bandaged but he was moving around more freely. His half-
grown ginger beard wasn't exactly glamorous, but it helped to
hide the chunky brown scabs down his face. He seemed
calmer, too. He had even ventured down the street a couple
of times to make phone calls at the bar on the corner. He
was just about ready, as he put it, to come out of quarantine.

"I tried to get in touch with you," he said. "The hotel said
you'd checked out suddenly one evening. Something about
. . . Lola, was it? Chasing tail, matey?"

"Sorry about that, Gus. Took a trip upcountry for a few
days. I didn't mean to leave you in the lurch or anything."

He held up a hand. The *sucito* stain on his thumb was like
a bright yellow blister. "Not a word, chum. You didn't come
all this way to do VSO on me. Just wanted to see how you
were getting on, that's all."

"Well, as a matter of fact, Gus, I've been getting on rather
well. I've got some dope on Snow White for you."

His eyes narrowed. "Good boy," he breathed. "Let's have
it."

I told him about Rikki and what he'd told me: the processing plant at Hacienda Alaska, the drop at the San Felipe
slaughter-house, the frozen meat export cover. He listened

intently. "Meat," he said steelily. "I was right. It *was* a bloody butcher's knife that bastard tried to rearrange me with."

Gus was pleased but he was also frustrated. If only I'd been able to get a name, a company, something to get the teeth into. "So what's our next move?" he asked himself quietly.

I felt it was time to tell him. "Look, sorry, Gus. I came to tell you this, but also I came to say goodbye. I'm driving up to the coast in a couple of days' time with some friends."

He looked aghast. "You don't mean you're dropping it? You're not walking out on this story *now*, are you? Look, we're three-quarters of the way there, but three-quarters of a story makes sweet fuck all. Nothing will come of nothing. Think again, Charlie, old cock."

"Well, I'm not quite sure what . . . I'm certain Rikki's told me everything. Anyway, I feel pretty bad about promising him all that money."

Gus swept this away with a fierce backhander of irritation. "Professional necessity, mate. Hack's honour. Absolutely un-avoidable."

"So what do you suggest?"

There was a baleful pause. He shook his head at me. He slapped himself playfully on the cheek to check he wasn't dreaming. "Christ," he said. "It's obvious, isn't it? You get your arse up to the Matadero San Felipe, and do some sniffing around!"

"But I told you," I protested, "I'm leaving for the coast."

"When are you going?"

"Friday."

"So? It's only—well, what day is it today, in fact?"

"Tuesday," I admitted.

"Exactly," he said, triumphantly. He was delving through the Who's Who now, clawing up heaps of dog-eared paper. I stood watching in dismay. An aircraft droned effortfully over-head.

"Christ, Gus. It's a slaughter-house. What could I possibly find there?"

He wasn't listening. "Gotcha!" he said, drawing out a sheaf of pale, low-grade photocopies. They were pages from some kind of trade directory. He ran a black-nailed finger down the list. "Here we go. This should about do it. FCPC. Colombian Meat Producers' Federation." He circled the address and phone number and handed me the page.

"I really don't think so, Gus. I *really*, really don't think so."

The San Felipe slaughter-house lay behind a supermarket in the nebulous northern outskirts of Bogotá, where the city laps around the old outlying villages of Suba and Nissa, depositing its flotsam of shopping malls and housing projects on the high green savannah. I presented myself at the gates and said I wished to see Señor Santander Gomez Cuartas, Junior Vice-Superintendent of the slaughter-house.

Getting this far had indeed been easy enough. A visit to the offices of the Colombian Meat Producers' Federation had secured, along with reams of information and statistics about the meat trade, the name of Señor Gomez. As Jefe de Relaciones Públicas at the slaughter-house, he was the official unfortunate delegated to deal with occasional visiting nuisances like myself. I flourished my business card at the security man. This describes me as a "consultant researcher," with a Mickey Mouse company address and telex number underneath, a useful tool in the nose-poking trade. Judging from the security man's blank gaze it might just as well have described me as an Egyptian rope-dancer, but the general effect was enough. He telephoned through to Gomez and told him he had a visitor at the front gate.

Presently Gomez appeared, a small, worried man with a goatee beard. He wore a white coat with splashes of blood on it, and carried another over his arm. Oozing plausibility, I explained my mission. I was compiling a "business opportunities" report on Colombia, was very interested in the meat business, had your name from Señor So-and-so at the Federacíon, and would be most grateful—esteemed *señor*—to be shown around this major meat-processing plant of yours. He said he would show me round with pleasure. He gave me the white coat to put on, and I was in. If Rikki was right, this was where the Snow White pipeline disgorged 100 kilos of cocaine a week. I didn't quite know what I was looking for, but surely something must show. I noted the trucks parked at one end of the abattoir, dusty flat-bed trucks and larger covered lorries that brought the cattle up from the lowland grazing plains of the east. There must have been thirty or forty trucks there. How to spot a few sacks of coke?

The job in hand, however, was my guided tour of the slaughter-house. I wasn't looking forward to this. We watched the cattle being herded into the corrals behind the abattoir. Most of them were *cebú* oxen—big, placid, humped, white beasts, South American versions of the Brahmin Ox, though unfortunately for them not sharing their Hindu cousins' immunity from slaughter. Gomez rubbed his hands and said that a stout, well-covered *cebú* bullock was worth upwards of 30,000 pesos. Each of these big fellows would weigh about 500 kilos and yield over half that weight in meat and assorted offals. Meat is measured in the traditional unit of *arrobas*—12.5 kilos—and a good animal is always said to yield *una arroba mas*, one *arroba* more than half its body weight.

As we walked round the back of the corrals, Gomez stopped. Gesturing me to follow him, he walked over to a group of three men standing round a station-wagon. A fourth was sitting in the opened back, pulling on a pair of rubber boots. Gomez introduced me to a tall, lugubrious man, the *matadero*'s Senior Vice-Superintendent, and to the young, bearded manager of the Cafam supermarket next to the abattoir. Small-talk was exchanged. Sixty million kilos of beef left the slaughter-house every year, I learned.

The small, elderly man in the back of the station-wagon was discussing something with a white-coated official—instructing him, it seemed, for now the official said, "Yes, *señor*, right away," and hurried off, checking his watch like

the White Rabbit. Gomez promptly launched into obse-
quious greetings. "What a pleasure it is to see you, Don
Rafael," he cried, ducking and bobbing like a courtier. He
plucked fussily at my sleeve. "May I present to you Señor
Rafael Vallejo Aragon? He is one of our most distinguished
and successful figures in the meat business."

The small man took this heralding as no more than his
due. He wore a smart tweedy suit, check shirt, heathery
woollen tie. His rubber boots were brand new: blue with
bright yellow soles. The whole gave a careful effect of well-
breeched country gent. He stood to shake hands. The palm
was hard and calloused, the figure beneath the squire's tweeds
stocky and powerful. He hadn't been born distinguished, I
guessed.

I fired in a couple of polite questions about his meat interests. His answers were vague and grand. He soon turned to
the others to discuss beef matters. Gomez hung in for a bit,
larded Vallejo with more compliments, then said, "We must
leave you, Don Rafael, you are a busy man." Vallejo said to
me, with mechanical largesse, "You must come to my stud-
farm in Cundinamarca one day, señor. I will tell you everything about the meat business in Colombia." He laughed a
gravelly laugh. "The meat business is very good. We are a
nation of carnivores!" He made a grimace, gnashed his teeth
comically. The others laughed fulsomely. Gomez cried, "It is
true, Don Rafael, it is true!" Vallejo frowned for a moment.
"In England you have these"—he searched for the word, and
spoke it with distaste—"vegetarianos. Not in Colombia. It is
not natural. For rabbits, maybe." There was a sudden bully-
ing note in his voice. He covered it with a loud, false laugh,
echoed once more by the entourage. Gomez writhed with
delight, but I saw his eyes flick over to me to see how I was
taking this slur on my homeland. I thought of making some
smart-ass riposte, but the odds were against me. For a moment, though, I found myself staring straight into the little
man's hard grey eyes.

"He's an important man, then?" I said to Gomez as we
walked on.

"*Millonario!*" whispered Gomez, pouting with pleasure at the thought.

From a raised walkway we could view the entire corral. In the corner was a pen with a few steers lying awkwardly, some moving and struggling. These animals, immobilized by sickness or injury, would be dispatched *in situ*. All the other animals were progressing, hour by hour, pen by pen, towards the *corriente*, the narrow black-railed ramp that led up into the abattoir proper. There a man in white overalls and a safety helmet prodded them up, in single file, with an electric goad wired up to a live overhead cable. The ramp led to an opening, with steel half-doors, like saloon doors in a Western. The patient oxen plodded up. The leading one glimpsed the scene inside, beyond the steel doors. If there is a bovine notion of hell, this was surely it. It skidded back, but the animals behind blocked its retreat, and the prod goaded it on.

Without really meaning to, I said, "He doesn't want to go in."

Gomez laughed, as if I had made some polite little joke. "It is sad, isn't it?" he said, unconvincingly. We walked on into the *matadero*, the killing place.

Just inside those swing doors, the steer came into a square well, about 20 feet long. A man stood high above it, wielding a long steel pole with a sharp spike at the end, like an elongated ski-stick. As the animal was released into the well, he held the *pica* vertical above him, two-handed, and brought it down in a swift, hard jab into the steer's neck, just behind the horns. The animal fell, stunned and helpless, eyes lolling, legs cavorting crazily. Another worker now nipped down into the well and slipped a heavy chain loop around its left hindleg. This was a deft operation, with half a ton of flesh and bones thrashing about on the floor. A third man, up on a level with the *picador*, pressed a button. The hoist clanked into action, winching the beast up, upside down. It hung swaying from the overhead rail. This rail ran on circuitously, like a ghost train, through the various departments of the slaughter-house. With a brisk, practised slash the man next to the *picador* cut the upended animal's throat. Blood poured out like water from a pail, thick crimson blood, splashing and steaming on the wet concrete floor. The next man sliced off the head and feet, a surprisingly easy operation with those big, scoured knives. The whole process, from living creature to headless carcass, took no more than half a minute. At the San Felipe slaughter-house 800 to 1,000 cattle are dispatched every day. When the darkness comes they switch on floodlights over the corrals, and the sacrifice continues.

The carcass continued along the overhead rail till it came to the skinners. Skinning is done with a kind of modified chain-saw. This sliced up the belly, and a hook was then passed through the skin at the back, and the chain-winch pulled upwards, bringing the whole hide with it. The skin was stretchy and pink on the inside, peeling off like a long pale glove. The guts piled out: strange coils and tubes, white, red and blue. The skins were carted off in one direction, the guts in another. In another room they were sorting great vats of the stuff—*viscera roja*, the offal; *viscera blanca*, the intestines, paunch, etc. Nothing will be wasted. The carcass now looked like a recognizable piece of butchers' meat, and off it went along the rail to the other half of the *matadero*, to be packed whole into cold-store trucks, or chopped and packaged ready for the butchers, restaurants, roadhouses and kitchens of this nation of carnivores.

Gomez was at my shoulder throughout, explaining it all, casual and precise, like Mephistopheles giving a guided tour of the inferno. When he judged I had seen enough, he took me to his office, up a few steps behind the gut room. When he closed the door I realized what a huge din had filled the slaughter-house. The whole gory business had made such an impact on my eyes that I had hardly noticed the noise. I felt sick and tired. I saw my knuckles whiten as I leant on the metal desk. There was a pile of S-shaped hooks and a wooden-handled knife sharpener in the in-tray.

Looking out of the barred window on to a small, enclosed
yard outside, I saw two men talking. One was the little meat
baron, Rafael Vallejo. He had his back to me, but the tweed
jacket and the white hair were unmistakable. The other was
the white-coated minion he had been talking to when I first
saw him. I watched with idle curiosity. Gomez was hunting
out some statistics for me, tetchily complaining of the lack of
a secretary to keep his papers in order. I heard a door opening into the yard. Vallejo turned. Another white-coated figure came into view, from some room next to Gomez's office.
There was something vaguely troubling about his back view.
The broad, slightly hunched shoulders, the square head of
spiky black hair. I had seen it before. With a jolt, I realized.
I had seen it walking out of The Place a couple of nights
earlier, clad in sky-blue. It was Oddjob.

Rikki was right, Snow White was real, and I was right slap
in the middle of it. Under no circumstances must Oddjob see
me here. He did not look like a man who had much time for
funny coincidences. I shrank back, grateful for the grimy film
over the window.

Gomez had found the figures, the annual tonnages and
percentage breakdowns so vital for my study of the meat business. He brought a few folders over to the desk and began to
drone out the data. I mechanically wrote as he spoke, but all
the while I was keeping an eye on the trio out in the yard.
Vallejo was talking, with jabbed gestures of emphasis. Oddjob was listening, head still, occasional sulky monosyllables
of agreement. The more I watched, the cosier it looked.
Could it be possible? Had I stumbled right up the ladder all
at once? Vallejo was no small-time spiv. If that was cocaine
talk going on in that yard, then the distinguished millionaire
and carnivore Don Rafael was something pretty big. The sun
glinted on his white hair. Was he the *capo*? Was he Snow
White himself?

In a pause between statistics, trying to sound casual, I said,
"Look, there's Señor Vallejo again. He does a lot of business
here, does he?"

"Oh yes. He has many cattle ranches in the *llanos*. We handle all his stock."

"And the meat itself? He had distribution networks, that sort of thing?"

"Of course. Transcarne. One of the biggest meat transportation companies in Colombia."

It was all falling into place. Out in the yard there was just Vallejo and Oddjob now. The third man had left. Oddjob's sleazy, slant-eyed, tom-cat's face was half-turned towards me. He was talking, with choppy, robotic gestures from his big paws. It was the first time I'd seen him utter a word. "Who's that Vallejo's talking to?" I asked.

Gomez had his glasses off for reading the figures and now had to fumble them out of his white coat. "That? Oh, that's one of our packing managers."

Somewhere a siren shrilled. Gomez looked at his watch, closed his folders. "Midday," he announced. "The end of the morning shift. You would like a beer?"

As in all the comedies, the booze was in the First Aid cabinet. He took out two bottles and two glasses. Vallejo and Oddjob were still conferring, but with a hasty, last-minute air now. Gomez was washing the glasses in a hand-basin. No: the glasses were on the desk—Gomez was washing two *more* glasses. He was walking to the door that led out into the yard. It opened with a squawk of metal on the stone floor. The two men outside wheeled round. Gomez bobbed in the doorway. "Don Rafael! Rodolfo! You will take a beer with us?" A curt wave from Vallejo, "How kind, Señor Gomez." A nod of assent from Oddjob, a.k.a. Rodolfo. Gomez fussed happily back into the room, polishing a glass on his coat-tail. "We will have a party," he chirped.

Fear is blank. Brain dazzled, body frozen, a rabbit caught in the headlights. I heard the fizz of beer, the thin clatter of bottle-tops on the metal desk. You bloody idiot, I thought. You've really done it this time. Vallejo was walking slowly towards us, still talking. Oddjob glided resentfully beside him. In a few seconds he would be here. He would recognize me, he would start asking questions, he would go on asking till he didn't need any more answers. Then he would probably hook me up on the overhead rail and loosen my guts with one of those skinning-saws.

There was only one way out: back into the slaughter-house. I hunched up, hand to my mouth, and blurted, "*Estoy enfermo! Voy a vomitar!*" Vallejo had just stepped in through the door as I rushed out of the office. The last thing I saw was Gomez's startled face, and the beer spilling past the glass as he looked up from pouring.

I sprinted down the steps, back into the mayhem of the killing-floor, through the gut-room, slowing to a trot, trying not to attract attention. I kept my hand over my mouth, so everyone would think the gringo *maricón* couldn't handle all the blood and death. I heard Gomez's voice behind me. "Señor Nee-col, this way! Not there, *señor!*" I dodged down a corridor, passed through an empty room with a long line of severed calves' feet dangling from chains, crossed a yard, and came into what was evidently the pig section of the *matadero*. There were squeals without, but in this room all was quiet. A man in a rubber apron was thoughtfully prodding a few dead porkers in a vat of hot water. Another, wearing a cap with a cloth down the back of his head like a legionnaire's képi, was scraping the hairs off a strung carcass. I slowed to a walk. White coat on, notebook in hand, just an official on his way from this door to that.

I came out into another yard. Pigs milling in slatted stalls, but no one around that I could see. I tried to get some bearings. There was a sort of fenced runway through which the pigs were herded into the stalls. Beyond it I saw trucks and cars parked: the back of the *matadero*, I reckoned, the opposite side from the one I'd come in at. If I could just get myself out through some back gate. I edged along the side of the stalls and was just about to break cover when I heard footsteps and voices. I shrank back, but I was still in full view if they came into the yard. The stall nearest me was empty. I clambered over the side and dropped silently into a rich mulch of straw and pig-shit. A few inches from my face, in the neighbouring stall, a dozen fear-crazed pigs bumped and snuffled against the slats. I crouched shivering while the voices passed.

Skulking at the edge of the truck park I saw that there was indeed a rear gate. A few yards away a man was closing up the back of an old flat-bed truck. He wore blue overalls and a battered straw hat: a pig-man, I supposed. He climbed into the cab and started the engine. He'll do, I thought. I stripped off my dung-smeared white coat, dumped it in a corner and trotted briskly up to the truck. "Excuse me, *señor*. Are you going? Can you give me a lift?"

The pig-man surveyed me, chewing on a toothpick. I was breathing heavily: fear at high altitude. There was muck on my hands, my tie, my notebook. He ran a hand over his grey stubble, amiable and puzzled. I tensed with impatience. Then he nodded slowly, and said something in a rich *campesino* brogue. It sounded like "I'm going to Zoggo."

"That'll do nicely," I said, and climbed up into the cab. He smiled a broad, toothless smile, fished out a crumpled pack of Pielroja, and offered me a cigarette. I fumbled for matches, trying to speed everything up. Any moment now Gomez and Oddjob were going to come round the corner and start the hue and cry. "My car won't start," I said. "I'm terribly late." He shook his head philosophically and said something else I couldn't understand. Lateness was not a concept that meant much to him. At last, clamping the cigarette in his mouth, he eased the pick-up into gear. The truck chugged off lazily down along the red-brick back of the *matadero*. My eyes darted around, looking for the familiar little-and-large figures. The truck seemed to be firing on about half a cylinder. Optimum speed was reached at 5 miles an hour. The pig-man slumped comfortably in his seat, elbow resting on the window. Jesus, I thought, jiggling futilely, I've picked a real winner here.

I regretted my move even more when we reached the roadway, and instead of turning towards the rear gate he swung the truck right, heading for the front of the *matadero*. This brought us right into the central thoroughfare: offices, canteen, lunch-hour crowds of white-coats, slaughterers, truckers. Almost immediately I spotted Gomez, talking to a security-looking man in a peaked cap. He was tugging at his little beard, puzzling away at the mystery of the vanishing journalist. Then, off to one side, I saw Oddjob, silently watching, his fat brown face ranging slowly round like a radar-dish. From where he stood he could see both exits from the *matadero*. He was waiting for me to break cover. He was bound to see me as we passed.

We chugged serenely to my doom. I squeezed my hands in mute supplication. In doing so I felt the box of matches still cradled in my sweating palm. With a swift, purposeful movement I spilt the contents on to the rusty floor at my feet. "*Maldita sea,*" I cursed, "how clumsy," and bent myself double to retrieve them. In this position, I fervently hoped, I was just out of view below the line of the window. "It's all right, *señor*, I have matches," said the pig-man. "No, no," I called up from my jack-knife position. "I'll get them." He shrugged. The truck hiccoughed on towards the gate. I scrabbled in the dust for the little waxy white matches. With this meagre camouflage I passed beneath and beyond the gaze of Oddjob.

When the truck stopped I straightened up, thinking we were at the gates. But we were still a good 20 yards short of them. The pig-man had stopped to talk to someone, another *campesino*, another crumpled hat. It was going to be one of those slow, mulled conversations full of pauses.

Craning round, I saw Gomez and the peaked-cap fellow walking purposefully up the roadway towards us. Clearly they were coming up to the gate. They were going to warn the security guard: a mad Englishman on the loose. The pig-man was talking about the price of pork, warming to his theme. I heard again the butcher's phrase Gomez had used, "*una arroba mas.*"

Oh yes, we're all after that little bit extra, that one *arroba* over the top. Only sometimes it costs us more than we can pay.

It was now or never. "Thanks for the ride," I said, and jumped out of the cab. The truck shielded me from Gomez. Those 20 yards to the gate were a fast walk through eternity. I waited for the shout behind me but none came. As I passed through the gate the security man waved. I saw him jot something down on a clip-board. One consultant researcher, business done, leaves the slaughter-house. He must be a busy man. Look how he's running . . .

14

MEDELLÍN

Back at the Cuadros's house, sipping tea, courting forget-fulness. When I walked in little Sam said, "Pooh! You pong." Now I had showered off the pig-shit, and the maid, a fourteen-year-old Boyacense girl named Maria Elena, had taken my soiled clothes away to wash. Everything was set for our departure for the coast the following morning. Lola's husband—mustachioed, practical, New England-born Luke—had slept off his jet-lag. Her brother Alberto was winding up his business affairs. I was feeling better already.

The phone rang. Lola said, "It's for you, Charlie." I guessed it was Gus: I had given him the number. I took the phone into another room.

"Mate?" said the familiar voice at the other end.

"OK, Gus, listen. There's a meat magnate by the name of Rafael Vall—"

"Forget it. We've got problems."

"Problems? Damn right. I nearly got my balls chopped off up at the *matadero.*"

"I'm at the airport." The idea of Gus being anywhere but in his moth-eaten old armchair at the crow's nest was star-tling. What had happened, I asked. "They've got to Julio Cesar," he said. "I knew it. They don't give up, they just wait till your sweat starts to cool. He managed to flannel them, said he thought I'd run off back to Europe, but it's only a question of time before they come knocking on the door."

"So where are you going?"

"That's just it, mate. I'm not going anywhere at present."

"No money," I said dully.

"Can you meet me? I'll be in the cafeteria. Green carnation in my buttonhole." He rang off.

Another taxi, through the darkening streets to Eldorado airport. Gus was there, in a creased navy blue suit shiny with use. The only luggage he had with him was the box containing the Who's Who. He was looking very jumpy, an alien figure among the black plastic and potted palms. "Thank Christ," he said. "Look, there's a flight leaves for Medellín in an hour. Can you stand me the ticket money?"

"Why Medellín?"

"I've got friends there," he said. "Also, I need to see a doctor, get some penicillin up my bum. My leg's got worse again, some infection I think. Just can't do it here in Bogotá. Bad climate, if you know what I mean." He broke off to survey a couple of new arrivals in the cafeteria. "There's someone else I want to see there too," he continued. "I'll tell you about him. But first, get me that ticket, will you?"

As I went off to the Avianca counter, he called me back. "Not McGregor, of course. Don't get the ticket in my name. You can never be quite sure who's talking to who round here. Any gringo name will do. Internal flight: they don't check."

I came back with the ticket. I had got it in the name of Malcolm Goodman. He stuffed it into his jacket pocket. "Now, tell me what you learnt today." I told him about Vallejo, the big wheel, the man with the cattle-ranches and the transportation company, the man seen chatting cosily with the known hood Oddjob or Rodolfo. "It all fits, Gus. He's got the connections all the way down the line. I reckon he's our man, Mr. Snow White."

"Could be, chum, could be. You did well. There's some people call themselves journalists who couldn't write 'Fuck' on a dusty window." I glowed under the praise of Ace McGregor. He may have been crazy, but he was still the old pro. "On the other hand," he ruminated, "it could be nothing at all. I mean, Vallejo could have been there for totally legit reasons. And this Rodolfo is a packing manager there, you say, even if he's also a hood."

"Sure," I said. "But all you're doing there is swallowing their cover story whole. I'm sure I'm right, Gus."

"We need the evidence, mate. We need more if we're going to make this story stick. And that's where this bloke in Medellín comes in. He's a bit of a dodgy customer, but he knows me. We go back a long way." His eyes clouded with some reminiscence, but he shook it off. "The thing about him is, he knows everything there is to know about cocaine *money*. As you know, Medellín is the racketeers' financial centre. The banks are chock-a-block with dirty dollars, and the industrial sector. It's one bloody great money-laundry up there. Well, Eduardo knows it all. You say to him: Vallejo. You say to him: Transcarne. He'll tell you all their nasty little secrets."

A tannoy crackled in to announce the departure of the flight for Medellín. A few people rose from their tables. I got up, but Gus held my arm. "You really ought to meet this bloke, mate. In fact, come to think of it, for this book of yours you can't afford *not* to."

"Yes. Well, give me his name and number, and I'll see if I can look him up."

Gus screwed up his ginger-pale face. "Don't think he'd be too keen on that. I mean, a girl like Rosalita's one thing—I don't mind giving you a name or two. But this guy's in another league. He wouldn't like to think I'd been flashing my address book around with him in it. No, I've got a better idea. Why don't we meet up in Medellín?"

"For God's sake, Gus, I told you. I'm leaving for the coast tomorrow with my friends."

"'Course you are. So you'll be coming through Medellín anyway. No problem." He fished out a scrap of paper from his jacket, and scribbled something on it. He handed it to me: it said "El Ave Perdida," with a street number. "Look. I'll be there at . . . shall we say midday on Saturday? You'll probably be in Medellín by tomorrow night, but we'll say Saturday. Let you get your beauty sleep. Your friends can drop you in Medellín, we'll go and have a chat with Eduardo, and then you can take a plane or bus on up, and meet your friends on the coast."

"I don't know, Gus. It got pretty heavy at the slaughterhouse today. I feel like a change of scene."

"Medellín," he cried. "City of Eternal Spring. Orchids in the back garden. What could be better?" Another announcement for the flight. We got up. "It's up to you, Charlie. I'll be there. Little Eddie's got a lot of stories to tell, and maybe he'll give us the story about Snow White. You've put in some leg-work on this one. You've had the luck. Ride with it, old cock, ride with it!"

The pretty girl at the check-in said, "*Buenas tardes*, Señor Goodman." Gus said to me, "Nothing like a ripe little bod in a blue uniform, eh, mate?" The girl handed the ticket back. "You like my uniform?" she said in perfect English. Gus wheezed and twinkled.

We shook hands. "Thanks for your help," he said. "You're a scholar and a gent. See you Saturday."

Twenty minutes later, from the Observation Lounge, I watched the thin line of passengers crossing the windswept tarmac to the Avianca DC-10. Gus's stooped, threadbare figure stood 6 inches taller than anyone else. He held the thin lapels of his jacket across his throat. The ace journalist, the *éminence grise* of the Great Cocaine Story. With his limp and his precious cardboard box, he looked more like a wino queuing up for a bunk in the doss-house.

From Bogotá to Medellín is no great distance, about 350 miles, but in the Andes, where one is even less like a crow flying than usual, this means little. The mountains run up through central Colombia like some ridged prehistoric spine, three ranges running roughly north–south, divided by the valleys of the Magdalena and Cauca rivers. Bogotá stands over 8,000 feet up in the Eastern Cordillera, Medellín 5,000 feet up in the Central Cordillera, and the only way between them is down the side of one mountain and up the side of the other. Alberto reckoned twelve hours, now the new road

was nearly finished. Further north, he said, there are places a
finger's pinch apart on the map that can take you a day's
hard travelling to get between them.

Alberto was in his mid-thirties, the eldest of Lola's brothers. With the father dead, he ran the family firm, Con-
strucciones Cuadros, building suppliers and contractors. The
ingredients that made up Lola's exquisite face, and his handsome younger brothers', had somehow not worked with Alberto. He had big, exophthalmic eyes, and a round, droopy
face off which a wispy black moustache drooped further.
Artful whorls of hair failed to conceal his imminent baldness.
He was quiet-spoken, intelligent and humorous, and—when
he needed to be—as stubborn as a *cebú* ox. He was perennially in search of a suitable wife, though his particular penchant seemed to be for youth and nubility. If Alberto had
had his way he would have flown straight to Cartagena and
spent his whole holiday lounging on Bocagrande beach eyeing up the *sardinas*. But Luke and I were family guests, we
wanted to see something on the way, and the duties of hospitality far outweighed the prickings of the flesh.

At last we were off, Alberto at the wheel of the family
Renault. We came through Facavita in a rainstorm, a hard
little highland town, and down past looming pine forests.
There were quarries and cement plants belching black smoke
into the Andean air. Luke, ecological, complained. Alberto,
patriotic, praised the excellence of Colombian cement. The
road steepened downwards. Quite suddenly we came out of
the rain-cloud into a different world. On the Andean roller-
coaster it is the transitions which are so stunning. There is a
point—it always seems sudden—when the starker upland
scenery softens and luxuriates into subtropical forest. They
call these upper reaches of the forest *la ceja de la selva*, the
eyebrow of the forest. This is the classic South America:
steep, steamy and baroque, a landscape of half-glimpsed valleys and strange conical tumps, everything matted with
greenery and fringed with wispy mists. On cleared slopes
were neat glossy rows of coffee-bushes, and by the roadside
were fruitsellers, and boys waving green packages at us—

white cheese wrapped in banana leaves. With each straggling village we were more and more definitely in the hotlands. A wooden shack with a hand-painted sign, "CAFÉ ASÍ ES LA VIDA"—The That's The Way It Goes Café. A policeman picking his teeth on a verandah. Straw hats, mules, dust. The little huts and farmhouses seemed to be *made* out of dust.

We stopped at a *gaseosa* stall outside Villeta. We had peeled off our Bogotá woollies, but stepping out of the car the vicious heat brought sudden needles of sweat. An impassive, coffee-coloured man in a Panama hat served us, his big face looking out of a small hatch like a disconsolate rabbit. He made a separate journey into the back of the store for each bottle, spinning out the morning's solitary event.

Still we wound on down, dusty banks above, hazy vistas below. And there was the Magdalena river, the artery of Colombia, running a thousand miles from the *páramos* of southern Cauca to the Caribbean Sea, here already wide and lazy and turgid brown—

> *Para brindarle amplio regazo,*
> *Se abre como un inmensa hoja de tobaco*

—it offers its broad lap to you, opening like a giant tobacco leaf. We crossed at the old town of La Honda, the deep place, the bottom. Brown tumbling waterfront, brown dug-out boats, brown boys fishing off the rocks. It was the beginning of the *subienda*, when the river rises and brings its harvest of fish.

We followed the left bank for a while, then crossed again at the steel bridge at La Dorada. The road ran straight, thin and hot along the valley floor, up to Puerto Libre and Puerto Triunfo, tall grass and scrubland on either side, shacks selling fishing nets, occasional glimpses of the tawny river. Odd, pillared outcrops of rock looked like the badlands in old TV Westerns. Luke and I reminisced: how Pancho in *The Cisco Kid* said "Let's went!", how Bronco Lane always drank milk—or was it sarsaparilla?—in saloons, and what was it exactly that *kimo-sabe* meant? By 3 o'clock we were ravening for lunch. We had passed hundreds of roadhouses, but Alberto refused to stop. They were unhealthy, he said, *muy insanos.* An unexpected hotel, a *club campestre* near Doradil, finally fitted the bill. They were building a safari park there. The hotelier told us proudly how they were bringing kangaroos from Australia, leopards from Africa, mountain deer from Scotland. The place was quite empty. Alberto asked, wasn't it a bit far from anywhere? Who would come to it? "We are developing the area," said the hotelier vaguely. Later I learned that the whole complex was owned by Pablo Escobar, a big, Medellín-based cocaine *capo.* Just another off-loading of narco-dollars. As Gus had said, the whole country has got snow in the blood.

At Puerto Libre we crossed the state line into Antioquia. Soon we were climbing the steeply forested slopes of the Central Cordillera, Alberto still at the wheel, still hoping to reach Medellín by nightfall. This was the new road he had spoken of, cutting five or six hours off the previous route via Manizales. It zigzagged off above us, an ugly red-earth scar blasted up through the trees. It was still far from finished—pitted and treacherous, with many trucks and clouds of dust. We made slow progress. We passed gangs of shovel-men at work. Sometimes they shouted and whistled as we passed. Once, while we waited for a digger to do a twelve-point turn, a group of shovel-men came strolling over, and Alberto made us roll up all the windows, which made us feel like rats in a cage. "They want our beer," he said grittily. The men stared at us sullenly—understandably so, I thought. One of them spat pointedly on the ground. He was old, too old for this work, scrawny ribs glistening with sweat under a red rag of shirt. He looked full-blooded Indian. He was staring straight at me, muttering. I felt very uncomfortable. A couple of the other men wore scarves over their mouths, bandit-style. Sam was impressed by that.

The light grew softer and pearlier. The sun set theatrically over the valleys and gorges, and after what seemed like a two-minute twilight it was dark. With the darkness we found

ourselves in the road-workers' camp, a shanty-town of wood
and polythene straggling down from a bluff above the road.
The men were returning from the day's labours. Gypsy-like
women stood in groups. Hurricane lamps, meat smoke, root-
ing pigs, barefoot children in the mud: the whole thing
looked like a medieval battle-camp. Here Alberto made his
first mistake at the wheel. With the darkness, and the mêlée
of the camp's tracks, he momentarily missed the curve of the
road. Swerving too late, we slewed off and subsided into a
broad ditch. There was a nasty scraping sound beneath us as
we went. Alberto swore. The baby cried. The car wouldn't
start. Alberto beat his hands against the steering wheel. Sam
woke up on Luke's lap, rubbed his eyes, and said, "Why are
we stopping here, Uncle Alberto?" I opened the door and
sank into a foot of mud and detritus. The temperature had
dropped, the sweat on my shirt chilled me. Lola sat, unflap-
pable, giving her breast to the baby, while we sized up the
situation by torchlight. It did not look good. The front off-
side wheel was submerged in mud. A pile of rubble—the
scraping sound—now propped up the underside of the car, so
that the back wheels were jacked up a foot off the ground.

No one seemed to have noticed our predicament, or if
they had they weren't rushing forward with help. We were in
semi-darkness, outside the arc of the lamps and fires. A couple of children stared at us, but as I walked towards them
they ran away. Cars and trucks rolled past with an indifferent sweep of headlights. Luke stayed with the car and his family,
while Alberto and I set off into the camp, a nervous delega-
tion, to ask for help. The men looked tuckered out, sitting in
groups, passing hootch-bottles around. Alberto hailed a tall
young mulatto and explained our problem. He came over to
look at the car with us. He laughed, and wiped his brow with
a cloth round his neck. "I can sell you four mules," he said.
He came back presently with half a dozen men, one of them
a giant of a man in a check shirt bulging like a breastplate.
He looked like he could lift the car out with one hand.

In the event, it took a gruelling half hour in the mud to
get the car back on the road. The only way to tow it out of

the ditch was backwards, and to do this the rubble had to be removed from underneath it. We divided into two gangs, one holding up the back of the car, while the other scrabbled beneath to clear and level the pile of rubble. It was all quite jolly. More workers and camp-followers clustered around, with lights and shouts of jocular advice. The children were fêted, Lola was stared at. I heard the word "gringos" amid the general banter. Once the back-wheels were at last resting on something solid, ropes were fetched. At first we tried to pull the car out like a tug-of-war team, with the big fellow at the head, digging his boot-heel into the mud, but it was no use. Someone went off for a vehicle. Alberto handed round cans of beer. The man came back with a dumper truck. With a few wrenches and groans, the car stood on terra firma, dejected and caked with mud. There was a cheer from the crowd. People now began to drift away, the best part of the show being over. It took another while to get the car started, mainly due to mud in the distributor, and even when it did roar into life—another sporadic cheer—new problems arose in the form of a jet of water spouting from a rip in the radiator-casing. This proved little to tax the bottomless improvisational skills of the Colombian mechanic. Several packets of Chiclets were ordered to be purchased from the camp *tienda*. We solemnly stood around masticating sticks of gum, Sam in seventh heaven as he went from one flavour to the next, and as soon as each piece was wet and pliable, it was added to the communal pile. A wad of *fique* fibre was tamped into the hole in the radiator, and the chewing gum thumbed in around it as putty. The mechanic assured us this would hold for a few hours' driving, enough to get us to a garage in Medellín. We thanked them all profusely. Alberto made to offer them money, but with gruff grace they refused.

Just as we were finally piling into the car, I saw in the crowd, with a jolt of recognition, the old Indian shovel-man we had wound our windows up against a few hours before. He was staring at me now, just as he had stared at me then, only this time he had a half-smile on his face, which gave him the bearing of a malevolent monkey. I felt a flush of shame over me. We, the rich, had refused them; they, the poor, had helped us; a bare biblical moral with us as the ones who wouldn't get to heaven. And with the shame came a touch of fear in the night. There was a gleam in that shadowed face, which was a look of satisfied revenge. And then, seeing myself and the others sodden with mud and smirched with oil, I was suddenly glad that the shovel-man's curse had paid us out like this. I inclined my head to him, as if to say "*touché!*". He made no movement in answer.

It was still two to three hours to Medellín, they said. Elated to be on the move again, with nothing worse than a couple of new rattles in the car, we settled down for the last leg. But the road, bad enough by day, was murder by night. Alberto hunched over the wheel, eyes straining through the fog of dust that swirled in the headlights. The road snaked to and fro, now tarmac, now pressed earth, now skiddy loose stones. I consulted the road-map by torch, but it was useless. It had been printed before this new road was begun. At some point we must hit an existing road, or a village, but where and when—*quién sabe?* We were somewhere in the Central Cordillera, crawling along a dark road in second gear, hungry, tired and dirty. The signpost, when it eventually came, seemed quite appropriate—"El Santuario, 2 km."

The "sanctuary" turned out to be a bustling Antioqueño village. We found rooms at the Hotel El Castillo, a large, run-down old colonial house, with a flagged patio and a balcony. The rooms were small, partitioned off by thin wainscot panels topped with a grille of chicken-wire. Gnarled strands of cobweb and dust hung from the wire. Alberto was very displeased—this kind of place was not what he had planned at all—but the rest of us were happy to be anywhere. For my own part I have a deep, furtive love for the shabby one-night hotels of the Colombian hinterland. There was no water, but we washed ourselves down well enough from buckets, and at an eating house round the corner we ate massive platters of *bandeja antioqueña*, a catch-all dish of steak, eggs, kidney beans, plantains, rice, potatoes and the big chunks of pork scratchings called *chicharrones*.

We coasted into Medellín the following morning, in time
for a late breakfast. Coming over the pass it lay far below us,
a sprawling Lego city of skyscrapers and suburbs, on a saddle
of rock between the dark, saw-toothed mountains. At a roadhouse on the outskirts we ate eggs, *arepas* and hot chocolate.
To buy cigarettes I was directed across the road, to a half-
finished breeze-block *chozuela*. A sullen black woman answered my knock. Inside the shack I could see beds,
crumpled piles of clothing, a couple of children, and a pair of
feet, presumably papa's, poking off the end of a bed. The
room was windowless. The floor was made of earth. *This* was
poverty: not the hard, bare life of the mountains, not the
scruffy indolence of the tropics, but this nondescript struggle
on the littered verge of an urban through-road. She brought
me my few pesos' change. I told her to keep it. She shrugged.
The feet on the bed stirred and rubbed one another. Nothing
to wake early for. The children played in a silent, watchful,
listless way, like small animals in a zoo, creatures with no
horizon.

At the roadhouse I took directions for a bus into the centre. I said goodbye to my friends, with arrangements to meet
in Cartagena in a couple of days' time. One last bit of business with Gus and I would be up on the coast. Or so I
thought.

Of Medellín I remember little, except an absurd impression
that the city was full of one-legged men. Patient monoped
street vendors stood on corners. Beggars loped through the
streets on crutches, some carrying those officially stamped accounts, even grisly photo-montages, which explain how their
disability was incurred in a *bona fide* industrial accident, or
while serving in the armed forces of the republic. In reality,
Medellín is a brash, uncomplicated city, its origins—an early
seventeenth-century settlement of refugee Spanish Jews—
lost among office blocks, modern churches, well-laid parks
and brightly-lit cafeterias. It is Colombia's industrial second
city, the Birmingham or Chicago of the Andes. It produces
three-quarters of the country's textiles; has steel mills, chemi-

cal plants, cement works, machine shops; glass, paint, food, cigarette and liquor factories. All this, grafted on to deep-rooted coffee, cattle and land wealth, has made it a banking and financial centre—and, as Gus pointed out, a laundering centre for narco-dollars. It is also Colombia's gay city: its 45th Street is like South America's Earls Court Road on a Saturday night, a streetlight promenade of pretty boys, rough traders, drag queens and leather-clad crypto-Nazis. "Remember," grinned Alberto, "if you drop a peso in Medellín, don't bend down to pick it up." As I left he was floundering for some explanation of this, under close questioning from Sam.

I liked the feel of the place: it had none of the sombre, dark-eaved quality of Bogotá. People are often nicest in these ordinary, unlovely cities. They do not expect you to be here, it seems, and so they are pleased that you are.

I took a room in a tall, tenement hotel near the bus terminals, and at quarter to midday I was sitting over a glass of brown Medellín rum, in the bar curiously named El Ave Perdida, the Lost Bird, waiting for Gus.

He arrived on the dot of midday. The moment I saw him I knew there was something wrong. He brought trouble into the bar like a smell. He was breathing fast and his limp seemed to be worse than before. He carried the Who's Who in one hand, and a rather smart blue plastic sports bag in the other. When he saw me he threaded through the bar in a hunched, low-profile way, as inconspicuous as a six-foot, ginger-haired gringo could get.

"Knew you'd be here," he gasped. He slumped into the chair next to me, stretching his damaged leg out straight, wincing. I saw a darker stain on the dark blue trouser leg. I raised my hand to call the waiter—a drink first, then the questions—but he grabbed my wrist back down to the table. "No time," he said. He looked under the table. "Where are your things?" I told him. "Let's go," he said.

"Where are we going? Are we going to meet Eduardo?"

"Tell you about it back at the hotel."

Outside the sun had broken through. The air was balmy—

that temperate "eternal spring" that the tourist brochures tell of. Office girls eating French-stick sandwiches in the Parque Bolívar, a folk-band playing Peruvian music, flower-sellers. Gus hobbled along, a trainee in Medellín one-leggedness. I carried the blue sports bag for him. It felt light, almost empty, but I could feel something sliding around in the bottom. I offered to carry the much heavier cardboard box. "No, no," he insisted, "you take the bag."

At the hotel the *señora* said, "No guests." I was even more surprised than she was when Gus pulled out a wedge of 1,000-peso bills. He slapped one down on the counter. She tried to pick it up, but his grubby fingers pressed it flat on the surface. "*Nunca me viste,*" he said softly. You never even saw me. The *señora* smiled reassuringly. "*Nunca, señor,*" she said. "There are no gringos here," she added, glancing significantly at me, in the hopes that I too was buying anonymity. She took Gus's bill, folded it up thin and slipped it under her watch-strap.

My room was on the second floor. There was no sight or sound of any other guests up here. A small barred window stared out at a blank grey wall opposite. Gus seemed to approve. He threw his carton down with a thud and sank gingerly on to the bed.

"OK, Gus," I said wearily. "What's the story this time?" He was rolling up his trouser leg. I winced as I saw the blood-soaked bandage. "For God's sake, what happened?"

"I fell," he said.

"Oh, sure."

"It's true," he cried. "Cub's honour." He stretched the leg out on the bed, smearing blood on the rough white ticking. Propped up against the wall, he began to rummage in his pockets, piling the contents on to the bed between his legs. My eyes widened as he brought out handfuls of crumpled paper money: pesos, dollars, even Venezuelan bolivars. They were all high denomination bills. I began to feel very nervous, and a little angry. "What the hell is going on, Gus? Where did you get this stuff?"

"Bit of a sorry story, mate, but needs must. I went to see

friend Eduardo this morning, at his apartment, very swish, up near the Union Club. And, well, to cut a long story short, there it was. All this loot, bloody oodles of it, stacked up in his office. I saw it through the door when I first walked in. So we're out on his balcony, taking *tinto*, having a chat. The phone rings. While he's on the phone, I say: 'Excuse me, Eduardo, where's the *baño?*' I nipped into his office, grabbed as much as I could get in my pockets, and split. It was Saturday morning, see. No one else around. I was going like a bitch down the stairs—he was up on the fifth floor—and I fell. That's how I buggered my leg again."

I stared at him. The eternal spring seemed to have turned into tropical summer. I tried to open the window, but it wouldn't budge. "This guy Eduardo," I said, trying to keep my voice calm, "he's a . . . cocaine financier, money launderer . . . right?"

"Well, sort of. He's into all sorts of dodges."

"But this could well be mafia money you've got here?"

"I told you, mate. There was enough money to buy an oilfield in there. This was just a skimming."

"How much have you got?"

"Don't know," he said, riffling the bills with his fingers. "Haven't had a chance to count it yet." His face split into a grin, a naughty boy's apple-scrumping grin. Only it wasn't an irate farmer we were dealing with here. There was a silence. I was pacing up and down the room: it only took five paces each way. Then Gus said, in a low, confessional voice, "It wasn't *just* the money, either."

"What?"

He gestured at the sports bag on the floor. I guessed right away, but I unzipped it all the same. A small, squat package wrapped in newspaper. "Peach?" He nodded. "How much?" He shrugged: half a kilo, a pound, he wasn't sure. It had been sitting on the desk in the office. It had practically got up on its hind legs and begged him to take it. "You stupid bloody fool," I said, though whether it was Gus or myself I was addressing I wasn't quite sure. I could have been halfway to the coast by now, cruising through the green hills of Antioquia with Lola and company. Instead, here I was in an air-less room on 45th Street, with a pile of hot money on the bed, a pound of stolen cocaine in the bag, and a halfcrippled lunatic sitting opposite me saying, "I've got it all worked out, mate, there's no way they're going to find us."

The stuffy room was making him sleepy. He had had a hard morning. He pushed his ill-gotten gains to one side, and set-tled more comfortably on the bed. In what way, I asked, had he got it "all worked out"? Out of another pocket in the unpleasant blue suit came a couple of slips of white paper. He handed them to me. They were bus tickets: Medellín to Quibdó.

"Quibdó?" I said. "But that's somewhere in the jungle, for Christ's sake."

"That's right. Slap-dab in the middle of the Chocó."

"But no one goes to the Chocó, Gus. It's a sweat-hole."

"Exactly right, mate. It's the last place anyone would think of looking. Look, face it, Eduardo's going to put the word out on me. I don't fancy trying to fly out of Medellín. I don't want to go back to Bogotá—nothing for me there. He'll have friends up on the coast. So—it's go west young man."

"And you want me to come with you?"

"Just as far as Quibdó," he implored. "I can't make it alone, not with my leg like this. I'll make it worth your while. Money, peach, whatever. I'll *give* you the Who's Who: what more can I say? Just one last ride, mate. You know what they say—two hearts are better than one . . ."

"And after Quibdó?"

"I'm going down to Buenaventura. It's goodbye Colombia, out the back-door. I can sell the peach there. With that and the loot I'll have more than enough for boat passage out of Buenaventura." He stretched luxuriously. "Ship up to Pan-ama . . . Mexico, maybe . . . Who knows, perhaps I'll go to Canada. Plenty of McGregors up there!"

I got out my road map of Colombia. The Chocó was a long swathe of emptiness between the brown swirls of the mountains and the blue of the Pacific Ocean. "For Christ's sake, Gus. Buenaventura's right down the other end of the Chocó. There aren't any roads. Look."

I pushed the map at him. He was settling down to sleep now. He didn't bother to look at it. "Blue ones," he yawned.

"What do you mean, blue ones?"

"The roads through the Chocó. They're blue." He cocked open an eye. "Rivers, matey, rivers. You can get boats down the San Juan river to Buenaventura. Don't worry! I told you: I've got it all worked out."

I stared at the map disconsolately for a minute or two. It was more or less true. The one and only road through the Chocó petered out at a small jungle-town called Istmina, but the blue line of the San Juan ran clear on down to the Pacific, debouching just a couple of map-inches above Buenaventura.

"But I don't want to go to the Chocó," I whined. "I want to go to the coast."

No answer came. Gus was asleep.

15

INTO THE CHOCÓ

The bus left at 6 in the morning. We stumbled through the dawn streets, heads full of snow. The bus was already full of chattering black Chocuano faces. Apart from a few vestigial Indian tribes—Waunana, Catio, Cuna—the inhabitants of the Chocó are almost exclusively negro, descendants of the slaves who worked the Spanish sugar plantations. The Chocó Indians still refer to the negroes as *los libres*, the freed slaves. To most Colombians the Chocó is synonymous with disease, poverty and underdevelopment, 30,000 square miles of jungle shading down to the mangrove swamps of the Pacific littoral. Its one redeeming feature is the presence of gold and platinum in the river gravels, though little comes out of there now.

We found seats, a few rows apart. I sat next to a ragged old black in a jumble-sale jacket. He was clasping the seat top in front of him before the bus even moved, thin black sticks of wrist with little white hairs on them. With much revving and trumpeting, and shouts of "Quibdó, Quibdó, *directo* Quibdó!" we set off. It was one of those classic Colombian buses, a patchwork of beaten tin built round a snub-nosed Ford 600 engine, "Flota El Progreso de Chocó" painted in curly, festive fairground lettering on the side. Religious trinkets danced above the windscreen. Grey tongues of smoke licked up through the floor.

I could see Gus's greasy ginger head over the seat-tops. He had borrowed a jumper from me and was resting on it as a pillow against the window. We had been up all night, sampling the ripped-off *perica*, and counting up the money: something over $2,500, including the pesos and bolivars. His face was grey, his movements were jagged and shaky. I was seriously worried about his health, and supposed that was why I was here, bound for the sweatlands, the green machine, the land of night-biting *zancudos* and wild-eyed old gold prospectors.

We came out through the posh southern suburbs of Medellín, bungalows in neat gardens with orchids growing as profusely as daffodils. We switchbacked down to the Cauca river, and began to climb the sparsely populated Western Cordillera. This was coffee country: precipitous plantations, beans drying on sacks by the roadside. Four hours out, still in the hills, we crossed the state-line into the department of Chocó. At El Cármen everyone was out to watch the cycle rally we had passed. The bus was not accorded its usual welcome. *El ciclísmo* is virtually Colombia's national sport: trained on these tough slopes, local heroes like Martín Ramirez and Pacho Rodríguez are proving to be world-beaters. We rattled on through the dusty outskirts, a face in every window, a lounger in every doorway, children running alongside. A last glimpse of the mountains—a wood-frame bus lurching up a hilly side-street, a woman hanging out of the crowded doorway, wind catching her bright dress, colours unfurling against the brooding hills—and then we saw the expanse of the Chocó, laid out below us like a hazy green sea.

With every minute of our descent the heat grew stronger, the air sat on us. The old man beside me was wilting. His mouth fell open, his eye glazed over. He had a wedge of *arepa* bread wrapped in tin foil. He picked at it listlessly, little chunks of damp dough, sparrow's mouthfuls. He had no teeth. Pieces fell on his lap, and mine. I gave him an orange, an *empanada*, some water. I smelt his stale, brackish sweat, a sickbed smell, *la catinga Chocuana*. I would smell it many times down in these low, swampy regions. He talked in sudden bursts. He was returning to Quibdó, his birthplace, to live with his sister. She was a school-mistress. He had been living in Medellín. How long? Too long, he said, with a toothless wheeze of laughter. In his younger days he had worked as a cow-hand, up on the cattle-plains of Córdoba, the great grasslands of the Magdalena delta. "When the sun shone, the *ganaderos* said it was hot. I said to them: 'You don't know the Chocó!' When the rains came, the *ganaderos* said it was wet. I said to them: 'You don't know the Chocó!'" He remembered the big sky filled with vultures. Flocks of white egrets followed the cattle, and perched on their humped backs. When the grass was flooded the cattle fed on wild hyacinths and lilies.

He lapsed back into his misty, old man's silence. He kept rummaging in his pocket for his ticket, looking at it, putting it back in another pocket.

We were down on the flat now. Little wood and thatch settlements punctuated the monotonous green scrub, the hacked-back hedge of forest. In another burst of lucidity, trawling it up from his Chocuano childhood, the old man enumerated the different kinds of palm tree used to build a house. *Chontaduro* for the posts and flooring, *guayacán* and *meme* for the woven wattle, *asaguara* for the leaf-thatch of the roof. I saw children's white eyes in the dark doorways, and an old black mama, smoking a wooden cob-pipe, a silent glimpse of the Blues.

Quibdó announced itself with a brief discord of tin roofs, overhead wires and fly-blown hoardings. We were quickly in the centre. There were a few picturesque streets of wood, old two-storey trading houses with teetering balconies, but most of the town was concrete, drab and smudged, looking like it was built in a hurry. Fruit and vegetable debris sat in the streets, a dank, mildewy smell, sharpened here and there by the piquancies of rotting fish. The mud of the jungle town, that charmless grey river-mud that looks like the deposits round a blocked-up drain, lay everywhere. In a mountain town you feel exposed and dazzled. In a jungle town you are threatened, compressed, sandwiched between the laden air and the mounting silt.

The bus finally came to a halt on the waterfront: the Atrato river, as wide as a lake. I woke Gus up. He had slept through the entire journey. He started up, stared at me blankly for a moment. "We're here," I said. I could feel the heat coming off him. He was sickening: the excitements of the last few days, the strains of the last few weeks, the excesses of the last few years: bad leg, bad diet, bad nerves: the list could go on. He had a whole lot of bodily debts to pay, and the Chocó was just the kind of place where your credit ran out.

The bus was empty now. The driver, small and bald, was waiting for us to leave. "We're here, Gus," I said again. "Quibdó."

"Quibdó," he faltered. "Keep dough. Keep dough safe." He twisted round to check his sports bag up on the luggage rack. He moved his lips trying to moisten his mouth. He made to settle back down in the seat. "Dough safe," he muttered. I put a hand under his arm to help him up. His armpit was burning with fever-heat.

As we climbed off the bus, a little black boy in baggy shorts danced up, crying, "Hotel? Hotel?" He took my bag and the Who's Who, and put them in a makeshift wooden barrow. He tried to take the sports bag off Gus. Gus, gaunt, confused and quavery, held on. An absurd tug of war ensued between these ill-matched opponents. I gently released Gus's grip. "He's taking us to a hotel, Gus," I explained in nurse-like tones.

A hundred yards down the waterfront, a small, rickety hotel—Residencias San Francisco—lurked in the shadow of the ugly grey Palacio Episcopal. In the lobby three black boys lounged in front of a large black and white TV. A church service through a haze of static. The rooms were little more than hutches, but they had a balcony of sorts, and a view over the river, and electric fans. The air was hot and wet. A faint breeze stirred off the river, but it too was hot and wet. Gus flopped on to the bed. "Give me whisky," he rasped. The best I could do was a bottle of beer from the lobby.

Another passenger from the bus had wound up at the Residencias San Francisco, a strange, pallid young man with lank, swept-back hair. As I walked down the corridor, leaving Gus asleep, he was sitting bare-chested on his bed a few doors down. *"Pues, paisa, qué tal?"* he called, in a rich Antioqueño accent—the rough equivalent of "Wotcha, mate!"— and gestured to me to join him. He was rolling a joint of dark *mango viche* grass. Wasn't he worried about being seen, with the door open and all? He bared his discoloured teeth in a sarcastic laugh. He had just sold some *marimba* to the black boys in the lobby. We sat smoking on his balcony, the wide smooth waters of the Atrato pinkish and benevolent in the late afternoon haze.

His name was Alonso and his primary purpose in Quibdó was to sell lottery tickets. He had stacks of them laid out on the bed. The lottery is a daily institution in Colombia, just about the only reliable form of national taxation. There are national lotteries like the Cruz Roja, state lotteries run by each department, and small local lotteries usually called Chance, pronounced "Chancay." A typical ticket costs something like 1,500 pesos, but most punters buy only a *fracción* or two—for instance, a 50-peso fraction of a 1,500-peso ticket entitles you to one thirtieth of the ticket's winnings. The winning number, the *premio mayor*, wins a small fortune—about 20 million pesos on a standard state lottery— and there are smaller prizes, *premios secos*, for the numbers before and after the winning number, and for *approximaciones*, which are tickets containing some of the figures of the winning number. The lottery-seller lives on his luck. Not only does he get 10 per cent of every ticket, or *fracción*, that he sells: he also gets 10 per cent of anything the ticket wins.

Alonso asked what brought me to Quibdó. I explained vaguely that my friend was sick, and that I was seeing him off on his way to Buenaventura. "He will go down the San Juan, then?" I nodded. "And you?" I said I was going back to Medellín, and then on up to Cartagena. "But you do not need to go back," said Alonso. "You can get a boat here, down the Atrato. It will take you to Cartagena." He gestured down along the waterfront. A group of scruffy cargo boats rocked gently in the pink water. This sounded like very good news. I have a deep dislike of retracing my steps: tramp-steamer passage down the Atrato river was much more like it. Perhaps, after all, I would get something out of this journey to the Chocó.

After dark, Alonso left to tout his lottery tickets round the bars of Quibdó. His *marimba* was strong. I went to lie down on my bed, thinking to take a rest before getting some supper. I promptly fell into a deep sleep. I dreamed I was sleeping beside a rushing white-water river, but when I woke it was only the dull roar of the electric fan. I watched the dawn come up, diaphanous drapes of grey-green mist rising off the waters. Slowly the river came to life. Tall negroes punted long thin dug-outs. Women, big breasts and bottoms crammed into gaily patterned dresses, sauntered along the river-front, tin dishes of fruit on their heads: green plantains, pomegranates, mamueys, pineapples.

I found Gus somewhat restored by his long sleep. His hair was matted, his face looked drained, but it was clear he had sweated out the worst of it. "What dreams I've had," he said. "You were in it, mate. I thought you were a *curandero*, you know, a bloody witch-doctor. They still have them round here, you know. I thought Old Papa Macumba was coming to get me."

I told him he must stay in bed for the day. I went to get some breakfast, and some bread and fruit for Gus. The heat was already massing. After five minutes' walking I was covered in that shrink-wrapping of sweat that comes in air so humid that your sweat can't evaporate. After breakfasting on eggs *pericos*—scrambled with tomato and onion—I strolled along the waterfront to check out the possibilities of a boat-ride downriver.

The boats floated gently on the rubbish-strewn water near the riverside market. They were single-mast, shallow-draught vessels, with a slight upward curve like an Arab *dhow*. The largest, about 100 feet, was called *La Gaviota*, the sea-gull. A group of blacks were lounging in the shade of the awning which covered the stern half of the boat. I walked up the gangplank. Beneath the *toldo* it smelt of hot wood, old fruit and engine oil. A big negro in a vest, middle-aged, crew-cut hair the colour of gun-metal, rose from the group. He was the captain. I asked if he was bound for Cartagena. He was. I asked how long the trip was. Inside a week, he said: three days down the Atrato, refuel at Turbo on the Urabá Gulf, another two to three days to Cartagena. I asked if he would take me. With pleasure, 3,500 pesos all in: hammock, meals and passage. I saw the crew tucking into a mushy brew in tin dishes. The skipper moved to block my view. "To you 3,000," he said.

So far, so good. Then I asked when they were leaving: there was no cargo aboard that I could see. His big head wavered non-committally. "*Depende*," he said. Depends on what? He rubbed his big hand over the back of his head: I heard the rasp of his crew-cut. "*Pues . . . depende de Dios*," he said. Well, of course. All things, no doubt including the departure of tramp-steamers down the Atrato river, depended on God. One of the crew, a tall, shifty-looking *mestizo*, strolled over. He sliced an orange in two with a Swiss Army knife, and handed me half. It depends, the skipper continued, on the rains. He looked philosophically at the sky. The rains were late, he said. The river was very low, down to 10 feet in some places, too shallow for the boat. They had been waiting for five days already. He gestured out at the middle of the river. Long mud-banks were visible. "How long must we wait?" I asked futilely. He shrugged. A day, a week, a month, *quién sabe*? I felt the sweat trickling down my chest. The *mestizo* held out his sucked-dry orange peel, stuck a splinter of wood in it, and said with a laugh, "You'll have to sail to Cartagena in this!"

I returned to the hotel disgruntled. I didn't fancy even a week, let alone a month, stuck in Quibdó waiting for the rains to come. Gus ate hungrily. The sun beat down from a dull washed-out blue. I lolled feebly in the draught of the fan.

"You look like you need some medicine, mate," said Gus, reaching under his bed for the sports bag. "Let's do some peach. Sharpen us up a bit."

I went off to buy some more warm beer from the boys in the lobby, but I hadn't gone far down the corridor when I heard a strange, strangled shout from back in the room, then a cry of "Fuck a priest!"—one of Gus's peculiar oaths. I doubled back into the room, to see Gus staggering backwards away from the bed. A look of horror-story disbelief racked his grey face.

"Gus! What's happened? What is it?"

His hand flailed weakly towards the bed. There I saw the packet of cocaine in its polythene and newspaper. At least it hadn't been stolen—a thought that had flashed through my mind. Then I saw. The fine white flake was grey, wet, clotted, a damp mulch—you could have plastered the walls with it. It was obvious what had happened. An extremely soluble powder, poorly packaged, in high percentage humidity. The jungle had claimed it—$5,000 worth of merchandise pulped into pottage.

"Oh dear, oh dear," I said weakly.

Gus's mouth was moving. A parched clicking in his throat. Some of the stuff was on his hands. He kneaded it, held it close up to his staring eyes. "Ruined," he croaked. "A pound of the finest. Ruined. *Ruined!*"

"Oh, come along, Gus," I said briskly. "I'm sure we can do something."

He sat down heavily. "Yeah," he said bitterly. "We can chuck it in that fucking millpond out there."

"No, I am sure we can dry it."

"Dry it? In this humidity? Look at the stuff. It looks like half a kilo of snot!"

I was trying to remember something—something Mario the cook had told me, that crazy night on Caracas Avenue. You dry it in the sun or *under light bulbs*. That was it. We could dry it under light bulbs. "I've got an idea, Gus. You wait here."

It was getting near midday. I had to move fast before everything seized up for the long lunch-and-siesta break. After a bit of sweaty work among the general stores of Quibdó, I returned with the requisites: a few metres of electric flex, some insulating tape and a couple of empty cartons. Each of our rooms had a single bulb, high up, festooned in cobwebs and insect corpses. With a chair on the bed, held by Gus, I could just reach high enough to sever the wire. I brought the bulb, in its socket, from my room into Gus's, and with a great deal of teetering and bodging, I fixed up a makeshift drying-box: two long wires leading off the overhead flex, two bulbs fastened into the base of a carton, which was then placed on top of the other carton containing the flattened wedge of damp cocaine. Praying that this wasn't going to blow out the entire electrical supply of Quibdó, we turned on the wallswitch. It worked. Through the long afternoon we watched and waited and sifted. Gradually the cocaine began to dry. By the time darkness fell it was just about recognizable again: lumpy, greyish, a bit sticky, but essentially workable, snortable peach. We were as high as kites from sniffing and smoking the stuff as we worked it. It probably wouldn't get a very good price in Buenaventura, where Gus intended to sell it, but total loss had been averted.

We spent the evening drinking gallons of beer in a rickety wooden bar called La Vírgen Negra, with Alonso the *lotero* and a shifting group of laughing Chocuanos and Chocuanas. We tacked back to the hotel, way past midnight, and had to holler in the street for the boys to unlock the door. "*Abre, abre, nos acalabazamos!*" shouted Gus. Open up, we're turning into pumpkins . . .

16

THE SHIT CREEK
SPECIAL

The following morning—sky brilliant blue, same boats moored on the waterfront, no sign of any rains—I decided it was time to cut my losses and backtrack by bus to Medellín. Gus was leaving that morning, south to Istmina where the road ran out, there to try his luck for a boat down the San Juan to Buenaventura. The San Juan was going to be low too, of course, but it was a much shorter distance from Istmina to the Pacific than it was from Quibdó to the Caribbean, and with luck he would be able to make the trip on some smaller boat, a fisherman's *lancha* or *panga*.

Gus felt honour-bound to offer me the Who's Who, as he had promised in Medellín, payment for whatever obscure moral support I had provided on his fugitive trail. But I could see the idea of parting with it was painful to him, and some residual goodness in my heart—"hack's honour," he would have called it—made me refuse. "You might need it," I said.

"Inside the Cocaine Underworld, eh?" he laughed. "Well, you never know, do you?"

We said goodbye on the waterfront, where the truck left each morning for Istmina. I wished him luck. "Don't worry about me, mate," he said. "I'll get through. It's the first law of jungle travel—where there's a Shit Creek, there's someone who'll sell you a paddle."

Sacks, chickens and children were loaded, and the truck

rolled off, a dozen black Chocuanos and the thin ginger man in their midst.

An hour or so later I strolled up to the row of sheds that served as the Quibdó bus depot, to buy my ticket for the midday bus to Medellín. The man behind the grille shook his head. *"No hay."*

No tickets for Medellín? The depot was nearly empty, the bus was standing in the street. How could this be? It was clearly some attempt to extract baksheesh from me: for a small consideration he could squeeze me in. I stood my ground.

"We have tickets, *señor*," he explained wearily, "but no buses are going to Medellín."

"Why the hell not?"

"Derrumbe." The word that all South American travellers learn to fear. Landslide. "It happened last night," he continued. "Near El Cármen. There is a bridge down too." My heart sank. In these remote regions, the blocking of roads and the breaking of bridges can mean days of delay.

I asked the pointless question, "How long?" and got the *mañana-mañana* shrug in reply.

There seemed no alternative but to fly. There was an airfield of sorts north of the town: perhaps I could get a flight direct to Cartagena. At the small Coturismo office downtown I found the news was bad. There was no flight to Cartagena, only to Medellín. I had missed one flight this morning: the next was not until Friday night.

I sat on a bench, hot, dejected and hungover. Stuck in Mosquito City. One river to the coast, no boats. One road to Medellín, no buses. One flight out, three days and eight hours away. I had just two options left: sweat it out in Quibdó, or take the one exit still open—south to Istmina, and join up with Gus for a river ride to Buenaventura. It took me just a few seconds to decide. When in doubt, *move*, even if it's in the wrong direction.

The next morning found me on the waterfront, piling into the truck to Istmina. It was a different truck from yesterday's. Wooden seats had been nailed onto the flat-bed, and a

curved tin roof covered us. It was murky and dwarfish inside.
It was like a fairground ride. Everyone was in place when the
driver had the last-minute brainwave of filling up with petrol,
and there was much ado with jerry-cans and syphons while
we deep-fried under the tin roof.

We lost Quibdó quickly and without regret, and lurched
along the thin, straight, red earth road. At Yuto an old
yellow ferry, no more than a motorized tray, took us across
the Atrato. Somewhere south of Certegui a tyre blew, an
inside tyre on one of the rear double wheels. A replacement,
as bald as a bathing cap, was unroped from the roof of the
cab, where it sat flanked by rusting silent klaxons. The
driver's assistant, who looked like an African warrior,
sweated beneath the truck with jacks and levers. The passengers encouraged him from the shady side of the road. At
Las Animas more passengers piled in. A child was plonked
on my lap: that sickbed smell again. The road climbed and
fell. The vague blue-green vistas to the west were the Baudo
region. This was once the stronghold of the legendary black
guerrillero, Carlos Quinta Abadía, who liberated the blacks
from Spanish slavery. The stories say he was a giant man
covered in hair, and that when the *blancos* sent in soldiers to
kill him, he caught their bullets in his mouth and spat them
back.

Istmina was two wooden streets and assorted alleys on a
bluff overlooking the San Juan river. There was one crumbling old hotel, hopefully named Hotel Turístico, run by a
crumbling old *mestizo*. His skin was greyish and flecked with
yellow liver-spots. His hair stood on end, so often had he run
his hand through it. His vest bore deep smudges where his
fingers scratched lazily at his paunch. The small erosions of
jungle-town life were etched on him.

I expected to find Gus bivouacked here, but the old *dueño*,
whose name was Lopez, had seen nothing of him. There had
been no gringos here for weeks, he said. Either Gus had hit
lucky and got a boat straightaway, or he was holed up somewhere else, despite Lopez's assurances that there were no
other hotels in Istmina.

I took a room out back, giving on to a balcony on stilts over the river, but the river was so low that the balcony looked down at a slate-grey bog of beached-up junk. Every time someone used the lavatory you could hear everything pouring 20 feet down into the mud. Lopez leaned in the doorway as I dumped my meagre baggage. Grimed with sweat and dust, I tried the taps in the basin. "You won't find any water there," he said, mildly amused at my naïvety. There was no running water. There were buckets and a big barrel, and—with a broad, proprietary sweep of the hand—"of course, the river." A hundred yards across, the bank shelved gently between grey waters and tall trees. People were bathing and washing clothes. Next to the water-barrel a huge blackish pig rooted in a pen, seemingly on guard. I thought of the pigs at the San Felipe slaughter-house. I thought of the Great Cocaine Story. I drowned these thoughts in the splash of cool water over my head, the glint of the river light through the chinked wooden walls of the baño.

There was only one other guest at the hotel—a small, vivacious Chocuana called Tabatha—and she seemed here by virtue of charity or obscure family connection. Her husband had been arrested after a knife-fight and was serving six months in the Istmina jailhouse. I shuddered at the thought. She was going back home, with her two little daughters, to the family house near Noanama. She was waiting for a boat downriver. No boats had gone for a week, she said, or only local boats hopping down a village or two. This was depressing news, but it also meant that Gus must be somewhere in town, after all. She was quite casual about it all, well-practised in the art of living in limbo.

I dined well on sobrebarriga of beef, with plantains and rice. Fresh fish, like running water, was oddly unavailable. Wherever I was, Lopez seemed to be leaning in a doorway, looking like he had just woken up. It was dark now, and he was half-drunk. Somewhere in the rambling wooden house a radio was playing: Cuban brass, Chocó soul, I couldn't tell quite what. The house had been built by German timber merchants, he said. He had lived here for thirty years. He laughed hollowly at the way life had gone. Thirty years in the Chocó! It was gold that brought him here—*el fiebre del oro*. He had prospected for twelve years out along the San Juan and its tributaries. He had eaten monkey stew, and seen men killed for a few grains of gold. *El mazamorreo*, they call it: the old technique of placer-mining, panning gold out of channels and pits cut off the river. He brought out his old prospector's tackle—a small, wooden-handled iron pick called an *almocafre*, a leaf-shaped wooden spatula called a *cacho*, and the *batea*, a shallow dish for panning off the gravel-wash. They were caked with dry, pale river mud. There is still gold out there today, and prospectors looking for it. In Quibdó or Istmina you can sell a *castellano* of gold, just under 5 grams, for 3,000 or 4,000 pesos. There is also much platinum, found in little grey flakes or grains in the river gravels. The big gold-workings down along the San Juan were once owned by gringo companies. Since being expropriated by the Colombian government they have lain idle. He sniggered gloomily. "We take back the gold and we leave it in the mud!" He spat down into the dark street.

Down at the waterfront the following morning there was no news of any boats going anywhere much. Nor was there any news of Gus. A fruit-seller said yes, she had seen a tall gringo looking for boats, but it transpired he was dark and handsome, and anyway this was about two months ago. In the Chocó, said Lopez, you walk on stepping-stones while time rolls past beneath you. I found a couple of houses that called themselves hotels, but they didn't harbour Gus either. I waited for the daily truck from Quibdó, but it wasn't the one Gus had travelled on, and the driver knew nothing. It was a mystery: he had done a complete vanishing trick somewhere between Quibdó and here.

In Istmina I sat and sweated and puzzled and waited. My pen left furry blotches on my notebook. My cigarettes drooped. The small store of cocaine Gus had given me grew smaller and sludgier. I scraped it on to cigarettes and took it as basuko. The quality was dulled. I took more, just to jazz things up at first, then just to keep me going at all—I could feel the hit running out like petrol from a ripped tank.

Then one morning I couldn't even sit up. This wasn't co-caine, this was fever. A hot ague had me by the back. My head ebbed and ached, my stomach turned to water: the Choco Choo-choo. Strange scenarios flew me away, brought me back. Six months in the hole . . . a gen'lman o' fortune, sir . . . crash on the levee, no boats gonna row.

Old Lopez was standing at my door. "You are sick, *señor?*" I requested mineral water: he brought Coca-Cola. Another time his wife was there, with a huge slab of papaya in her hand. She told me to eat the seeds, a sovereign remedy against fevers. The seeds were black and intensely bitter, al-most impossible to swallow. It was like an expiation, a myrrh. I crushed them with the bottle and washed them down with Coca-Cola.

Another time, night-time, I was terrorized by a giant black flying beetle. It crashed in angrily through the torn netting at the window. I swatted at it with my notebook, missed. It traced a few circles in the air, gathered its wits, and came hurtling down at my pillow in a low, deadly arc. A dreadful, chivalric struggle ensued, which I finally won by slamming the door on it. Its carcass stuck in the door-jamb, orange slime oozing from its shattered carapace. Should I drink this too, sovereign remedy against all fears?

The second day of the fever. The play of the river light, the patterns of notched wood. Inside a bowl of bird calls and children's voices I curled asleep. Women at the creek laughed and slapped at their washing.

That night I heard it drumming on the tin roof over the balcony. Rain. I looked at my watch for the first time in two days: it was gone 3 in the morning. I stumbled out on to the balcony. There were no lights, no movement, only a met-alled gleam of water, a vague collision of greys where the trees met the cloud. But I didn't need to see. I could feel it on my face and my chest, tiny drops, specks of coolness, like stars coming out all over my skin. A cracked laugh of sup-plication may or may not have escaped my lips.

In the morning I rose from my sweat-bed, showered down with pails. Señora Lopez was cooking *arepas* on a charcoal griddle on top of an oil-drum. The air was clearer after the rain. It couldn't have made much difference to the height of the river, but it seemed like a good omen. And sure enough, while I was breakfasting, in walked a tubby, cheerful man in a small, peaked yachting cap. With him was a mulatto boy, about ten. The man carried heavy cartons done up with packing string. He looked like he was going somewhere. I inquired. His name was Manuel, the boy was his son Henry, and they were going down the San Juan river, as far as Capoma. I hardly dared ask anymore. Some catch, surely: they were going in April, they were *walking* there. But no. They were going in a fishing boat, piloted by a negro from the coast called Mico, and provided Mico hadn't drunk himself to death last night the boat would be leaving around midday.

It was not the ragged, picturesque old river-boat I had envisaged. It was a low fibreglass *lancha*, 20 feet long, white with orange fittings, and a Yamaha 40 motor. It didn't even have a name. It was, of course, faster and more convenient than a tramp-steamer. The "picturesque" is an aesthetic often based on other people's inconvenience. The main point was it was going, and for 2,000 pesos Mico would take me all the way to the Pacific Ocean in it. He was a tough, simian man, about thirty I guessed, quick to anger and quick to laugh. I could tell his price was high by the way Manuel suddenly started looking at the ceiling and whistling carelessly when the figure was mentioned. But Mico had seen the fear in my eye. He knew I'd pay twice that, so all in all it seemed fair. The Shit Creek Special was sailing at last.

It was afternoon before we finally set off, and then we stopped for another while at Andagoya, just ten minutes downriver from Istmina, while Mico went off for petrol. I waded ashore, among the stilted, tin-roofed wooden houses, and bought some *chontaduros* from a woman in a red bandanna. *Chontaduro* is a very nourishing palm fruit. It looks like a small mango, or a hardened Victoria plum, and has a savoury, almost cheesy meat inside. Among the debris on the river bank I saw a polythene bag with a dead kitten half-spilled out of it. The rictus of little teeth, the blue jelly eyes, told the story.

At Andagoya we were joined by a jovial negress with hair plaited close down her scalp. She was the district nurse, carrying medical supplies to villages downriver. This brought our complement to eight: Mico the pilot, and his co-pilot, Federico, a ferrety *mestizo* in a baseball cap; Tabatha, the prisoner's wife, and her two little daughters, prim in lacy bonnets; chubby Manuel and his son Harry, the mulatto boy; the district nurse; and the gringo. And so the little fibre-glass Ship of Fools set off for the Pacific Ocean.

Progress was slow because of the river's lowness. Federico the ferret knew every inch of the river. He stood up at the stern of the boat, scanning the bright water, directing Mico at the tiller. Now to the left, now to the right. "Here it is good . . . Here it is a whore." Often the propeller hit bottom, the boat juddered, Mico cut the engine, and we floated amid the whoops and screeches and comic arpeggios of the jungle birds. At a sharp elbow of river, overhung with predatory vegetation, the channel was so narrow that we had to disembark entirely, and carry boat, motor, baggage and children 100 metres across to where the stream broadened again. Federico's machete flashed. Some unseen animal—by the sound of it small but quite weighty, a peccary perhaps—hastened through the underbrush as our odd procession passed. Later there was another rainstorm. Mico handed out polythene sheets, but we were all soaked by the time we had rigged them up—all except for the district nurse, who had a black umbrella, a providential brolly. Tilting it at her feet, and crouching behind it, she was the only one of us who stayed dry.

Towards evening we saw some Waunana Indians, tall, bronze, broad-shouldered men, naked except for a small cloth jock-strap, and with that distinctive pudding-basin hairstyle. Their canoes glided on the rich evening water. Little children poled little canoes. A cluster of palm-thatched huts stood above a small creek, some with steep conical roofs, some with long ridge-pole roofs. Bare-breasted women stood in doorways, or rocked children in hammocks. Manuel said to me, *"Cuidado con los Indios!"* Take care with Indians. "Their arrows are sharp, and their curses are strong. I knew a man who shot an Indian: he drowned in a gold-pit three days later. The shaman had put a *madre de agua* on him. The curse of a water-mother. It brings death and misfortune by water."

We ploughed on west. Everything turned scarlet and orange and then it was dark. The immense, comfortless trill of frogs and insects settled in behind the whine of our motor.

Two hours after dark, cold and wet, we came to a scattering of wooden shacks. The village of Capoma was a little way inland, I learned. This was Manuel's destination. He was going to leave his son Harry with some cousin or aunt, then travel on down to Buenaventura to look for work. Harry was the half-caste product of Manuel's days as a gay-dog bar pianist up on the tourist island of San Andres. When Manuel came back to the Chocó, Harry came too. They had run a store in Quibdó for two years, selling boat-gear, but the business had folded, and now they had to part.

The new-built house by the riverside was the school-house, convenient for pupils that commute by canoe. The district nurse knew the school-mistress well, and it was decreed that we could shelter the night here. We scrambled up the steep muddy bank.

The school-mistress greeted us warmly. Here, at last, I got news of Gus. "You're the second gringo we've seen here in a week," she told me. Tall? Red-headed? *Poco loco?* She nodded. He was travelling with a couple of desperate characters, *mestizos*. She thought they were gold prospectors. She didn't know where they'd come from or where they were going. To Buenaventura perhaps? She shook her head. "They were travelling *upriver*," she said.

Inside the school-house, the pungent, turpentinish smell of freshly sized wood made me think of a tennis hut in an English garden: another place, another life. Soon we were tucking into fried mortadella and plantains, ranged improbably round the little school desks. I handed round a half-bottle of rum. We nested down on benches or the floor. I was too tired to ponder long on Gus's whereabouts. I drifted off to the sound of the three women out back, in the *maestra*'s little kitchen, talking and laughing late into the night.

A dream of amorous escapades in the tennis hut was rendered uneasy by the machete-wielding negroes and ill-intentioned shamans who were vaguely glimpsed in the sunny rose-garden outside. No sooner had the dream begun than one of the blacks was in the hut, pulling me away, pinning me down, and then I recognized his face to be that of Mico the *lanchero*. He was pushing at my shoulder, and even as I shouted at him I found myself awake in the Chocó school-house, with my fellow-travellers laughing, openly but kindly, at the mad gringo gabbling up from his bed on the floor. We drank *tinto* coffee, thanked our hostess, and said goodbye to Manuel and Harry. The imminent sadness of their own parting made our more casual parting sad.

On the river the air was grey, misty and chill. The motor coughed a few times, then caught. A river bird, some giant, leisurely jungle heron, flapped off into the steaming trees. I handed round the rum: a slug of morning fire. Federico drained the last, threw the bottle into the mud and said, "A quien madruga Dios le ayuda." God helps those who rise with the dawn.

By midday it was just Mico and me. We had dropped off the others, Tabatha, the nurse, Federico, one by one, at huts or villages that meant much to them and nothing to me. There had been other stops, to deliver letters and to buy provisions—rice, salt, *panela*, toothpaste and petrol—from an Indian trader. Now the river widened, and the tall trees gave way to stunted deltas of mangrove, and I tasted the salt on my lips.

Mico's family house stood in a cove out near Charambirá Point. We were still in the maze of inlets around the San Juan estuary, out of the Chocó, but not quite at the Pacific.

The family were all there, easy and distant, potentially fierce, tidal people. Mico's father whittled wood for a machete handle, a sister rocked in a net hammock, brothers ranged from approximate ages eight to thirty-five. I was treated to fish soup and *agua de panela,* plied with questions about England, and good-humouredly grilled to ensure that I thought the Chocó the most beautiful part of Colombia. "It is tranquil here," said the elder brother, a smaller, more philosophical edition of Mico. "The sea, the forest, the fish, the birds, the animals, the Indians and . . . us." He was listing these out, counting them off on his hand. When the list stopped, he looked at his fingers, half-surprised. "That's all there is here," he laughed. "Seven things!"

I made the final leg to Buenaventura in another fishing boat, belonging to a neighbour of Mico's. Two young black fishermen took me: the tall, quiet one had a long, livid pink scar down his cheek; the younger, more impish one sported an unexpected pink shirt with a frill down the front, like a Carnaby Street dandy of twenty years ago. Scarface's young wife and daughter came too. She carried her handbag and high-heeled sneakers in a polythene bag. They were taking in three days' worth of fishing to sell. The fish was in the central hold, packed in ice and polythene, with fresh-cut branches on the top to keep off the sun. Inside was hake, striped tunny, a shark-like fish they called *gata,* and—the *pièce de résistance*—a giant sea-bass, 150 lb without the head, which would provide the delicious fish-steaks, *chuletas de mera.* All this, they hoped, would fetch around 30,000 pesos.

For an hour we threaded the mangrove mazes of the Bocas de San Juan, passing other boats amid the silence and the claustrophobic tangles of air-feeding roots. Out on the open sea the wind got up. The boat pitched. The wife and daughter huddled under plastic sheets. The coastline was wild and beautiful, high shelving cliffs fringed with dense forest. We cut close to the Islas de Palma, uninhabited islets, very spooky and piratical, with pelicans massing over the crags.

It was late afternoon when we rounded the last point and glimpsed the tiny grey mass of Buenaventura, nestling deep in its inlet like an abscess down a tooth-socket. Few people speak well of Buenaventura—hot, dirty and expensive—but right then it meant a bed and a meal. I had been on the water, face into the wind, motor gunning, for twelve hours. The inlet containing Buenaventura is some 10 miles deep, and it was another twenty minutes before we were down near the wharves, and then—one last *longueur* to test the spirit— the engine cut out, and we pitched silently in the growing darkness while Scarface, never once losing his cool, coaxed and adjusted it back to life. We cruised into the fisherman's wharf: lit windows, oily waters, a gaggle of shanty houses on stilted walkways high above the water. A black docker shouted to us to get alongside. Scarface put us the wrong side of the jetty. The docker jumped down and angrily paddled us round. In the midst of his jabber I heard the words "fucking people," universal dockside *patios*. We climbed the slippery ladder to the wharf. The docker threw up our bags. A little gangway led to the street: two Chinamen at a table, fish and salt smells, small dogs nosing the gutter. The fishermen had asked 400 pesos for my passage. I went across the street to change a 1,000-peso note. The old black mama took a little brown phial from under the bar. She dropped a spot or two onto the bill. It was iodine, she explained. If the ink on the bill turned black when the iodine hit, it was counterfeit. "*Buen ojo, buen aventura,*" she said, a cryptic remark which meant both "A sharp eye brings good fortune" and "Watch out in Buenaventura."

I said goodbye to the Chocuanos and checked into the first flophouse I could find, Hotel Mónaco, 300 a night. Black tarts with red hennaed hair patrolled the street, cockroaches patrolled the bedroom. My clothes were drenched and brackish, and those in my bag not much better. This vague nebula of jungle-must wafted along with me all evening. It hung in the smart, silent restaurant where I ate pork *a la mejicana*—smothered in hot chili and kidney-beans—and it pursued me down to the bar where I drank Johnny Walker Black to celebrate, or perhaps to drown, my return to civilization.

Whatever happened to Gus McGregor—last seen heading up the San Juan river in dubious company—remains a mystery. Maybe he's swinging in a hammock somewhere in the Chocó, waited on by nubile Waunana maidens. Maybe he's up in Canada, hobnobbing with the other McGregors—clan motto, he liked to remember, "E'en do, and spare nought." Maybe his luck, the *buenaventura* he stretched for so long, finally ran out. If you ever see his by-line, pay your penny and read his story.

Back at the Hotel Mónaco, I fished out the last remains of Gus's cocaine, the stolen, troublesome *perica* whose siren charms I had sailed too close to. The fever, and the journey, had rescued me, but now . . . As I stood there debating, a trade-wind broke in through the shutters, blew through the room and scattered the cocaine to white dust on the floor. I shrugged. So long to the White Lady. So long to Gus. All night the cockroaches seemed unduly active. For a few more sleepless hours Gus's spirit lingered with me, in the skittering and scratching of cocaine-crazed roaches.

17

TERREMOTO!

Surfacing in Buenaventura I discovered that time had marched on to the beginning of Semana Santa, the Holy Week leading up to Easter. In the mountains some three hours inland from Buenaventura, connected by good roads, lay the town of Popayán. Popayán is *the* classic place to spend Semana Santa in Colombia. The nightly candlelit processions of holy images are famous throughout the Catholic world, and the town is briefly inundated with pilgrims, tourists, Paez Indians and pickpockets. Prescribing myself a short dose of innocent tourism, feeling that I was so far adrift of any meaningful schedule that a few more days wouldn't matter, I set off.

They call Popayán *la joya blanca*, the white jewel of Colombia. It is—or was—one of the loveliest towns in all Latin America. Founded in 1536 by Sebastian de Belalcazar, one of Pizarro's henchmen, on his trek north from Peru in search of Eldorado, it stands in a temperate mountain valley, altitude a little over 5,000 feet. Below are the cane-fields of the hot Cauca valley, above are the rugged green Andean highlands. I remember my first impression of it twelve years ago—the rinsed mountain air, the cobbled streets, the rococo colonial buildings, the seventeenth-century university, the chic restaurants, the leather shops, all bright white against the surrounding green hills, and all very much alive, no museum piece. I suppose Popayán is the Oxford or Cambridge of Colombia, but even this comparison underrates its special place here. Europe is studded with historic university towns, but in the harsher circumstances of Latin America preservation is luxury not often afforded.

It was late on Wednesday night when I arrived on the bus from Buenaventura. I had missed the first part of the festival, including the Palm Sunday procession when they bring down the images—Christ the Master, Our Lady of the Sorrows, Death—from the hilltop chapel of Belen, but I was still in time for the climactic Easter processions. The hotels were full, but I found a room at the Residencias Viajero, a non-descript hotel in a workaday part of town. The room was in a long annex out back, with metal doors and an odd, tinny corridor. It was like being below decks on a ship. But the rooms had private bathrooms, and out of the shower there gushed, as if in some biblical miracle, piping hot water. I sluiced away the last grime of the Chocó, and sat up late planning elegant historical itineraries for the morrow.

I should have been reading my bible: "Boast not thyself of tomorrow, for thou knowest not what a day may bring forth." The following morning, Jueves Santo, the last day of March 1983, at a time later fixed by the newspapers as 8.17 a.m., I was dozing in my bed at the Hotel Viajero, when I heard a soft, deep rumble. I thought at first it was thunder, and then, because I could feel the vibrations of it running up through the metal-frame bed, I sleepily reasoned that it must be some enormous truck gunning its motor below my window. The noise stopped. I nuzzled back into the pillow. But there was no mistaking the second one. It started loud and it got louder, an evil grumbling that swiftly became a roar, and it couldn't be trucks, and it couldn't even be another Colombian civil war in progress, because the roaring sound was my own room. The walls, windows, door were shuddering around me. The light-bulb swayed sluggishly. It was as if some giant pair of hands had grabbed the room by the lapels and was shaking it back and forth. Still in bed, half up, I was thinking: It's going to stop now, because if it doesn't stop something big is going to break and fall on top of me. Cracks sprouted up the wall. A fine meal of plaster floated down on my head. I leapt out of bed. The room pitched angrily. The floor was swampy with movement. It was contravening all the rules that govern floors. Fairground rides are like this, and inebriate efforts to go up a down escalator. The shuddering beneath my feet was like a low, sinister voltage of electricity. I threw myself beneath the bed and lay there with my arms over my head, sneezing amid the fluff and butt-ends.

I know the facts now. It was an earthquake which lasted eighteen seconds, measured 5.5 on the Richter scale, and had its epicentre near the village of El Tambo, some 15 kilometres west of Popayán. Right then, as I levered myself out from under the bed, all I knew and cared about was that it had stopped. A chilly silence ensued, and the first thing to break it was the sound of a door slamming and a woman laughing. I went out into the corridor. A young couple were down the far end, heading out. "What the hell was *that*?" I called. *"Un temblor, hombre! Un temblor!"* I felt let down—the man's shrug, the woman's laugh. He called it a *temblor*, a tremor, not a full-bore, earth-moving *terremoto*. I returned to my room feeling foolish. Had I really hurled myself under the bed? Had I really thought I was going to disappear down one of those lightning-shaped chasms with red-hot lava sloshing about at the bottom? How silly. It was only a *temblor*. They probably have to sweep this plaster-dust up every day.

I dressed quickly. There was no water in the bathroom. The porter, a diminutive, sanguine fellow called Miguelito, was in the lobby. He hadn't been out—the lone night-porter never leaves his post—but he'd been in the doorway, and the street telegraph had been buzzing. There were houses down, he said, and some churches. A woman had been badly hurt round the corner, maybe some dead in the cathedral.

Out in the street there was rubble and broken tiles on the sidewalk, but you could find that any morning of the week on any Colombian street. It wasn't until I turned the corner, heading towards the old heart of the town, that I began to see the real signs: whole roofs caved in, shattered shop windows, broken guttering swaying in the breeze. The nearer I got to the centre, the worse it became. Now I realized my luck—partly because I was staying in a down-market, newish part of town, and partly through geological factors unknown, I had weathered the quake in one of the few parts of town scarcely affected by it.

A crowd milled in front of an elegant town-house whose entire front wall was now a mound of broken masonry in the street. The rather chic upstairs room—a sofa, a standard lamp, an oval mirror with photos and cards tucked in the frame—looked absurdly like a stage-set for some discreet Ibsenesque drama. Our gaze invaded its small, complex privacies. A vase of hibiscus flowers teetered on the carpeted edge of a void.

There was a shout, and from behind us a low rustling rumble. A batch of stone and lath tumbled down onto the sidewalk. A woman screamed and put her hand to her face. I saw blood welling out over the fingers. Another woman held her up, shouted to get back, give her air. She was hit by a piece of wood, a man said. No, said the woman, it was glass. She had seen bits of glass shoot through the air like bullets. A soldier was going past. He was breathless from running. The crowd lapped around him, firing questions, but all he would say was that everyone should stick to the middle of the street for fear of more subsidence.

I pressed on towards the centre. A pall of dust hung in the air. Amid the dereliction I heard sirens, a woman calling hysterically, "Octavio! Octavio!" Men were coming away from the centre with white dust in their hair and all up their arms. More white dust, but now from a bakery, where broken sacks of flour were being pitched into the street. Somewhere else I came on two old men picking at a huge pile of rubble. There was someone somewhere under there. It was strangely silent in this street. The town had lost its connections, the grid was broken, and one stumbled into these little quiet tributaries. I started in to help, tossing up stones and bricks. We wrestled with a huge wooden cross-beam. The hopeless, Sisyphean task became apparent. Then more people arrived, it became crowded and disordered. A thrown tile hurt a small boy. Someone shouted to form a line. I ducked out and walked on, moving from stall to stall in this carnival of destruction.

The old colonial heart of Popayán looked like a bomb-site. The churches, the cloistered university, the Hotel Monasterio were all in ruins. By the time I got there they had cordoned off the centre, with soldiers at every corner a block away from the cathedral square, Parque Caldas. I talked my way in past a wide-eyed young conscript. In human terms, the epicentre of the disaster was the cathedral. The entire roof, the famous domed cupola, had caved in on a churchful of people celebrating morning mass. They had been pulling the dead out for an hour now. A long line of soldiers and *campesinos* ferried stones out of the shattered building. They wore bandannas over their faces, bandit-style, against the fog of dust. I saw a dead body brought out on a stretcher, head covered with a blanket. A pair of white ankle-socks and sandals stuck out—a little girl in her church best, with a few grazes on her skin that her mother could have medicated in a moment.

They were also bringing the holy images out of the cathedral: amputated, lopsided, dust-covered figures, yet paradoxically more human than ever, as if they too had been walking and talking until the clock reached 8.17 a.m. They carried away the Christ down the smoky street, borne high on a running, straggling crowd. Perhaps this was nearer to Calvary than the regular pomps of Holy Week ever got.

In the tree-filled square, where the hawkers and cigarette-boys and lottery-sellers should be, Red Cross workers were setting up little stalls of drugs and bandages. Every uniformed man from miles around was here—firemen from Silvia, Civil Defence from Buga, boy scouts, *carabineros* in their green cowboy hats. Soldiers rested silently on the sidewalk, cigarettes cupped in dusty hands.

The TV cameras had arrived from Cali. A man in jeans was poking a microphone at an army officer, but a surge of people bearing another stretcher out of the cathedral knocked him to the ground. There was an old man on the stretcher. He was looking around him, head cocking up out of the blanket with busy, birdlike movements. Someone ran after, carrying a trilby, and plonked it on the old man's head. He said something—I couldn't hear it—and there was a moment of brusque laughter. There is so much laughter in Colombia, so much grace under pressure, so much marvellous, rickety improvisation—all of it never more tested than today.

The rumours flared and multiplied: thirty dead, fifty dead, a hundred dead. There were radios everywhere. People cupped them anxiously to their ears, huddled round them in groups, listened in at open car doors. The commentators brayed and babbled. They knew no more than anyone else. By the afternoon the death-toll was said to have reached 200, and this was the figure we subsequently read in the press—a special edition of *El Pueblo* of Cali was the first paper to filter in to Popayán late that night. But even this was well short of the final count: 490 lives were lost on Holy Thursday, and some 35,000 people were left homeless. Outside Popayán, whole villages—El Tambo, Cajibío, Piendamó—had been virtually flattened.

Down at the park near the Humilladero bridge, a tent-city of dispossessed families had sprung up. Throughout the afternoon, keeping the panic simmering, small tremors were felt, distant whispered reminders that froze people in attitudes of vigilance and fear for a few seconds, then passed. Fundamentalists were calling the quake *el castigo de Dios*, God's scourge, for turning the passions of Holy Week into a tourist jamboree. A bizarre side-note was the effect on the town cemetery. The vaults had cracked and pitched skeletons and corpses out into the open. "*Para hacer sitio a los recién llegados*" was the grim comment: to make room for all the new arrivals.

All day I wandered the broken city, with that hollow feeling inside which is really fear, but which feels like a sadness. By late afternoon, like an exhausted body, the town seemed to sway through a sudden oscillation of mood. There was a defiant surge of adrenalin in the air. The street vendors and roadside cooks had sprouted back out like irrepressible weeds.

Café owners set up soft-drink stands outside on the sidewalk.
A few bakers were baking, a few restaurants were producing
food on open-range fires: nothing fancy—soup, rice, meat—
but food. Darkness fell. The emergency lights flashed red and
blue. People took to the bars and drank away the dust from
their throats.

Then later this fragile mood faded and there was just ex-
haustion. And with it came the worst realization of all. This
wasn't just a dreadful day, a nightmare from which they
would awake next morning. The *terremoto* was here to stay.
Tomorrow their houses would still be in pieces, their live-
lihoods buried. There would still be no electricity, no water,
no sanitation, no telecommunications. Food and fuel supplies
would be stretched. Drugs, blood plasma, bandages—those
pathetic little pyramids on the Red Cross stalls—would be
running out. Looters and profiteers would be out on the
streets. Cold night rains would beat on the plastic shelters.
Gastro-enteritis would prey on the children.

This wasn't the United States or Europe, ready to switch
into a vast, co-ordinated rescue operation. Here the supply
lines are poor, the resources stretched. The only main road
into and out of Popayán—the Pan-American highway leading north to Cali, south to Ecuador—was already impossibly
clogged by the outbound traffic of tourists and refugees. President Betancur might thump his tub and say, "*Vamos a recon-
struir Popayán*," but it would take time. Tomorrow, next
month, next year, they would still be putting the broken city
together again.

That night everyone slept out in the street for fear of another tremor. Miguelito, the little porter at the hotel, as-
serted that one was due at midnight. He had quickly assumed
an expertise in seismic matters. He had heard—and I think
he was right—that the earthquake had been a superficial
one, only 20 kilometres below the surface. In terms of anything on the surface, towns for instance, superficial earthquakes are the worst. A couple of faint murmurs were heard,
but midnight came and went uneventfully.

All night, fires burned at the street corners and trucks

rolled through the dark town. There was a general curfew: any attempt to move more than a block encountered tired, suspicious soldiers who sent you back. It was like a city under siege. The air was filled with the smoke of the bonfires, and the smothering taste of masonry dust as the fall-out continued.

On Good Friday morning I joined the thin stream of refugees heading for the new bus station on the edge of town. There I found more scenes of chaos, and a degree of urgency owing to the rumour that all the gas stations in town would soon be out of fuel, and then no more buses would be going. A bus was leaving for Cali as I got there, but it was already jam-packed, and the driver was turning people away. Another bus came, but it was for Pasto, due south. I was buying some provisions in the depot store when another Cali bus came in, and I was again too late to squeeze in. I was beginning to feel the panic of being stuck, Chocó despairs revisited, and when a fourth bus rolled in, dusty and dilapidated, driven by a check-shirted *campesino* who looked like Charles Laughton, I piled in hastily with the first surge of people, and was well ensconced in the aisle at the back before I'd even learned where the bus was bound. For La Vega and Valencia, I was told. Where were they, I asked, wedged in too tight to consult my road-map. In the mountains, *señor*. As the bus headed out, I began to wonder if I was being wise. There wasn't a single tourist aboard. There must have been eighty people in that rattle-trap old bus, and it looked like every one of them was going up into the mountains because they *lived* there.

During a hot, honking, two-hour queue for petrol, I had ample time to reconsider. The map quickly confirmed my suspicions. A thin dotted line—"Carrera Transitable" according to the legend—represented the road up to La Vega, south-east of Popayán. At La Vega it appeared to stop. They had said the bus was going to Valencia, but this wasn't marked on the map at all. I asked one of the passengers.

"Valencia is *el último pueblito,*" he said mysteriously. The last village before what? "Before the *páramo,*" he said.

This did not sound promising. A dirt road up to the *páramo,* the bleak heaths of the Andean highlands, was to all intents and purposes a dead end. The only way out would be straight back down again.

I was about to cut my losses and head back into town, when a young man, bright-eyed and earnest, said to me, "Up around Valencia it is very beautiful."

"I'm sure it is," I said, "but there's no way on. I must get north." The time for sightseeing was over.

"But you can," he cried. "The road runs out at Valencia, but there is a trail that goes on, right across the *páramo,* and down into Huila department. It is the old pilgrim way, the *camino real,* between San Agustín and Popayán. From Valencia it is three days by foot to San Agustín, or perhaps you will be able to get a mule to ride. From San Agustín, of course, there are buses."

We consulted the map. He put a cross where Valencia should be, and ran a pencil line due east across to San Agustín. One map inch, about 50 kilometres, across the Páramo de las Papas, height 11,000 feet. It seemed a long, cold way round to Bogotá, but it also seemed a lot better than getting my bag out and traipsing back into the stricken city in the dimming hope of getting transport up to Cali. When the bus finally set off, I was still on it. The young man, Otaviel, chatted informatively. He was a student and had walked all around these southern mountains, doing survey work for the Agustín Codazzi Geographic Institute in Bogotá.

The pale, brilliant green of the Cauca valley—cane-fields, rice-paddies, bamboo groves—slowly changed to the deep, burnished green of the mountains. At La Sierra we stopped for snacks: *empanadas* and hardboiled eggs. A lot of people left the bus at La Sierra and I got a seat. A wizened old Páez lady threaded barefoot along the aisle selling the tiny sweet bananas they call *manzanitas,* little apples. Otaviel got off at San Miguel. We switchbacked up through forest and rocks.

La Vega was a high, pale village, with a wide square full of light. A blind man sat under a tree, with a guitar leant up beside him, and an enormous bunch of marguerite daisies on his lap. The bus was almost empty when we made the last stretch to Valencia: two brown-faced, slant-eyed Páez, the worldly-wise ten-year-old boy who was riding shotgun, and the big, gruff *campesino* at the wheel, who reminded me of Lola's uncle Juan and his drowned *rápido*.

The boy put on music. Grupo Miramar: spiky rhythms and heavy Sir-Douglas-style keyboards. The light was fading now. I sprawled in the back seat. An array of peaks, canyons and valleys stretched away behind us until they turned a deep sapphire blue. We lurched on up the dirt-road to the last village.

Valencia was a straggling, one-street village, thirty families, *campesinos* and Páez hill-farmers, subsisting on cold-climate crops and the sale of milk to the dairies that supply Popayán. The air at dusk was chill and rare. Fifty pesos bought a musty bed for the night in a house that served as the village inn. Across the street, the low-built wooden church was filling up for a Good Friday evening service: candles and lamps, bright paper decorations, a small boy in a bishop's hat made of newspaper. Inside the benches were crowded, everyone muffled in woollen *ruanas*, a low murmur of conversation and crying babies. It was not so much a service as a Sunday school lecture, conducted by a nun and a priest, on the theme of Las Siete Palabras, the seven utterances of Christ on the cross. The sharp-faced sister compared Christ's offer of redemption to someone giving you a free ticket to the cinema: you would be snubbing Him if you took the ticket and didn't go to the movie. She was pale, bossy and bespectacled, the expert on spiritual hygiene. The Indians in their ponchos stared at her, slant-eyed, open-mouthed. The mumbled credos echoed in the cold mountain air.

In the morning the sky was grey. There were horsemen in the street, wood-smoke in the air, milk churns waiting to be trucked down the mountain. I learned that I could hire a

mule at the house of Gustavo Papamija. This was easy to
find, I was told. It was *la última casa*. So out of the last
village I went, walking east, up to the last house. It was an
hour's easy going on a trail bordered by stubby trees and
green meadows. On the way I met an old, pixie-like Páez
man in a woolly hat. I stopped for the mandatory exchange
of cordialities, and to check that I was still en route for Papamija's house. He insisted I rest and eat with him in his hut
beside the trail. It was dark and smoky inside. Old clothes
and horse-tack hung from the mud walls. A watery grey
broth simmered on the *candela*, the low wood fire which is
never allowed to go out. The soup—maize and cabbage, both
growing in the plot outside the door—tasted thin, stalky and
saltless. I brought out white cheese, bread and aguardiente.
We ate out of black pots, mostly in silence. It was a gentle,
tonic silence, full of birdsong. It is *sano* here, he said—a
word often used by the country folk of Colombia—sane and
healthy, not like the other Colombia of *mala fama*, bad
name. I reflected guiltily that it was precisely the country's
mala fama that had brought me here in the first place. As I
was leaving, beside his crooked gate, he pointed at an orange
lump, about 6 inches long, nestling on the earth of the bank.
I thought it was some mushroom or fungus. Then I looked
closer and saw that it was a creature with fine, fox-red fur,
some kind of large mountain dormouse, perhaps. The old
Páez gently touched it with a stick and to my surprise it suddenly unfurled its legs and flew silently away over the
thatched roof. It was a bat. "They're blind," I said. "No," he
corrected, "they see in a different way."

Gustavo Papamija's house was low, white and tin-roofed,
huddled in the lee of the hill 100 metres below the tree-line.
Gustavo was not at home, but his wife was—a small, tubby
Indian, wearing trousers under her dress—and his two big
sons, and a black-haired, beautiful girl, about twenty, called
Anilia, and assorted kids, dogs, chickens, and a goat. They
plied me with questions about the *terremoto*. There was a
long period of haggling on the porch with the two thick-set
sons, Gilberto and Raúl. A mule was available, but it would

have to be fetched from another farm. We agreed on a price: room and board for the night, and the hire of the mule to a village called Puerto Quinchana, all in for 2,000 pesos. At Quinchana I could catch a truck to San Agustín.

Gustavo came back that evening: a small, smooth-faced, nut-brown man, with a leather-sheathed machete at his side. He had Indian blood but was not pure Páez. His full name was Gustavo Papamija Guardialínea—his family had lived here so long that they had taken the honorary title of "Guardians of the State-line." The frontier between the departments of Huila and Cauca ran across the *páramo* near here. In the old days the Guardians of the Line patrolled for bandits and insurgent Páez, but nowadays it just meant keeping the trail open and well shored up against the bogs of the *páramo*.

After a sunset like the going down of Valhalla I was given supper in the little kitchen: mutton soup and maize bread. The two boys had gone off to buy provisions in Valencia, and to fetch the mule back. I now met another brother whom I hadn't seen before, a thin, whey-faced young man whose mouth hung open. This was Adolfo, the family simpleton. He stared amiably into the fire, perfectly still, like the Fool on the Hill.

After supper I watched them making sausages. Herbs, onion and rice were frying in a pan. Over the *candela*, iron hooks were suspended at different heights from the fire. Anilia and her mother argued over which height the pan should be. The *señora* rooted out some meat. Dismembered bits of sheep were stashed all round the smoky kitchen. Strips of meat hung from the rafters. An entire leg dangled on a hook in the corner, red and white, bones and joints. She flicked among the hanging strips, as if browsing through a rack of summer dresses, until she found one that pleased her. She tore off chunks of mutton fat and threw them into the pan. All the while Anilia was kneading away at a vatful of blood and innards, a rich gruel the colour of raw liver. It sloshed over her hands and up her wrists. She was wearing royal blue wool, a black skirt and white ankle-socks. The skirt rode up over her smooth brown knees as she worked. The contents of the frying-pan were now mixed in with the blood, and heated slightly. In another dish lay a pile of white gut, *viscera blanca*. Anilia began to squeeze and tamp the mauve mulch down into the tubing of white skin. Papamija tore off bits of sacking and knotted them tightly round lengths of filled skin. Slowly a string of blood-pudding sausages took shape. The usual word for sausages is *chorizos*, but when I used this word I was corrected. These were *rellenas*, said Papamija. Simple Adolfo seemed to find my mistake hilarious and dwelt on it through the evening. When a silence fell he would chuckle and shake his head, and murmur *"Chorizos!"* over and over again in his soft, sluggish voice. And everyone would laugh gently along, exchanging knowing looks, enjoying this obscure little parable of the Fool, the Stranger and the Sausages.

Outside the arc of the *candela* it was cold, but inside my eyes stung and watered from the smoke. Out of the west-facing window the last streaks of sunset hung on a white sea of mist. The boys should be back soon. The *señora* shooed away a dog that was nosing at the sausages. She talked at it in the strange, glottal whispers of the Páez tongue. She switched on the radio and sat over it at the table with a candle, and through a haze of static came name after name, the dead, the injured and the missing from the Popayán earthquake.

Around 9 o'clock on the morning of Easter Sunday, I breasted the Páramo de las Papas aboard the wide, sure, slow back of Michaka the mule. She was fourteen years old, chestnut brown with a black streak down her rump. I was assured she was *muy mancita*, gentle and tractable. I had directions to leave her with a Señora Paz in Quinchana, a day and a half's ride from Papamija's house.

The *páramo* was a blanket of swirling cloud and driving horizontal rain, through which a grim heath of yellowish bog-grass and stunted *frailejones* could occasionally be glimpsed. It was only an hour's ride across the *páramo*, I was told—the trail crossed it at the shortest point—but it was going to be a cold, wet hour. Away to my left I saw what Papamija had told me to look out for: the Laguna de Magdalena, a small lake glinting through the mist like tarnished pewter. This was the source of the Magdalena river. I persuaded a reluctant Michaka off down a side-path towards it, and found the stream issuing from the lake. There was nothing much to see, a thin black trickle through yellow tussocks, but it was something to know that this same water was going to run right up through Colombia, fatten into a 2-kilometre-wide river, and flow into the Caribbean Sea 1,000 miles away. In fact I suddenly found this very encouraging. "Coastbound!" I shouted into the rain. "From now on, coastbound," I said more gently to Michaka. She looked unimpressed, and turned back up towards the trail.

Once the sun had dried me, I decided that there could be few pleasanter ways of spending Easter Sunday than coming down through the stupendous forested gorges of the Huila highlands on the back of a mule. The local populace seemed to have other ideas, for I didn't see a soul on the trail all day, only rocks and stones and trees, and tangles of wild fuchsia, and the constant purling presence of the infant Magdalena. I learned the ways of Michaka the mule—very set ways, as she knew the trail intimately. She knew where a certain broad-leaved plant grew, and no amount of shouting and cuffing could dissuade her from stopping for a few mouthfuls. She knew where the track ran too steep and stony, and refused to budge until I dismounted. When I wanted to dismount for some reason, however, she knew it was unnecessary, and ambled implacably on while I tugged at the reins. I talked to her about this and that. She signalled mysteriously with her ears. I quickly developed a deep respect for her, but was never quite sure if the feeling was mutual.

Towards evening we came to a cluster of farms in a green valley, with the stubble of recent clearance on the slopes. At one of these I found a bed for the night, and grazing for Michaka. I dined regally on fresh trout from the Magdalena and warm milk spiked with aguardiente. My host was a thin, shifty man in a cap, with the nasal Huilense accent. He had a small herd of cows and took cheese to San Agustín twice a week. There was a spring to wash in and a candle beside my bed.

The next day—more vistas and silence, more echoing wooden bridges across the Magdalena, a rain-shower, a growing sense of hotter, spiky vegetation—we made it at around 2 o'clock to the dusty, one-horse village of Puerto Quinchana. I found Señora Paz, said goodbye to Michaka, and a couple of hours later I was rolling out to San Agustín in an open-sided bus. There was only a handful of passengers, which was just as well, because at Villafatima the wood seats were all taken out and stacked on the roof, and a consignment of timber was slotted in. On the outskirts of Villafatima a *campesino* ran up, pulling his horse, and flagged us down. There was a big tyre roped to the horse, and the man wanted it pumped up. The mustachioed driver fed the air-line out from the bus. He grinned and said he'd put it up the horse's arse to fatten it up. The *campesino* said to put it in his purse, to make *that* fatter. It was dark before we got to San Agustín. The driver joked with the timber-man. I could see his teeth flashing in the rear-view mirror.

I lingered a day and two nights in San Agustín, famous for its extraordinary collection of pre-Columbian statuary, strange brooding figures scattered among the woods and hills around the village like petrified extra-terrestrials. From San Agustín, still running with the Magdalena, I got a bus to Neiva, a hot, unremarkable town in the lowlands. I remember just one incident there. I went in for a beer at a bar near the bus terminal, but the man behind the bar frowned and cocked his head when I spoke. "Where are you from?" he said. From Britain, I told him. "I don't serve British," he said, jutting his stubbly chin at me. Then I saw the sign above the drink-tariff: "CAFÉ-BAR LAS MALVINAS." Of all the gin-joints in Neiva I had to walk into one called "The Falkland Islands." It was a year since the brief flurry of war in the South Atlantic, but it was clearly recent enough to the barman, who was Argentinian and proud of it. I thought of appropriate things to say, dissociations and mollifications, but I was new in town, and he was a brawny bloke with his arms folded over his check shirt, and I soon decided that tactical retreat was called for. No beach-heads for me today. On the sidewalk a man joined me. "*Argentino,*" he said, jerking his head towards the bar. "We don't like them either. You know what we say? If you want to make a few quick pesos, you buy an Argentinian for what he's worth, and you sell him for what he says he's worth."

From Neiva I flew to Bogotá, and so the whole crazy tangent became a circle, and I was back where I'd started three weeks ago. I didn't leave Eldorado airport this time. I sat tight and waited for the next flight to the coast. It left at dawn, for Santa Marta. There were no breakdowns, no hijacks, no side-doors. By breakfast time I was on the coast at last. *La costa del caribe!*

18

BACK AT THE
FRUIT PALACE

Back in Santa Marta, "the pearl of the Americas," everything was in place. The same scruffy waterfront, with its promenade of coconut palms. The same carpet of tiny orange petals fallen from the guaiac trees. The same banana boats lying off on the glazed sea. The same seafront cafés doing their slow morning business, the raunchy Rincón Francés, El Molino in a new coat of paint, the Manhattan ice-cream parlour. And there was the Pan-American, a neon cocktail glass fitfully flickering in the shadow of the awning. I had a *tinto* there for old time's sake. The waiter said no, they didn't have bands playing there on Saturday nights.

I cut up across the Parque Bolívar, away from the sea, and into the grid of hot side-streets that ran up towards the *mercado popular*. The scrubby, sandy foothills beyond the town looked parched. The streets were pale, bleached with sun, sliced with shadows, the low houses predominantly white-washed, but here and there daubed with pastels, faded Mediterranean tones of pink, blue and pistachio-green. I bought cigarettes in a tiny *tienda* with half-filled shelves, briskly served by a boy who hadn't been born last time I was here. Opposite, an old man was being shaved in a barber's shop the size of a cupboard, with flyblown old line-drawings advertising James Dean hairstyles. Next door was the Siete Rojo pool-hall, somnambulant figures moving in the dimness inside.

I turned into 10th Street. Looking at where the whitewashed frontage and grilled windows of the Fruit Palace should be, I realized I had come on to the street too high. I walked back down a couple of blocks, towards the thin band of sea. I was on the right part of the street now, but I still couldn't see the Fruit Palace, and it took me a moment to shake off my expectations, and see that the house was still there, much the same as before, only the signboard had been taken down, and instead there was painted boldly on the wall, "Restaurante y Mercados EL PROGRESO."

Inside, the counter was in a different place, and the burly man behind it was definitely not Julio. Otherwise everything was much the same. I noticed the carved wood on the door, the criss-cross of rafters on the high ceiling, the private table behind the arch. The archetypal Colombian café services were the same too, all kinds of drink, simple *comida corriente* meals, a few random provisions and toiletries, only the range of *jugos* was not as it had been in Julio's day. The place was empty, as ever.

I ordered a sapodilla juice. We traded a few pleasantries. He was surly but not unresponsive. The sun streamed in from the yard where I had lived with my hammock and parrot cage. From the edge of the new counter I could see right down the yard. Where there had been saplings in the dust there was now a tall young honey-berry tree, and behind a line of washing there was the hen-house, where poor old Harvey had ended up on that night of fiasco all those years ago.

"This place was once called the Fruit Palace, wasn't it?"

The man looked up from the blender with a squint of suspicion. He admitted that it was.

"I stayed here for a while, a few years ago, in the little room out back."

His face relaxed. "No, *señor*, I am sorry. We do not rent out the room any more." He served up my sapodilla in a dirty glass and added with a rueful shrug, "The family gets bigger."

"That's all right. I was really hoping to find the man who used to run the Fruit Palace, Julio. He was a very good friend of mine."

He shook his head. No, he didn't know anything about Julio. He had bought the Fruit Palace from someone called Luis, four or five years ago. Luis had gone to Sincelejo, he said. His wife came in from the room that had been Julio's bedroom. There was a bead curtain over the door now. She carried a little boy in the crook of her arm. She looked not unlike Julio's *muchacha*, Miriam—black hair combed back, plump body in a tight turquoise dress, bare feet on the stone floor.

The man asked her if she knew anything about this *tipo* Julio, but she shook her head, and said much the same as her husband, only this time it was Valledupar that Luis had gone to. They argued listlessly on the subject for a while.

I drank my *jugo*. The radio played an unexpectedly sad Tolimense ballad. There were two caged birds above the door: yellow and black *toque*, scarlet *sangre de toros*. The man stood in the doorway, sucking reflectively at his teeth, looking out down the bleached street. His greasy hair, flattened back over his head, came down into a fringe of tight greying curls at the back of his neck. The bright rectangle of the door showed a broken dusty sidewalk, the bonnet and bumper of a Dodge pick-up, a cream wall and a pale blue door, and next to it—a new addition to the view—the bright plastic frontage of a "Rico Pollo" fried chicken emporium. The woman came up and nestled against him, put her arm around his broad shoulders. He scarcely moved, just kept on looking down the street, letting her hang off him. She sat down at one of the tables and took the slide out to let her long, coarse, crow-black hair down. The toddler crawled by the counter. There was a guinea-pig running loose, fattening up on café dust before going into the pot. The little boy tried to chase it, but it hid behind a crate of empty beer bottles. The radio suddenly went silent. The man clicked his teeth, said, "We must get that shitty radio fixed," but neither of them moved. A deep silence fell over the room. Tacked on to one of the shelves was a humorous notice: "Credit will only be given if you are over eighty-nine years old, and accompanied by your father."

There weren't even any ghosts here. La Loca had swept them all away. Now another dreamer leant in the doorway, another *chulita* combed out her hair, and the town got on with its business, its leisurely stroll past the daily landmarks. It was so quiet in the Progress Restaurant and Stores that I could hear the dry, scaly rattle in the corner, as the guinea-pig snuffled at the corpse of a cockroach.

At the Hotel Corona—a converted monastery on 12th Street, very run-down, recommended by the man at El Progreso—I took an upstairs room, 300 pesos a night, no meals. It was scruffy but clean: a flagged floor, a low bed, a ceiling fan, a cubicle with a shower—or at least an overhead tap—and a lavatory. The long shuttered window opened on to the hotel courtyard, but the fruit trees in the patio were bushy enough to keep the room private. The desk boy, Omar, was a friendly, handsome creole, about eighteen. He was from the village of Caracoles, in the plains south of Fundación. Other people involved in the running of the hotel—vague *administradores*, porters, maids—were sometimes there, but Omar was always there, lounging at the desk, pottering in the courtyard, or lying on his bed in the back-room ready to poke his head out. He listened all day long to *vallenatos* on the radio—Radio Galeón—and read his way slowly through a huge pile of Venezuelan trash-mags. These cartoon penny-dreadfuls—*un cine en su bolsillo*, a movie in your pocket—are staple reading for Colombians of all ages. There are horror strips like *Posesión Diabolica*; and detective strips like *Adelita*, full of leggy ladies in vaguely sado-masochistic situations; and a heroic Indian, Lonely Eagle, who battles with swarthy, rock-jawed *guaqueros*; and a curious, downmarket Latin Superman, El Enmascarado de Plata, the Man in the Silver Mask, who so clearly has right on his side that even the Archangel Michael appears from time to time to get him out of scrapes.

Also staying at the Corona, just down the balcony from me, was a travelling couple, Renate and Renaldo. She was a languid, blousy, *jolie laide* Swiss, he a Titianesque Venetian with a fierce black moustache and long black hair, out of which a small plaited pigtail emerged piratically. Neither of them spoke English, so we talked in Spanish. Renate droned through travellers' yarns, burble burble, *me entiendes*, burble burble. Renaldo was quieter, more mercurial. They had been travelling round South America for five years. They had beautiful things, *las frutas del viaje*, the white woven hammock from the Mato Grosso, the drinking horn from Paraguay, leather-sheathed machetes, amethyst necklaces, and of course our treasured pipe, given us by Shipibo Indians in the jungles near Pucallpa, the bowl of blackwood, the stem of monkey's bone, especial good luck.

They hadn't been in Santa Marta long, but had slid with ease into its nonchalant rhythms. Santa Marta pampers your vices so attentively they begin to feel like virtues. Renate slept late in the mornings, but Renaldo was always up around six-thirty, while the sky was still pink, and down to the town beach. He would jog along the crescent-shaped bay, a good fifteen minutes' trot there and back, do some exercises, swim and return, purchasing the morning paper on the way back. After a shower he was ready for his Santa Marta breakfast, the *blanco y negro*, two generous rails of cocaine and two stiff cups of *tinto*. The *tintos* were brought by Omar, over whom he held a mysterious sway. Thus torqued up, he would attend to the day's small businesses—purchases, money-changing, and so on. Everything seems to run smoothest in the early morning in Santa Marta. After about 10.30 the sun gets too high, and people start thinking about lunch-time. He would aim to have his business finished by then, with the *blanco y negro* starting to wear off anyway, and then it was back to the Corona, where Renate was raising a sleepy head, or reading in bed. They would shower, share a joint of *punto rojo*, and then take a long, leisurely breakfast proper at one of the seafront cafés—eggs *pericos*, perhaps a shrimp *ceviche*, bread and guava jelly, coffee, *jugos*. Breakfast would slide effortlessly into the lunch-time promenade, a couple of beers here, a chat and a deal there: lottery-sellers, street vendors, gringos, Samarios, they seemed to know them all. Renaldo had that same singsong Italian Spanish that I remembered in Alessandro, Gus's friend, and the *costeños* found it captivating. After this came the siesta, ritually observed, then around 4 o'clock the day's second segment would begin, another period of activity, often their time for receiving people in their room. They had a profitable little side-line in drugs, selling discreet batches of slightly overpriced *perica* to gringos who didn't want the hassle of scoring off the street. Around 5.30, just as the sun was beginning to cool, they took another swim at the town beach, and returned to the Corona to prepare for the evening's festivities.

Sometimes the festivities would include a dinner of red snapper and Chilean Riesling at a small seafront restaurant called El Molino. The manager, Señor Santander, was a tall, melancholy man, fiftyish, with long, pale hands that always trembled slightly. I was surprised when, on learning that I was British, he asked: "*Usted es* Scowse?" I said I wasn't, but I knew Liverpool a bit. So, it transpired, did he. One night he told me his story. He was from Cartagena originally. During La Violencia, the civil war of the 1950s, when Liberal and Conservative factions were shooting each other in the streets, he had to leave town fast—he was a radical Gaitanista. He came to Barranquilla, signed up as a merchant seaman and sailed to Spain. For many years he was captain of an old tramp-steamer running cargo out of Bilbao, and often he sailed to Liverpool, carrying oranges, grapes and oil. There he met and wooed a Taiwanese girl, Lily, who lived in Liverpool's dockside Chinatown. Twenty years ago he married her—"It rained, as always," he said. Lily had been brought up in Liverpool. She was a great lover of what Santander called *el Merci-Bee*, and which I eventually understood to be "the Mersey-beat." It was incredible: Santander had actually seen Los Beatles playing at the Cavern, when there were still five of them, and he had seen Gerry y los Pacemakers, and Wayne Fontana y los . . . los . . .

"Los Mindbenders?"

"*Eso es*. Mindbenders!"

He stared off sadly towards the port. A container ship was being loaded under floodlights. His Chinatown Lily had died giving birth to their son. He had been back in Colombia ten years now. He had run pleasure cruises to the Rosarios Islands for a while, and now he lived in Santa Marta, with a new wife and a little daughter, and a good enough job here at El Molino. His son still lived in Liverpool, where he had been brought up by his Taiwanese grandparents. He would be about eighteen now. He was called John, as Lily had intended, after John Lennon.

The actual owner of El Molino was an unpleasant character called Silvio, a smooth-skinned young wheeler-dealer with a sneer of self-congratulation on his face and a little lip of paunch pouting over his expensive slacks. He did nothing in the restaurant itself, simply hung around from time to time, attended by various liggers and *guardespaldas*. One of these we christened the Lone Ranger, because he always rode his gleaming Yamaha motorbike, as if with a hearty "Hi-oh, Silver!", up on to the sidewalk and down the aisle of the restaurant to the back. Next door to El Molino was a bingo stall, Bingo El Portal, which Silvio also owned. This was run by two men, a fat chain-smoker who kept the till and administered the prize money (basic prize 1,000 pesos), and a thin, dandified man who called the numbers. His deep, deadpan voice, raggedly amplified, could be heard halfway down the beach drag. Between games these two would sit with Silvio and his cronies at their reserved table.

One night there was a fight at El Molino. Silvio was lounging around as usual, with his bowling shirt and aviator sunglasses and little leather handbag. He was huddled in conference with an older man I had not seen before, when on to the scene came an angry, half-drunk *costeño* in beach shorts. He made straight for Silvio, leaned his knotty arms on the table and started to harangue him in low, angry tones. I heard the words *plata* and *marimba*—money and dope, what else? Silvio craned nervously round for his cronies, but they were off inside the restaurant watching a video of *Starsky y Hutch*. Silvio started to back away. The *costeño*, sweating, came after him, shouting about money he was owed, 10,000 pesos, how he had nothing to feed his wife and little *chinos* on, while Silvio, the *gordo maricón* Silvio, sat like a frog on his stinking money, getting fatter every day. Then a full pushing, punching, kicking scuffle started, but the waiters and *guardespaldas* were out now, pulling the *costeño* away. Señor Santander flapped around the edge of the mêlée like a nervy flamingo. The Lone Ranger and a couple of waiters calmed the *costeño* down, pushing him gently but firmly away on to the sidewalk. They acted as if they knew him well, a recalcitrant regular nuisance. But the *costeño* still stood at the edge of the tables, swaying dangerously, spittle on his chin, shouting hoarse obscenities into the restaurant where Silvio stood in a huddle of ministering servants. Santander was dabbing at Silvio's bloodied nose. Silvio had hurt his arm: they poured water on it. He cursed like a child and lashed out at one of the waiters for pouring water on his Seiko watch. To my alarm the *costeño* now turned to us. There were other occupied tables, but it was ours he happened to focus on. He appealed to us with big gestures. Ten thousand he was owed, he shouted. And then he explained, quite clearly, how "*este hijo de puta compra la marimba y no paga nada*"—the son-of-a-bitch buys grass off me and pays me nothing. This kind of public announcement did not please the Silvio faction. I saw the Lone Ranger and another coming out, fast and mean, but before they had got to him the *bingero* had nipped around—the tall one, who called the numbers—and he was buffeting the *costeño* back with a series of hard jabs to the shoulder. I saw his hand slip in under his jacket. He showed something to the *costeño*—his back was to us, but it was obviously a gun. The *costeño* started backing off pretty smartly, and had soon pushed off out of sight through the crowd on the sidewalk. Everyone breathed a sigh of relief. The waiters laughed nervously. "Please, *señores y señoras*, a regrettable incident, please continue." The crowd melted away, the bingo-players returned to their seats, the antique ball-fountain creaked into action. "Y el veintiuno suertero," boomed the deep calm voice. Lucky twenty-one, and everything back under control.

There was a sequel to this little incident. A few nights later we came back for another dinner. It was Friday night. We expected quite a crowd, but all we found was a couple of waiters standing round sheepishly, and Señor Santander looking even more mournful than usual. There had been a burglary last night, he explained. The refrigerator had been stolen. It had been a tryingly hot day: a seafront restaurant with no cold beer was like a tea-shoppe with no fancies. There was no fish on the menu, either. It had gone off. It was, curiously, only the fridge that the thieves had taken.

"Why didn't they take the TV, or the hi-fi, or something more valuable?" asked Renate.

A slight change came over the funereal manager's face—yes, it was the ghost of a smile. "I think," he said mysteriously, "that would have been too much."

"Too much for a Colombian thief?" snorted Renate.

"I asked around," Santander replied. "On the black market you can sell a good fridge like that for around 10,000. You remember the other night? Ten thousand pesos?"

We pressed him for more details of this vendetta, but he shook his head and put a long forefinger to his lips. "The boss prefers we say nothing. We get a new fridge tomorrow. There'll be red snapper and cold beer tomorrow night."

19

CHILEAN PACKAGES

It was time to get the bit between my teeth, not an activity much encouraged by Santa Marta in the hot days of April. The pace of life was slow, not dull but slow, a lazy adagio punctuated by sudden scherzos of small-town drama, and by the insistent undertone of villainy that ran through the place. Nothing happened, nothing was done, but always in the most entertaining way. Everyone was waiting on someone or something else. The big deal, the mother-lode, the *gran chipola,* was just around the corner. The Samarios, with their strong black African and Moorish Arab strains, are by nature nonproductive. They value themselves as *hombres de negocios:* trading, broking, dealing, smuggling. The essential benevolence of *costeño* life—sun, sea and fertile earth—permits the pursuit of these vocations right down to the raggedest economic level. From the millionaire *marimberos* in the Country Club to the shaven-headed *gamines* touting Chiclets down the beach drag, Santa Marta is one great big service-economy.

But pleasant though it was to let the clock run slow, and sit in the sun, and have time bring you scenes as a breeze brings scents, I had a job to do. I was here to write a story, and I knew that Santa Marta, if anywhere, was the place to do it. I was going to forget all about Bogotá, Gus, basuko addicts, slaughter-houses and earthquakes. This was Santa Marta, *la costa.* I was back in the smugglers' den, the good-

time town, the rock 'n' roll South America. At last I was
going to get this story off the ground.

I had a plan of sorts. Part of the problem in Bogotá had
been my own approach. It was no use expecting to bustle in
with my pen and notebook, and cobble it up from a few
second-hand stories. The people that matter in the drug
racket like, as Gus had pointed out, to keep everything off
the record—and the people that don't will tell their secrets
to any Mrs. Henry who looks their way and pumps them a
few. I had been two months in Colombia, spent most of my
money, been jacked full of cocaine and basuko, and had still
yet to meet anyone that mattered. I had *possibly* shaken
hands with a cocaine baron—Don Rafael Vallejo at the San
Felipe slaughter-house, who *may* have been Gus's mysterious
Snow White—but that could hardly count as the scoop of
the decade. It was time to tuck my notebook under my pillow and enter Phase Two. Surely Gus was right when he said
one night in his crow's nest: "The only way to get into this
story is to become a part of it."

My plan was, in a nutshell, to pose as a would-be buyer of
a consignment of cocaine. Ten kilos seemed a nice round
number: a middle-sized amount, serious enough to require
proper smuggling rather than a simple mule-run through
customs, but without getting up into the industrial volumes
being moved by the big mafia syndicates. I wanted to keep it
on a human scale, and see just how far into the Santa Marta
smuggling circuit I could talk myself.

One problem about posing as a buyer was cash, or the lack
of it. Here in Santa Marta a kilo of cocaine cost around
$15,000, a little more than in Bogotá or Cali, because that
bit closer to the retail market. There tends to be little bulk
discounting in big drug purchases, so 10 kilos was going to
carry a price-tag of something like $150,000. For a few wild
moments I entertained the notion of cabling Malcolm for the
money, but quickly realized that not only was this futile, it
was unnecessary. I didn't actually need the money, as I
wasn't actually going to buy any cocaine. All I needed was

the appearance of having—or of being able to get hold of—
the money. I needed, in short, collateral.

Accordingly, soon after arriving in Santa Marta, I telephoned Malcolm in London. A secretary, a tinkling double-
barrelled voice from another planet, told me to hold on a
minute. The minute ticked away expensively. "Sorry, he
seems to have just popped out." More minutes. Then at last
the distant, flushed voice of Malcolm. "Charles! Super!
How's it going?" I assured him it was all going wonderfully,
piping hot stories at every turn, practically writing itself, and
so on.

"Listen, Malcolm, I'm calling because I think I'm going to
need a bit of back-up."

Over all those miles of cable I heard him wince. "Pretty
difficult, Charles," he brayed. "End of the tax year. They're
pretty sticky up in Accounts at the moment."

"I don't mean money, though Christ knows, I could use
some. I want you to do me a favour, that's all. I want collateral."

"Could you be more specific?"

"OK. In a few days' time I'm probably going to send you a
cable, all right? I'm not sure what it'll say, but when you get
it I want you to cable straight back to me. What you'll say is:
"Price is good, but check all transport before proceeding."
That's all, nothing else. Have you got that?"

"Yes, I've got that."

"Good. Send it to me at the Corona Hotel, Santa Marta."

"Yes, all right. But, you know, what's all this in aid of?"

"Call it a sprat to catch a smuggler. Look, I must go." I
ran through it one last time. "You will do it, won't you,
Malcolm? Oh, and Malcolm, one last thing. For Christ's sake
don't sign it, will you? No names. What? Yes, of course it's
all above board. Yes, totally kosher. 'Bye now!"

The next stage was to find someone with 10 kilos to sell. I
did not anticipate many problems here. The coke runneth
over in Santa Marta. It's impossible to say what proportion of

Colombian cocaine actually leaves from the Caribbean coast-line, or from the airstrips along the Guajira peninsula, but even if it's only half, that still makes a throughput of about 500 kilos a week. Most of that is in transit, rather than for sale, but in general there's no shortage of snow on the coast, and no shortage of people anxious to sell it to you. It is well-known that in Santa Marta it is easier to buy a kilo of *coco* than a gram.

I decided to try Waldino. He was the black-bearded Mr Fixit so warmly praised by Jairo, the Samario I had met with Julio Cesar that night on Caracas Avenue. I thought this was probably better than asking Renate and Renaldo for a con-tact. They doubtless had several, but it seemed likely that if they thought I was buying in volume, they would want to get in on it, become the middle-men and take their "drink," their slice of *perica* or pesos for services rendered. With 10 kilos the drinks were tasty. That would, of course, destroy the whole point of this charade, which was to get *myself* to the people that mattered. Besides, I liked them. I was going to have to do an awful lot of lying, and I didn't want to do it to them. So I was glad in a way when they left the Corona for a spell of sightseeing in Cartagena. They thought they would be back in a few days, but we said our goodbyes seri-ously, they because nothing is for certain on the road, and I because there was going to come a point when I and my phantom cocaine deal were going to have to disappear on the instant.

It didn't take long to rouse Waldino. Availability was his *métier*. The desk-boy at the Corona, Omar, knew him by sight. He suggested I ask for him at La Casona, a bar near the waterfront. There I was directed to a stationery shop off 5th Avenue, the town's main shopping and business street. In the cluttered, slightly funereal shop, a black-bearded man was serving a pair of schoolgirls with exercise books and pen-cils. It seemed an unlikely venue for starting up a cocaine deal, but when the girls left, I walked nervously up to the

counter, clutching a roll of Sellotape, and asked if he was
Waldino.

He wasn't, but he could find him. Waldino was one of his
partners. He handed me a pen, and a promotional note-pad,
and said to write my name and where I could be contacted. I
didn't like giving out the name of my hotel, but figured that
anyway it wouldn't take Waldino ten minutes, in this small,
nosy town, to find out where I was staying. I wrote my Christian name and my hotel. The pen had a picture of Spiderman on it.

"OK, mister," the man said briskly. "Waldino will find
you."

It all seemed unbelievably slick and easy. But a few hours
later, towards the end of siesta-time, slight complications began to creep in. There was a soft knock at my door, Omar's
voice saying, "You have a visitor downstairs." It was the man
from the stationery shop.

"I have spoken with Waldino, señor. Unfortunately he is
detained for a few days in Cartagena. He says if your business
is urgent you must meet him there."

Anxious to get things moving, I said, yes, I would meet
him in Cartagena. The man said I should be outside the Paragua café at 3 o'clock tomorrow. This was down in
Bocagrande, the beach resort part of Cartagena. Once again
he assured me, "Waldino will find you."

I told the man I would fly to Cartagena, to give a businesslike impression, but my resources were getting low, and it
was in fact Flota La Velocidad—the Velocity Bus Company—that took me to Cartagena the next morning. It was a
hot, cloudless day. We trailed dust and vallenato accordions
out of Santa Marta, south to Ciénaga, and across the narrow
causeway between the Caribbean and the swampy lagoons of
the Ciénaga Grande, dotted with floating villages of mangrove wood. At every stop the bus was besieged by vendors—
fruit, sweetmeats, tamarind juice, fried chicken. You can eat
well out of a Colombian bus window. Barranquilla loomed
up, sprawling along the mouth of the Magdalena, a dirty

great armadillo of dockside derricks and tacky skyscrapers, with a thick shell of shanty-town *tugurias*. At a stop on the outskirts I was offered, in quick succession, an electric toothbrush, a pair of ladies' high-heeled shoes, and a job lot of Eng Aung Tong Tiger Balm, all doubtless off the back of a cargo ship.

Barranquilla is Colombia's major industrial port, a hot, noisy, fly-blown city which seems almost proud of its lack of redeeming virtues. The first time I had landed here, I recalled, was by chance on the last day of carnival. Everyone had been drinking for five days solid. Rivers of urine ran past the beer tents on Paseo Bolívar. The city was locked in a spasm of dancing, music, jungle masks, ragged costumes. I wandered through it, drenched in flour and water, totally bewildered, unable to understand anything. Drunken Barranquilleros speak a Spanish faster and stranger than any known tongue. By the end of the day I was just about torqued up enough, but then there came a strange, half-understood ceremony, the Death of Jose Carnivalito, and then we were all running after the Carnival Queen in her big shiny Cadillac, and then suddenly it was over, and everyone was strolling around in their workaday clothes, and I was the only one still covered in flour and waving my carnival-issue plastic bottle of rum. There is no one more out of step than a novice on the last day of carnival.

This time round I was just passing through. The Cartagena road cut inland, a hot, undulating terrain of dry grass, low acacias, thirsty horses, cane-grinding sheds, mango-shaded *fincas*. Not long after midday we were nosing through the dusty white outskirts of Cartagena. On a wall a graffito read, "TU ESQUELETO ES VIVO"—your skeleton is alive. Of that I was certain, if of little else.

The bus disembarked us near the San Felipe fortress. I took a town bus down to Bocagrande. This is Colombia's most fashionable beach resort, a long, thin isthmus jutting out south from the old walled town, fringed with beaches and gridded with hotels, boutiques and pavement cafés. At the far end, a late addition to the city's many fortresses, stands the Cartagena Hilton. Locals call the area "Miami Chiquita"—Little Miami—and that about sums it up.

In the lobby of the Hotel Succar, where I went in to buy a street map, a bespectacled American, sweating profusely, was carefully consigning his money, passport, air tickets and watch to the hotel safe. The *portero*'s eyes glinted as the money was counted out—$2,500 in American Express cheques and a few hundred more in bills. I grinned at the American. He scowled back. "If I wasn't such a trusting guy, I'd put my goddamn shirt in there as well!" It transpired that he had arrived that morning from Panama City, tried to change some dollars where he shouldn't have, and ended up with that local speciality, *el paquete chileno*. A "Chilean package"—for reasons obscure—signifies any raw deal, any crockful of short change: a bagful of oregano instead of grass, a gram of borax instead of coke, or in this man's case, an envelope containing a neat wad tied up in a rubber band, with a 1,000-peso bill uppermost and every other sheet blank paper. He had that hot, haunted look, a big man running his hand through his hair. I thought of Harvey, hopelessly out-pointed by events that night at the Fruit Palace. There's something about this place: the heat, the ceiling fans, the smilers with knives. Beware the Chilean package! *La costa* means the cost as well as the coast.

At 3 o'clock, as arranged, I was waiting outside the Paragua, a big pavement café on a corner of 2nd Avenue. It was quiet, siesta-time. A few people moved slowly on the shady side of the street. Tonight it would be full, with lights strung among the palm trees and street-musicians playing. I was wondering what the next few hours would bring. It occurred to me that Waldino knew nothing of what I wanted—not a word had been mentioned about cocaine. For all I knew he might be hoping to sell me a gross of Spiderman biros.

3.15, 3.20, no one came. I stopped patrolling and sweated in a patch of shade. A waiter cleaning tables near me started to chat. Then I saw someone strolling purposefully across the street towards us, a small man in a floppy yellow T-shirt. I had seen him over the other side, in the Presto fast-food joint, drinking something out of a paper cup. Now he joined me on the sidewalk, hand stretched out. "Hey, my friend. Where you from? You been in Cartagena before? You gonna be glad you come. *Con mucho gusto!*" We shook hands. "Luis," he said, then repeated it for my benefit in the form of "Louey." He cocked his head to one side like a parrot, waiting for my name in return. *"Perfecto!"* he cried, "I have a real good friend called Charlie. From Estados Unidos. Man, you'd like that guy!" He spoke fast, slurring, half in the gabble of *costeño* Spanish, half in grating greengo-Eenglish. He was small, grubby and unshaven, and looked like he had shrunk inside his clothes. As he spoke he was leading me gently towards the street, drawing me away from the chatty waiter. The waiter shrugged and shook his head philosophically. He'd seen it all before. Just another Bocagrande street-boy fastening on to another dollar-rich gringo. They feed on them like fruit-flies here. I was beginning to think exactly the same. "No," I said, pulling away from his grip. "I don't want anything. I'm waiting for a friend." We were out of the waiter's earshot now. *"Claro, hombre,"* said Louey. "Your friend Waldino, my friend Waldino. He sent me to fetch you. We go just a couple of blocks, this way."

The couple of blocks turned out to be more like twenty. We hopped aboard a bus which took us out of Bocagrande and up to the walls of the old town. Louey didn't pay, just gave the driver a curt wave of greeting and pushed through the turnstile. He ushered me through, also mysteriously gratis. "Everyone in Cartagena knows Louey," he explained, and settled his scrawny frame in the seat, very casual, legs loosely crossed, ankle on knee. He spent the journey looking out the window, dreamily fingering his stubble.

He was watching me, I thought. All the while I was waiting he was there, checking my credentials, seeing if I had anyone with me, sniffing my scent. I was in at the business

end at last. I'd need more than a street map if I lost my way
now.

From Bocagrande you can see the old walled town, clamped
on to the headland like a limpet, with a rounded carapace of
roofs and cupolas rising up from the huge sea-walls. Cartagena de Indias—the Carthage of the New World—was
founded and fortified in the early sixteenth century, the chief
port on the Spanish Main for the shipment of plundered gold
and jewels back to Spain. Sir Francis Drake came to sack the
city in 1586. They paid him 10 million pesos to spare them
from the torch—the receipt he signed can still be seen in the
Palace of the Inquisition. The town is ringed by 7 miles of
wall, in some places up to 50 feet thick. It is said that the
walls were built with a mortar mixed with bulls' blood.
    Inside the old town everything is very tall, narrow and
close. It is beautiful, but sombre and inquisitorial: dirty white
walls, deep eaves, cobbled streets, huge wooden doors studded with iron nails. Sultry eyes watch from grilled windows
and luxuriant balconies. In the quiet parts it is like a spooky,
run-down Seville, in the trading areas more like a Moorish
kasbah. The touristic parts of the old town, El Centro and
San Diego, are where the governors, priests and merchants
lived, but there is another, rougher quarter called Getsemani, a warren of white one-storey houses, *casas bajas*,
once inhabited by artisans and soldiers and street traders, the
flotsam of the *conquista*. Into this we now plunged. Louey led
the way with a long, jaunty stride, calling out greetings every
few yards. I followed behind like his pet dog. The streets
were steep, some just wide enough for a car, some so narrow
you could touch both walls as you passed. We turned this way
and that. I had no idea where I was or where I was going.
The sun was hot but hazy, a dull iridescence in the close
streets. It was the end of siesta-time. People stood talking in
the street, lounged in dark doorways. They stared as I passed,
brown faces, white shirts, that aloof Arab look. And there
were the girls, *las costeñas*, those heart-stopping, carnival-

eyed creole belles, whose sleek sexuality is made all the more piquant by their utter indifference to honky white gringos.

Louey dipped into a narrow, tiled café: a few chairs, a few beer-crates, a few desiccated *empanadas*. Behind the counter a boy was bent over a sports page. The place was called, improbably, La Reina Victoria. The Queen Victoria Café. Louey called for two cold beers, walking straight down the café, not looking at the boy. Down the far end of the counter stood a short, wide, stocky man, a *mestizo* in his sallow colouring, a negro in the bones of his face and the wide, flattened nose. His beard was, as promised, black and profuse. His eyebrows and hair were negroid and wiry. He looked like a pirate, but—and I felt twin pangs of relief and disappointment—like a comic pirate. Give him an eye-patch and he would have been a dead ringer for Cut-throat Jake. So who did that make me? Captain Pugwash, about to embark on another addle-brained adventure?

Louey walked up to him, said something I didn't hear, scraped a chair round and settled himself astride it. The man put out his hand. "*Señor, qué tal?*" he said pleasantly. "I am Waldino." The boy brought the beers and a *tinto* for Waldino. I slaked my thirst too fast, and hiccoughed.

"Who gave you my name?" asked Waldino.

"A Samario called Jairo. I met him in Bogotá."

His small eyes flickered, looking for the face to fit the name. He found it. "Ah! Jairo." Rich, feckless Jairo. Not an impeccable reference, I guessed from his face, but at least genuine.

There was a short spell of aimless pleasantries. Waldino was a Guajiro, I learned, from San Júan del Cesar, a small town halfway between the Sierra Nevada mountains and the Venezuelan border, doubtless a good breeding ground for *contrabandistas*. I found myself keeping the conversation going with inane, cocktail-party comments. Eventually a silence fell, and there was nowhere else to go but down to business. I looked around. A couple more people had come into the café. "Can we talk here?" I said.

"Perhaps you would like to go out back," said Waldino. "I'll show you the view."

We walked out through a store-room, Louey following, and into a little backyard. Waldino had an oddly dainty way of moving, considering his swarthy looks. Short, busy steps, pointed black leather shoes. I wondered vaguely if he was gay. The view was stupendous—a tumbling scree of tiled roofs, a grove of masts in the Bahia de las Animas, the blue sea stretching off into the haze. The yard was a mess. An outbuilding had recently been demolished, but there was a straggling catalpa tree giving shade, and a chair, an upturned crate and a pile of rubble provided us with seats. We arranged ourselves hierarchically: Waldino, me and Louey. Louey unzipped his jeans—a flash of yellowed Y-fronts—and drew out a twist of brown paper from a pocket sewn inside the waistband. He began to roll a joint, and I began to make my pitch.

"Jairo tells me you're a good person to do business with, Waldino."

He received the compliment graciously, but somehow at arm's length.

"What kind of business are we talking about?"

I dabbed the side of my nose with my forefinger.

"Ah! *Negocios blancos, no?*"

"Yes, white business."

"And are we talking here about little business or big business?"

"If the price is right and the quality is good, we're talking about 10 kilos. Is that little business or big business?"

His eyes narrowed. He scratched his beard watchfully, his eyes penetrating me with the crystal-ball gaze of the Colombian dealer, whose livelihood—perhaps his life—depends on the swift sizing up of potential customers. The good, the bad and the just plain crazy: which compartment did I fall into? "Ten kilos," he said, with a modest shrug. "This is no problem. I can get it." I nodded, my mouth downturned in a businesslike way. He knitted his pudgy fingers, rested them on his thigh, and staring at them intently he said, "You got money?"

I took a deep breath. "At this precise moment . . . No." He was still looking down at his hands, but a single shaggy eyebrow cocked up challengingly. "Let me explain, Waldino. I am here, essentially, as a *representante*." He opened his eyes wide for a moment, gave a little wary sigh, "Ah!" This description of myself seemed to have explained the situation a little without in any way improving it. I hastened on. "I am here on behalf of certain . . . friends, in London. They wish me to establish a connection, work out the arrangements. Once everything is worked out—good *perica*, good price, good set-up—I will cable to them in London. They will have the money transferred to me."

He pursed his lips. "You going to carry the *mercancia* out yourself?"

"Of course not," I said. "That will have to be worked out between us. I'm sure you must have—"

"*Sí, sí, hombre,*" he said, waving aside any doubts. "Transportation no problem." He stood up, hands in pockets, looking out to sea. The sounds of the city floated up on the sullen air. The sun was sneaking round the edge of the catalpa tree, melting the shade on me. Louey handed me the joint. I smelt the fresh, resinous smoke, like minty hay smouldering on a summer's day. "Gold?" I asked. "*Claro, hombre,*" said Louey, "*la rubiecita,* the little blonde girl, just arrived in from Santa Marta. You want to buy some?" The smoke licked round my skull, the sun toasted my face. I handed the reefer to Waldino but he shook his head, and I instantly regretted having taken some. This silence was too long. I must fill it.

"My friends in London," I volunteered. "They are very keen to make a connection here. They have dealt mainly in hashish from the Middle East. If you can provide the right service, they will want to place regular orders, big volumes. I think we could both do very well out of this."

He looked impressed. I wanted to make it sound big, but even more I wanted to keep it all matey between us. You and me, Waldino, the honest brokers. You can get the gear, I can get the money: let's tango! But Waldino was still demurring, still worrying at my weak points. "You don't even have a little money to put up front?" he said. "Not even a *pocito*?" His finger and thumb measured out the thinnest wedge of bills that a self-respecting *contrabandista* could imagine.

I shook my head. "It's up to you, Waldino. I assure you the money is no problem, but only when I know exactly what's happening. Of course," I added, "I could front you 1,000 pesos for a little *muestra*, but I'm sure you don't need me to do that. We're talking about a serious deal here. My friends in London are . . . well, they're big *capos.*"

As I said this I had a brief, unsettling vision of Malcolm, ruddy and bespectacled, the phantom Mr. Big in a Bloomsbury bow-tie.

Waldino checked at his watch. "OK," he said. "I have to make a phone call. You wait here." He tripped busily back into the café.

Louey sagged dreamily, having smoked the rest of the gold. *"Soy maduro como un queso,"* he smiled. He was as ripe as a cheese. He rallied himself to see if he could sell me anything: grass, basuko, girls. "You like girls? No *putas*, real clean girls. We go out to a night-club, you and me, Charlie, *gozar un poco.*"

I paced around the little yard, smoking a cigarette. Who was Waldino phoning? What did he think of me? What would he do if he knew? Perhaps he was already calling his friends in the F-2. Soon they would be there in the café, he'd come and slip the package of coke in my pocket, they'd be waiting for his signal—*"Lo tiene, jefe,"* the gringo's carrying, you can come in now. I sat back down. Just that one toke of gold had stoned me. Everything was ambiguous. In a corner a lizard moved across hot masonry, yellow and black, darting and waiting. Somewhere far away I heard a girl's voice. It sounded like she was calling, "Charlie! Charlie!" But that couldn't be. No one was calling for me. I was flying solo, on these clouds laced with anxiety.

Waldino returned. "I have spoken with one of my associates in Santa Marta," he said. "I think I can help you with this." I nodded. For a moment my throat was too dry to speak. "I have other matters to attend to here in Cartagena," he continued. "I shall be back in Santa Marta on Friday, two days. You are at the Corona, no? I will find you there. We will talk about this *very* carefully."

The interview was over. The hook really seemed to have caught. Louey guided me back through the labyrinth, back to where there were crowds and buses and reality. Surely it had all been a dream. Gethsemane, the Queen Victoria, Louey, Waldino. I hadn't really just opened up negotiations for a 10-kilo move. I hadn't really just sold them my very own little Chilean package.

20

WALDINO CAN GET IT

I returned to Santa Marta. I swam, I wrote, I waited. I found at last a *jugeria* whose juices measured up near enough to my memories of the Fruit Palace, and here I reacquainted myself, working systematically down the tariff, with the marvellous range of tropical fruits.

We know a few of these in Europe—mangoes, paw-paws, passion-fruit, and so on—but this is only a tiny corner of the tropical orchard. In this lush, hallucinatory landscape grow star-apples and marmalade-plums, tree-tomatoes and honey-berries. Every *afficionado* has his special favourite—the silky, elusive *curuba*, perhaps; or the stringent *lulo*; or the noble *zapote*, or sapodilla, so unpromisingly turnip-like on the outside, but inside rich, orange and fleshy. For my part, I remained faithful to my first teacher, Julio. For him Nature's master-work, plucked from the highest branches of the Fruit Tree of Life, was the *guanabana*. I can see him now, enunciating that word, each syllable in itself a succulent morsel, *guah-nah-bah-nah*. To botanists this fruit is the *anona muricata*—it is the "muricate" member of the fruit family known in Spanish as *añon*. "Muricate" means studded with short, hard excrescences or points, like the shellfish *murex*. This, together with such English names as "alligator-pear" and "bullock's heart," conveys the fruit's demeanour well enough. It is not a looker. It dangles awkwardly from an undistinguished tree, long and bulbous, with a ridged green-ish-black rind like alligator hide. But inside—*qué rica, qué sabrosa!*—its white meat packed around black seeds tastes like some celestial version of wild strawberries and cream. The various *añones* are also known as "sop" fruits—because their white, mushy flesh looks like sops of soaked bread—and "custard" fruits. The *guanabana* is the "sour-sop" and the "custard-pear," while the related *chirimoya* is known as the "sweet-sop" and the "custard-apple." For the *guanabana*, I remember, Julio favoured a *crema*, made with all milk and the merest zest of sugar. On his tariff all the other *jugos* were 3 pesos a glass, but *crema de guanabana* was a princely 5 pesos.

Thus fortified with exotic strains of Vitamin C, I awaited Waldino. On the Saturday afternoon, three days after our meeting in Getsemani, he came. I walked out of the shower in my room at the Corona to find him standing in the open doorway. He murmured an apology as I fumbled a towel round my waist.

"I have brought it, Charlie," he said. He was carrying two large plastic bags. I felt a stab of panic. Sweet Jesus, I thought, he's bringing me the deal *now*. The fool's got it all wrong.

"Brought it?" I said. I stared at the bulging carrier-bags. He bustled in and laid them on the bed. "I think you will like it. I know you will like it. You want to try some now?" I stammered without meaning. "Señor Charlie," he said, with a broad, reproachful grin. "This is primo grade merchandise. What I tell you? Waldino can get it, no problem. *Max*-imum quality. *Muy puro.*" He spat out the phrases with relish.

"But, Waldino, I don't want the stuff now!"

He stared at me, nonplussed. The gap between his eyebrows and his beard momentarily widened, like a trapdoor long covered with undergrowth, then it clamped shut again into a petulant, bullish frown which I didn't like one little bit. He said quietly, "You do not want to try the *muestra* I have brought for you?"

"*Muestra?*"

The bags were nothing to do with it. He had only brought me a sample. Watching me closely he reached into his shirt-pocket, and drew out the familiar little rectangle of paper. "It is only a little, of course. I can get more, plenty more, but . . ." He cupped his hand at me, rubbing thumb and forefinger. "To get any further the engine needs a bit of gas, *me entiendes?*"

"Yes. No, that's fine, Waldino. Thank you." I cursed my stupid, clumsy paranoia. Jumping to the wrong conclusion could be fatal. There wouldn't always be a chance to jump back again.

I took the proferred *muestra* and tried to settle into the cool professionalism that I felt the situation demanded. I poked and sifted the white crystal. Waldino fidgeted around the room, anxiously muttering his ad-man's phrases. I peered and dabbed and tasted, pulled a face or two, demurred like a wine-buff. *"Reluce demasiado, no?"* I said. Too much glitter in it.

"Amigo," he came back earnestly. "That is good. The snow is sparkling. You try it and see." He gave a high-pitched titter which came oddly from the piratical face. He was nervous. He really wanted me to like it.

I laid out a rail on my shaving mirror and took it up through a 100-peso note. It was good. *Muestras* usually are, I thought, remembering the Harvey fiasco. Waldino hovered by. I complimented him on his powder. There was no doubt about it. It was cool as a mountain stream, as they used to say about Consulate menthol cigarettes. I offered him some, but he declined. "It's for you, Charlie." I took another snort up the other nostril. My brain put on its sailing shoes. Somewhere out in the street I heard a bell ringing. Probably the egg-man, who pushed a cart through the streets ringing a hand-bell. I remember Julio holding up an egg and delivering one of his maxims. *El mundo vale un huevo*—the world is worth an egg.

"You can get this stuff in quantity?"

"Of course."

"And the price?"

He scratched his head and seemed to wrestle with complex currency calculations, though of course he had the price in

his head all along. "Twenty thousand US a kilo," he said. I
knew this was high, so we haggled a bit. It was all absurdly
genial. I might have been shaving a few pesos off a bunch of
fruit at the market. We eventually agreed on $17,000 per
kilo. That this was not an especially good price didn't much
matter to me. I wanted only to keep the ball rolling, and I
figured that giving them a good mark-up would serve this
purpose better than trying to knock him down.

I then broached the all-important question of transportation. Who was going to do the smuggling, and how?

There were two options open, said Waldino. The first was
to use his connections inside the Santa Marta docks, and get
the merchandise on board a ship bound for Europe. The second—and the one he recommended—was to use a *barco pri-
vado*, a small private boat. He knew a *trasportista* who offered
a tidy, all-in service, running dope and cocaine to the Dutch
Antilles, about 400 kilometres north-east of Santa Marta.
There it was transferred on to a cargo ship bound for the
Netherlands. They would have someone to nurse it through.
It could be delivered for pick-up at Rotterdam or Amsterdam. This pipeline worked like a dream, he said. It was run
by a "very special friend." The cost of this service was
$30,000, non-negotiable, bringing the total money required
up-front, for 10 kilos of pure cocaine delivered in Amsterdam, to $200,000. At the dollar exchange-rate then prevail-
ing this was about £140,000. Add in another £10,000 for
out-of-pocket expenses, and your 10 kilos would represent an
investment of £150,000, which would immediately be worth
about £350,000 on the wholesale market in London. If you
were to run your luck once every two or three months, your
little syndicate would be netting a profit of around £1 million
per annum, tax-free. This is the sort of bottom line that explains the risks cocaine-runners take.

I said I thought the price would be acceptable. "Of
course," I added—and now I came to the lynch-pin of the
whole scam—"I will have to check all this out, Waldino. I
will need to meet your *trasportistas*, discuss everything with
them."

Waldino looked pained. "Charlie. This is difficult. These people are professionals. I work with them many times. They trust me. You must trust me, Charlie. I told you, Waldino takes care of everything."

"Of course I trust you, Waldino. But you must understand, this is my job here. I too work for professionals. They want me to know exactly what's happening before they put any money in."

Waldino continued to stall. Naturally I had anticipated this. As the middleman, he had considerable vested interest in keeping the links in the pipeline separate. He existed in the space between me and the others. This was the whole point of my arrangement with Malcolm. His cable was going to force Waldino to take me to them.

As we talked there came a knock at the door. Before I was even on my feet Waldino had scooped up the *muestra* off the mirror, and was ready to toss it out the window. I heard a familiar voice call my name. *"Tranquilo,"* I said, staying his arm. "She's a friend."

I opened the door, and there stood Renate. "Hello, we're back," she said, languid against the door-jamb, sunglasses and thin white blouse. Waldino's manner shifted abruptly. *"Buenas tardes, señorita,"* he said, smirking like a tango-singer. Renate eyed him coldly. *"Señora,"* she corrected, untruthfully, a reflex action after five years on the road with every small-town stud in South America bidding to get into her knickers. She was not beautiful, but she had one of those ripe, pale, faintly corrupt bodies—a touch of the Rubens—that seem to fill the swarthy Latin with anticipations of sexual *delicias*.

I introduced them. She said, "We thought you'd like to come over for a drink, Charlie." Then to Waldino, "You want a drink too? You can meet my husband."

Waldino thanked her. "Another time perhaps." We had a quick conference out on the balcony. We arranged to meet the next morning at the Telecom. I would cable my "friends" in London, telling them of the price, and we would await their reply. He was just about to go when he remembered his carrier-bags, still sitting on the bed.

"By the way," I said, recalling my earlier mistake. "What is in your bags?"

"*Bollos*," he said. "Here, have a couple." *Bollos* are small puddings, made of maize and milk, wrapped in plantain leaves. "They're for my little daughter," he explained. "She loves them."

"You have a daughter?"

"No, *hombre*," he laughed. "I have three, and a son also." He gave a silky little bow to Renate—"*Hasta luego, señora*"—and tripped off along the balcony. So Waldino was a family man. I found this vaguely unsettling.

I spent a couple of hours drinking and smoking with Renate and Renaldo. On the whole I was well pleased with the afternoon's business. The siren went over the docks. We strolled out, the evening promenade. The sky turned amethyst and lilac, and then it was the twilight hour, *entre dos luces*. We sat beneath the coconut palms. Renate murmured lines from her favourite poet, Baudelaire—

> *Voici le soir charmant, ami du criminel,*
> *Il vient comme un complice, à pas de loup.*

The next morning I met Waldino outside the Telecom on 5th Avenue. I made great play of the cable. It must be sent in code, of course, Waldino. Our code is real estate. (I had cooked this up in bed last night.) The telegram read: "TEN HECTARES IN EXCELLENT POSITION STOP TWO HUNDRED THOUSAND DOLLARS ALL SERVICES INCLUDED STOP AWAIT INSTRUCTION." I explained it all carefully to Waldino, and translated it into Spanish for him. I even showed him the words in my little pocket dictionary. What was it Rosalita had said? One big lie with lots of little truths around it. He watched me write the address, but it didn't mean much to him. "Business front," I said. He nodded sagely. He was definitely impressed. He didn't even mind when I had to borrow a few pesos off him to pay for the telegram. "Sure, Charlie. You and me, we deal in the big numbers, no?"

I sweated the next thirty-six hours, perming the endless possibilities of cock-up at Malcolm's end. Then the answer arrived, bristling with authentic London digits, and bearing the prearranged message: "PRICE IS GOOD BUT CHECK ALL TRANSPORT BEFORE PROCEEDING." Malcolm had got it right. The hook was baited.

"You see, Waldino? I told you. I have to check it all out, the whole move, before they come up with the dollars." I tried to sound resigned rather than triumphant.

He took it well, stubby hands raised in mock submission. "OK, OK, OK. I will talk with the *trasportistas*. They will show you everything, explain everything. Then we get this thing moving, OK?" Off he went, tubby figure squeezed into a shiny, palmtree-print beach shirt, an almost palpable little cloud of worry over his head. All these big numbers floating around, all these little problems in the way.

I jittered in the sunny doorway, watching him go down towards the waterfront. At last I was going to meet some real live cocaine smugglers.

Two, three, five days went by, and nothing happened. I met Waldino a few times, but he seemed evasive and tetchy. He was a busy man, plenty of other pots on the fire. He was having difficulty getting in touch with his friends, they too were busy men. We must be patient, Charlie. A few twinges of doubt began to steal in. Was Waldino busking too? Were his cocaine-runners as chimerical as my big London *capos*? We could go on sparring like this for weeks. The rhythms of Santa Marta grew daily more torpid, and I grew daily more certain that nothing at all was going to happen, that the Great Cocaine Story was finally going to sink, like the sieve of empty promises it had always been. And whenever this fear relented it was smartly replaced by the other, opposite fear—that the whole thing was getting too damn *real*, that these were real smugglers I was going to meet, hard men with cats' eyes to pry into my secrets. "The only way you're going to get inside the cocaine underworld is after it's chewed you up and swallowed you"—A. McGregor.

The days were hot, the nights filled with noises, and even while nothing happened the game grew more serious. There was no doubt about it. I was getting paranoid.

One night, sleepless beneath the ceiling fan, I became utterly convinced that Waldino was a narc. The place was supposed to be crawling with them, F-2s and DAS and local *agents provocateurs* working with US drug agencies. Of course. He's got the evidence, he's got the telegram. He's reeling me in: *I'm* the mackerel! There would be long interrogations, screaming-fits in the cells—"We got a live one here, *jefe*, he says he made the whole thing up for a *story!*" There would be frantic cables to Malcolm for bribe-money. There would be stickiness in Accounts, stickiness in the hole. They'd let me out in ten years, bearded and half-blind with prison-pox.

I spent a lot of time with Renate and Renaldo, shutters open, door open, sliding gracefully downhill. It was the *blanco y negro* for breakfast, *punto rojo* for lunch, *ron coco* for tea. Of these *ron coco* is not the least. This simple, sweet and deadly drink is prepared as follows: Take a ripe brown coconut, slice off the top, drain some of the milk, pour in a generous slug of rum, white or brown to taste, replace the top, and leave to steep for a day or so. Cocktail books would doubtless recommend it served with crushed ice, but there was no ice at the Corona, and anyway the best way to take *ron coco* is straight out of the shell, passed round like a pipe of peace, with reinforcements of rum to top it up with compound interest. In Santa Marta they call this way of drinking rum *chupando el mono*, sucking the monkey.

It was at the end of a long afternoon session with them that a boy came with a message from Waldino to meet him that evening at the Rincón Francés. It took me a while, surfacing through tropical mists of dope, to realize that this could mean business.

Soon after dark, rather the worse for wear, I tacked along

to the French Corner, a low, opensided beer and cheap food *chingana* at the other end of the waterfront. There were American sailors in town, big men in white, with cigarette packs tucked into the tight sleeves of their T-shirts. There was a group of them outside the Pan-American, joshing loudly. A blond boy, chewing gum, shouted to a *costeña*, "Hey, baby, let's you and me go get weird!" The night was hot, and the Yankee presence made the town uneasy.

Waldino was at a corner table, well-placed for keeping an eye on the comings and goings of the beach drag. He was with another man whom I recognized, with a start, to be the tall *bingero*, the one who had moved with such deadly grace that night of the fight at El Molino. One is always trying to make sense of these places that live by different laws, and unexpected interconnections like this are unsettling. Was the El Molino crowd—Silvio, the Lone Ranger, the *bingeros*—mixed up in this deal? Were they Waldino's *trasportistas*? No, that was unlikely. They could well be his suppliers, though. The possibility jarred me, but I had already been spotted by Waldino, and had no more time to think before joining them at the table.

Waldino introduced the *bingero* as Alfonso. We shook hands. I'd seen him at Bingo El Portal, I said, and I'd heard him all along the seafront. He laughed, deep and sonorous. His voice was as slow and deadpan as it was calling the numbers over the microphone. He had a long thin scar down his left cheek, showing pinkish on the teak-coloured skin. He wore a trilby-style straw hat, perched at a raffish angle, and the same maroon jacket I had seen him in before. Underneath it, no doubt, was the gun he had flashed at the troublesome *costeño* that night.

I looked to Waldino for some cue, some indication that Alfonso was here regarding our business, but none came. We chatted aimlessly for a while. Alfonso was a Vallenato—"valley born"—from the lowlands of Cesar, round Valledupar. He asked me about London, about the four seasons, about the prices: all the usual chit-chat. There were plenty of opportunities to slide into the subject of cocaine, but none were taken. After a couple of beers he rose to leave. He looked me in the eyes and said *"Buena suerte,"* good luck, and I wondered if this meant I would need it. Waldino walked out with him to the sidewalk. They conversed for a while, Alfonso slow and emphatic, stooping as he talked to Waldino, straightening up and looking out to sea as Waldino in turn talked to him. They seemed to be arguing about something. I had the feeling that Waldino was the inferior, the deferential one, but then deference is generally due to a big Vallenato with a gun under his coat.

Waldino rejoined me, a picture of false, shifty-eyed bonhomie. "So," I said. "What did you want to meet about?"

"Ah yes. Very good news, Charlie."

"What?"

"We go meet the *trasportistas,* very soon, maybe tomorrow."

"Maybe?"

He shrugged. "I told you, it is difficult to be sure." He fiddled with his beard. I heard the distant boom of Alfonso's voice, as another session started at Bingo El Portal.

"You wanted me to meet you just to tell me that, Waldino? Come on. You've been telling me that for a week now. Maybe tomorrow. *Mañana, mañana . . ."*

"Charlie, I'm trying. Have another beer."

"You sure it was just that? What about Alfonso—is he something to do with it? I think you got me here so he could look me over."

He assumed the exaggerated air of surprise which Colombians fondly imagine will allay suspicions, and usually only increases them. "Charlie! Alfonso's no *contrabandista.* He's a *bingero,* Charlie." He gestured vaguely down the drag to where Alfonso was intoning, *"Ochenta y ocho, los dos culebras!"*

"I know a bit about Alfonso," I said. Waldino's eyes narrowed. "He's with Silvio, isn't he, the guy who owns—"

"Hey, Charlie, *amigo!* You want to be careful here." He leaned forward and laid his hand on my arm. "OK. Look.

Alfonso and I have certain . . . mutual connections. No more."

"Are they who you get your *perica* from? Is that it?"

Waldino was suddenly angry. "*Hijo de puta!* We said no questions, not a word about where it comes from. *I'm* your supplier, *amigo*. You remember that. Waldino can get it: that's all you need to know."

I was blundering, offending protocol. My damn fool inquisitiveness was going to blow everything. I sat back, ran my hand over my face. The beers were mixing badly with the *ron coco*, and I was coming down off the afternoon's cocaine into that dangerous, jagged hinterland. I felt sluggish and uneasy. I didn't like this intrusion of guns. I thought again of Alfonso dispatching the *costeño*, the sleek, sneering face of Silvio. My little game took another twist of seriousness.

Some of the American sailors, those sober enough to make it this far from the docks, drifted in, shouting, "*Cervezas pronto*, you honkies." After a few minutes the tarts began to muster, like gulls following a school of fish. The purlieu of the French Corner was one of their stamping grounds anyway, and the nights the US Navy was in town they came out in force. There was a group quite near us, lounging against the low wall that separated the tables from the sidewalk. The sailors called to them, motioned them over. A few peeled off from the group, and sauntered purposefully over to their table. Two girls remained. I eyed them with vague, theoretical lust. Waldino followed my gaze. "You like the *niñas*?" he said, in a jolly, let's-change-the-subject voice. I shrugged. "I can get them," he said automatically. "Of course you can," I sighed, and before I could stop him he was tipping his chair back to lean over the wall, and calling, "*Ola, chiquitas! Piropo! Vengan por aca!*" Over they came. The tall, blondish one swung her handbag like a Charleston flapper. She seemed to recognize Waldino. He looked up at her, said something I didn't catch. He put his arm right round her waist, and made to worm his pudgy hand down the front of her tight white jeans.

"This is Rosa," he said. He leaned forward to me and

whispered loudly, "I hope she isn't as tight as her pants, you know what I mean?"

Rosa's hand snaked around Waldino's bushy head. She pressed it against her hip. Waldino winked at me. He puffed and pouted in a parody of lascivious pleasure. His hand began to delve below her waist-band. Then I saw Rosa's hand pressing tighter, the muscles in her arm tensing, and Waldino's face beginning to squash up against her tough flank. He broke away from her grip with a grunt of pain.

"Take it easy, monkey," she said, her brassy smile turned to a sneer. "Any lower and you have to pay."

A tall young black, wafting *eau de cologne*, sat down at the next table. He pushed an empty chair out with a foot shod in alligator skin. "Sit down, Rosa," he said quietly. She turned her back on us and sat down. Waldino, crestfallen, rubbed his sore ear. The other girl was still standing beside the table. She was short and dark, chewing gum. Her breasts jutted impressively under her T-shirt: *tout le monde sur le balcon*.

Waldino rallied his battle-weary machismo. "And what's your name, little girl?" he asked silkily.

"Mabella."

"Take a seat, Mabella." She had to squeeze behind me to get to the vacant chair. I felt first one thigh, then the other, and something soft and ephemeral in between.

"You want a drink?" he asked. She gave a quick, nervy shrug that made her breasts judder, and chewed even harder on her gum. She had a young girl's face on a woman's body. Waldino called for three beers. The waiter spilt some on Mabella's trousers, tight, bright green and shiny. She swore and scowled as he roughly dabbed it dry with a cloth.

"I've brought you a nice juicy gringo," said Waldino, with that high-pitched titter of his.

"*Carajo!*" she said, without much obvious enthusiasm.

I heard my slurred voice saying "Hang on a minute." I had a headful of catarrh from too much *perica*. The best part of me wanted to wish them goodnight, head back to the hotel, and tuck up with a good book. Renaldo had lent me a leather-bound edition of Charles Waterton's *Wanderings in*

South America, a trove of lore on preparing *curare* poison, removing ticks and chiggers, recognizing sloth's droppings, and much else. For bodily health in these "remote and dreary wilds" he recommends quinine bark, laudanum, calomel and jalap. For the soul, a small volume of the Odes of Horace. He says nothing about cocaine and black-eyed corner-girls.

So why am I still sitting here? As the poet says, *Video meliora proboque, deteriora sequor.* I see and approve the good, I follow the bad. Twenty minutes later the three of us were walking back up the beach-drag, past the sailors, past El Molino and the bingo stall, my arm around Mabella's shoulders, hers around my waist, our hips jostling.

At the Corona, leering like a pantomime pimp, Waldino patted us on the bottoms and ushered us in. Omar winked as he handed me the room key. They stood together, smiling encouragingly, thoroughly approving this time-honoured transaction. We walked hand in hand up the wide stone steps to my balcony room.

Inside, the dull air of the closed room made me feel ill. She locked the door behind her, leant against it, hands behind her back. Her breasts pointed accusingly at me.

"What do you want?" she asked.

I felt a headache plant itself above my right eye. "Well . . . How much is it?"

"Two thousand five hundred."

I echoed her, aghast. "You must be joking. I don't have that much."

"Two thousand five hundred to stay all night," she said.

I sat down on the bed. "I don't want you to stay all night," I said wearily. "Anyway, I can sleep all night for free."

She shrugged, then recited the rest of the tariff like a sulky waitress. Fifteen hundred pesos for a "fucky-fucky," two thousand for a *chupuda.*

"Chupuda?"

She looked at me pityingly. "Blo-joe," she said, *"el modo francés."* She sucked once or twice at an imaginary lollipop to make it quite clear.

I was sweating heavily. I wanted to lie down and go to

sleep. I went to turn on the ceiling fan. She thought I was
coming at her, and dodged away. "No, you must pay first."
Down in the courtyard I heard Waldino and Omar laughing
together. I felt trapped. I couldn't just send her away. The
absurd codes of machismo must be honoured. I thought of
tom-cats sitting round on a wall, while one of their number
services a hot mog.

After a bit of joyless haggling we settled on 1,000 pesos for
a "fucky-fucky." She pocketed the note and immediately
peeled off her T-shirt. Her breasts were brown and pen-
dulous, with big, dark coffee-coloured aureoles. They made
her look top-heavy. I suddenly thought how childish she
looked.

"How old are you?" I asked. Unzipping her green trousers,
she looked up in surprise. The breath of the ceiling fan
caught her fine hair.

"Fifteen," she said sulkily. Whatever catch-all desire I had
felt for her ebbed away in an instant, and in washed a tired,
desperate and useless pity.

"Fifteen? No more? So young, *jovencita!*"

"I don't think so," she said, and pulled down her knickers.
The stocky shoulders, the ripe breasts, the neat black triangle
between her legs—these belonged to the *puta,* but the rest of
her was just another undernourished young girl, with her
starch-fed belly and bum rounding out in different directions.
She lay on the bed, idly tweaking a nipple. "Hurry up," she
said. "A thousand pesos, twenty minutes, no more."

"Hang on!" I fished out a twist of cocaine from the drawer
in the table. "Do you want . . . ?" She shook her head. "I
think I'll just . . ." I heard again the laughter in the courtyard. My hands were clumsy with booze and sweat. A bit of
crystal fluttered to the floor. I snorted the rest straight out of
the paper, felt the slipstream surge, trying to push through
the fogs of despair, failing. My headache was worse. I began
to undress. I couldn't get the stud on my jeans through the
buttonhole. Finally I was naked, tacking irresolutely towards
the bed, where my pot-bellied Lolita, *mi muñeca de carne,* lay
eyeing me with mild curiosity.

It was not a success, not a *nuit de passion* to linger in the memory. She lay inert and passive. I lay dutifully active. I pressed and fondled. I made one or two requests, in the hope of gingering things up a bit, but these apparently were not on the schedule. A "fucky-fucky" was the basic economy model. She was anatomically available, and that was it: a glove of warm flesh to slip into for a few minutes. Perhaps this is what turns on the average Colombian Joe. It didn't turn me on. I felt limper and guiltier with each minute that passed. It didn't even occur to me to kiss her.

In the end we lay side by side, in a sheepish parody of post-coital glow. I made excuses—too much of this, not enough of that, wait a few minutes and I'll be raring. She looked at her watch. Time was almost up. We talked a bit. She was from Bucaramanga, down in the Eastern Cordillera. She had been on the game for a year, ever since her father had died. She had worked the bus stations in Bucaramanga. It was all in the family: her uncle pimped for her. One day she took the train to Santa Marta, to get away from him. She had been here six months, sleeping by day in a little *residencias* near the Gobernacion, working the Rodadero bars and the dockside by night. She didn't like drugs because her uncle had made her take them. Basuko, pills, and a funny black powder which you mixed with cobwebs, and which made you stupid, and you lay on the bed like you were para . . . para . . . yes, *paralizada*, while the johns came in and did their business on top of you.

I watched her get dressed. In that absurd way of things, I felt the twinges of desire return when she stood, wearing just her brief lacy knickers, and for the first time since I had met her, she smiled at me.

"It's OK, gringo. It happens."

"Come back to bed," I said.

She shook her head: she had to go back to the beach. Tomorrow night, maybe. I heard her sandals slapping down the staircase, then a burble of raucous comments from the pair down at the desk. They talked for a bit, then the street door was bolted, and all was silent.

She must have felt I was owed something for my 1,000 pesos, though. Next morning, with a sore, disgruntled head, I was greeted downstairs by Omar wearing an even wider grin than usual. Here we go, I thought. The gringo who can't even get it up with a *puta* . . .

"So you had a good time last night?" he crowed. I shrugged non-committally. "That's what the *niña* says," he continued. "She says he may be a gringo, but he sure is one hot lover."

21

SEA BREEZE FARM

So what had I so far got out of Mr. Fixit Waldino? A smidgin of *perica*, half an hour with a street girl, a few words with a gun-toting *bingero* who may also have been a trafficker: not a lot to show for ten days' work. Then one morning I returned to the Corona from breakfast at the seafront to find him leaning at the desk. He greeted me warmly and asked if I had anything planned for the day.

"Nothing special."

"OK then, let's go!" He steered me back out of the door, into the street.

"Where are we going?"

"To see a man about a boat."

Outside, parked up on the kerb of the narrow street, was a brand-new maroon Sierra station-wagon, glinting in the sun. A couple of *gamines* were peering into it. Waldino shooed them away officiously. They had shaven heads, which meant they had been pulled into the police station once too often. With a jocular bow, Waldino opened the passenger door and ushered me in.

"Very impressive, Waldino," I said. The new seats, baked in the morning sun, gave off a pungent plastic aroma. "Is this yours?"

"It belongs to one of my partners," he said. With a crunch of gears we bounced off the kerb and down towards 5th Avenue. He drove slowly down the avenue, a hirsute arm resting casually on the open window. He called out and waved at friends. He looked very pleased with life, eyes twinkling amid the black undergrowth. In the kudos language of Santa Marta, a brand-new station-wagon spoke loud and clear.

We were going to Taganga, he explained, a small fishing village just round the headland from Santa Marta. We were going to meet a man called Agaton. Other than that he wouldn't tell me anything. I asked if this Agaton was the *trasportista*, but he only said "not exactly," and when I started asking something else he growled amiably, "No more questions. I'll take you there, I'll do the talking. You sit back and enjoy the ride."

We headed out past the market, through the rind of wooden shacks at the edge of town, and up into the scrub hills. Santa Marta lay below us, the streets trapped in a hot, chalky haze. Twenty minutes later we were in Taganga. There was not a lot to the place: a few sand-streets gridded up from the sea, a few boats bobbing in the bay, a few fishermen at their chores. We stopped the car in shade and strolled around the shore for a bit. Agaton was not here, as far as I could gather. We drank a beer at one of the stalls by the beach. Waldino began checking his watch. It was getting near lunch-time. He went to talk with a fisherman mending a net strung between almond trees. He came bustling back. His shirt had half untucked itself from his waistband. He looked scruffy, hot and a little worried.

"Let's go," he said.

"Where?"

"To Negangue."

"But isn't Agaton going to meet us here?"

"I don't think so."

We climbed back into the car. The seat burnt my back. "Look, Waldino," I said. "Does Agaton know we're coming today?"

He gave that wavering, quiddity-laden "*Si-i-i-i*" which most often means "No."

"For Christ's sake, does he know we're coming or not?"

"No. I know *he* is coming." I stared at him. Even Waldino had to admit he owed me an explanation. "I know Agaton's bringing the boat in today. He's meeting someone. Sometimes he comes in at Taganga, sometimes Negangue. They're hard to get hold of, *hombre*. You have to *find* them, and the best time is when they come in."

"Come in from where?"

"From their place, Charlie. Their *ranchito*. They don't often use the road. It's quicker and quieter by boat. OK, enough questions. We go to Negangue."

Negangue was a few inlets further east. We had to drive up on to the main road, the Troncal de Caribe that runs all along the coast from Cartagena to Riohacha, and then back down a winding track through dry, buff-coloured hills dotted with *mesquite* and fuzzy black thorn-scrub. At the bottom lay a deserted crescent bay and a single dilapidated wooden farmstead. There an old man was sitting, shaving bits of kindling for the range. Four freshly caught iguanas lay outside. They had their front legs tied behind their backs, the claws knotted with wire. Only the biggest moved, about 3 feet long, yellow and black. It leered at me with a baleful red eye, puffed out its scaly dewlap, gnashed its small, prehistoric teeth. Iguana stew is a favourite dish in the tropical outlands, and iguana eggs a delicacy. Waldino asked if Agaton had been seen here today. No, he hadn't. He asked if there was any chance of some lunch—most houses will sell you fried fish and *patacones* for a couple of hundred pesos. But not today. The boys weren't back with the catch yet. The beach was hot, the sand greyish. We sat on rocks beneath a stand of almond trees at the eastern end of the bay, and we waited, smoking cigarettes and getting hungrier.

Around 3 o'clock I was surprised to see a taxi skidding down the track to the bay. It drove right down on to the sand, and kept on going as far as it could, which was to the rocks where we were sitting. A woman got out, a big handsome woman in a cotton dress with a bold black and white pattern. She took out some large parcels, wrapped in polythene and newspaper. The taxi went off back up the track, streaming a plume of dust behind it. She joined us in our patch of shade.

"What you got there?" asked Waldino pleasantly.

"Ice."

"You've come to cool us down then?"

"I've come to meet my husband, *tonto*. He'll cool you down if you like." Poor old Waldino. Every time he looked at a woman she started talking about her husband.

At last we heard the sound we'd been waiting for. At first it was just a faint counterpoint to the gentle whisper of the waves. Then it was definitely the chug and whine of an outboard engine. The boat appeared round the headland. There were two men in it, one black, one *mestizo*.

"There's Agaton," cried Waldino.

"There's my husband," said the woman.

Agaton was a big, flat-faced negro, with eyes that reminded me of the iguana at the farmstead. He looked like Sonny Liston in a bad humour, though differing in one essential respect—he only had one hand. His right arm ended in a gnarled stump, mauvish in colour. He had blown his hand off with dynamite, I later learned, part of the fisherman's lot. He could stun a 100-lb tuna with one blow from this natural club.

He waded ashore, greeted Waldino with a gruff grunt and a cuff on the shoulder. The woman kissed him on the cheek. His hand briefly cupped her rump. He nodded at me. The boat was hauled a little way on to the sand. The woman nuzzled up to the *mestizo*, who wore a baseball cap. I wondered which of them was her husband.

Agaton tramped up the sand, sat down in the shade and lit a cigarette. Waldino skipped along in his wake. They conversed, Waldino voluble, Agaton implacable and ursine, blowing great spouts of tobacco smoke out of his nostrils. Waldino was explaining me, I realized: Agaton didn't know the first thing about me. I could tell from the way Waldino's hands were working. Agaton kept glancing over at me. I kicked around at the water's edge, hoping he was gaining a good impression of me. The woman was loading her cargo of ice on to the boat, helped by the little *mestizo*. He was wiry and unshaven, wearing a vest and long, frayed denim shorts. His cap bore the legend "Pittsburgh Pirates." I admired the woman's plump contours as she bent and straightened to hand up the packages. I could see the line of her knickers under the flimsy cotton dress.

Now Waldino and Agaton were walking down towards me. Waldino hardly came up to his shoulders. Waldino said, "This is Charlie." Agaton held out his good hand. This being his left, I took it in my left. This unfamiliar motion, in my nervousness, became a clumsy and elaborate clasp.

"Waldino tells me you need help with some cargo?"

I nodded, uncertain exactly what Waldino had told him, anxious not to get any wires crossed at this delicate stage.

"It can be arranged," he continued. His deep, smooth voice was almost hypnotic. I felt empty in my belly. The light bounced off the wavelets. His face was inscrutable, but there was a glint in it—not quite friendliness, perhaps, but yes, a glint of amusement. "We have good contacts with Europe," he said. He looked off into the distance, as though Europe might actually be glimpsed on the horizon.

"And this is the boat?" I asked, for something to say. He shook his head. The boat was called *El Problema*.

"We have another," he said. "In this one we fish. In the other we handle the exports."

He turned away. The interview seemed to be over. He had a few more words with Waldino, then they walked off towards the farmstead. They conferred with the old man. Waldino went and climbed into the station-wagon. For a moment I thought he was going, leaving me here at the end of the line with this dubious trio, but he was only moving it to park it up close to the palm-thatch shelter which served as the farmhouse kitchen.

"What's happening, Waldino?" I asked.

"We're going for a ride in the boat."

"Where to?"

"To see the boss, of course." He was jaunty again now. "Hey, *amigo*, don't look so worried. You are among friends.

This is Waldino!" He thumbed at his chest. "Any friend of
Waldino's is welcome with these people."

He strolled over to talk to the *mestizo* and the woman. He
did not seem to know them, but soon they were joking
matily together. The woman threw her head back when she
laughed. Her elbow rested loosely on the little *mestizo*'s
shoulder. He had a cigarette butt, unlit, between his lips.
Waldino motioned me over and introduced us. The *mestizo*
was called Miguelito, the woman Rita. Miguelito shook my
hand, quickly, wordlessly. He leapt up into the boat, moving
like a monkey, and began to tinker with the engine. Rita
leaned against the side, running her eyes up and down me.
She had a way of chewing her lower lip, and a half-smile
which seemed to be a suppressed giggle. Her hair, coarse and
glossy, jet-black, was piled untidily on her head. The skin on
her face was bad: pock-marked and oily, with a perceptible
shadow of moustache, but it was a strong, animated face.
Her lipstick looked like last night's. Her arms were smooth as
teak. I couldn't quite place her: part *costeña*, certainly, but
with something else mingled in, something which made her
taller, more aquiline, more mongrel. "So," she said, smiling
at me, "you are coming with us to Finca Las Brisas."

I looked at Waldino. He nodded his head encouragingly.
"I believe I am," I said, and she laughed her big, throaty,
slightly cruel laugh.

We pushed the boat back down into the shallows. *El Problema* was a 12-foot *pesquero*, a dusty, muted blue on the
outside, the colour of ink on blotting-paper, and the traditional fisherman's orange on the inside. The gunnel was
picked out in white. The boat was a simple dug-out, probably
made from the trunk of a *ceiba* tree.

We arranged ourselves on the plank-seats: Agaton at the
bow, Waldino and I in the middle, Rita behind us, with
Miguelito standing beside her, working the tiller. The sun
was just beginning to lose its bite. Its softening light gave the
headland waters a rich, creamy appearance. Miguelito started
the engine first pull. We were off to Finca Las Brisas, Sea

Breeze Farm, to meet the Boss. I gave myself up to the animal pleasures—the sun, the boat, the moll's sudden laughter—but none of it quite removed the knot of adrenalin in my gut. As we left Negangue and rounded the headland into open sea, I pondered the advice of the popular song—

> *Cuando se danza con diablo*
> *No se da un paso falso . . .*

When you're dancing with the devil, make sure you get the steps right.

No one spoke much during the trip. We scudded along, always within sight of the shore. The dry scrubland around Taganga and Negangue gave way to a plusher, greener, wilder landscape. Steep forested hills rose up behind the beaches and bouldered coves. Drapes of grey Spanish moss hung from the trees like mouldering lace. The hilltops disappeared into plump, smoke-coloured clouds, so local and defined they seemed to be impaled on the sharp peaks. Much of this stretch of Caribbean shoreline is a protected national park, the Parque Tairona, so-named after the Indians that once lived in these foothills. I recognized some of these beaches: Guachaquita, Arrecifes, Cañaveral. I had spent time here when I was in Santa Marta last time. There had been four of us: two Americans, an Italian girl and me. We frolicked naked in the surf, hiked through the magical valleys, subsisted on a happy diet of fruit, *punto rojo* and the works of Carlos Castaneda. Somewhere up there, in a valley cupped in the forest, are the remains of a Tairona settlement, probably the one referred to by the *cronistas* as Chairama, but nowadays simply called Pueblito, the village. An old stone highway leads up from the sea to Pueblito, entered by a concealed doorway, climbing steeply, every step catered for by ingenious contrivances of rock, root and earth. Gringos—I think only the gringos—called it the Stairway to Heaven.

After about three-quarters of an hour Miguelito began to guide the boat inshore. I couldn't see anything except a wild-looking headland, with huge white boulders packed in earth. As we cut close to this promontory pelicans flew up above us. Then I saw the bay, and the ragged settlement of wood and palm-thatch buildings, huddled between the sand and the steep rise of forest behind it. Gangling coconut palms swayed like feather dusters high above the roofs. The buildings looked tiny beneath them. The low sun gilded the water all the way into the bay. It looked like the classic tropical hideaway. If Gauguin had stopped off here he would never have made it to Tahiti.

Coasting in there was a small incident. Waldino had spent the voyage in an apparent trance of content, trailing his hand through the water, looking—as he had looked that morning, driving the station-wagon—like one whose diligent labour had reaped its just rewards. Now he suddenly leapt up, shouted, "Ay! *Mierda!* Stop, stop!" and started lurching back to the stern of the boat, seeming to catch at something in the water. He tumbled into a tangle with Rita, who squawked and cried "Help! He's after me!" But he wasn't trying to ravish Rita, or to catch a fish with his bare hands. It was his watch. In the choppy water round the headland, it had worked off his wrist into the slipstream. With a quick, practised twirl of the rudder, Miguelito brought the boat round. We bobbed idling in the golden water. Waldino moaned and groaned about how much it had cost him; it was quartz, it was digital, it was Japanese. We edged back to roughly where the watch had sunk, and peered rather hopelessly over the edge. Agaton rubbed the back of his head. His stony face split into a droll, red-eyed grin. "We can't leave it there," he said. "The fish will know what time it is, and then we'll never catch them!" Miguelito told Agaton to take the tiller. Agaton moved past us, swift and limber for a big man with one hand. Miguelito crouched down, bony hands gripping the white gunnel. He took off his baseball cap, threw away his cigarette butt, dropped off the boat in a crouch, and dived down. He went up and down four or five times. He could touch bottom but he couldn't see the watch. Rita, indifferent to the tragedy, sat arranging her hair, slide between her teeth, arms up, rings of wet sweat on her dress, thick tangles of black hair in her armpits.

Miguelito climbed back in, water streaming off his skinny body. "No luck," he said. "You'll have to buy another one." We headed into the bay, Agaton at the tiller. Waldino hunched in disgruntlement. A flashy Japanese watch is an essential item in the Colombian hustler's wardrobe. As we neared the shore I heard dogs barking. Miguelito hopped out into the shallows, hauled on the rope. Agaton cut the engine. *El Problema* bumped and scraped ashore. Black drifts of mica glistened in the wet sand. "Welcome to Finca Las Brisas," said Rita, and laid her hand on my shoulder to steady herself as she climbed out of the boat.

An old black woman, a patterned scarf round her head, a tin dish in her hand, came out of an open-sided building. I saw in it the glow of a wood-fire. Agaton went up to meet her, leaving giant footprints in the wet sand. I heard him call her "Mama." An old brown dog fussed around Rita, who was clearly his favourite. Back through the buildings, where the farmyard petered out among the palms, I saw two knotty, bare-chested *costeños*, either side of a giant pile of coconuts, machetes in their hands.

I helped Miguelito unload the stores from the boat. Agaton showed me and Waldino to an open-sided wooden outbuilding. A pair of big, mangy hammocks hung down from a side-rafter. We fixed them up and sank gratefully into their strong embrace. My skin was hot where the sun had been on it, and gave off a baked scent which mingled with the brackish, musty aroma of the hammock. We rocked in silence. The sun set. I wondered when we were going to meet "the Boss" and where he was. I asked Waldino.

"He's not here just now. He's in Riohacha. Agaton says he will be back tomorrow. He will discuss everything with you."

"Who is he, Waldino?"

"He's called Ariel"—pronounced Arry-el—"He's one of the best, Charlie, top drawer *contrabandista.*"

"He doesn't know anything about me, does he? I could tell, back at the beach—"

"I told you, he's hard to get hold of. OK, I haven't seen him for a while, but I know he'll do it. I've worked with him before."

After a while we were summoned down to the kitchen. Kerosene lamps hung from the palm-wood rafters. Waldino and I were given chairs at the little table, places of honour. Agaton perched on an oil-drum, Miguelito sat on the stoop, and Rita, not eating until after the men, leaned in the doorway smoking. Mama served up huge bowls of *mondongo*—a murky broth of odds and ends: offal, fish and grey, granite-hard plantains—with a dish of coconut rice and *patacones* on the side. The talk was desultory, through mouthfuls, mostly about the fishing. They were taking *El Problema* out the next day, for snapper, swordfish and fat-eye. They would be gone two days, selling their catch in Santa Marta at dawn. There was talk too of a *cosecha de marimba*—literally a harvest, but in this case a consignment, of marijuana—which was due in soon. There was no effort to hide anything from me. Their life of fishing, farming and smuggling seemed as elemental as the breeze and the breakers outside, and the immense mono-tone of frogs and cicadas which sang me to sleep.

The following day Agaton and Miguelito—the *muchachos*, as Mama called them—had left before I woke. I breakfasted on eggs, rice and greasy *tinto*. Waldino snored late in his ham-mock. Rita was nowhere to be seen. Mama prepared the day's stew. Strips of greyish meat hung on a line outside the kitchen, curing in the salt breeze.

There were many dogs, of which the nicest was the aged brown fellow who had greated Rita. He was called Leoncito, the little lion. He was lean and warty and silver-whiskered, and his eye shone with the deep animal savvy of an old dog who has lived on his wits. He took a shine to the soft-hearted Englishman, and padded along after me as I strolled round. The farmyard straggled down to the beach, ruled—by virtue of sheer bulk—by a huge black pig, a tropical Empress of Blandings. The geese were hostile, the turkeys baroque,

the cats pregnant, and the hens so hungry they even squab-
bled over sea-shells.

The two workers I had seen when we landed lived in a
little shack the other side of the banana grove. They were
called Flaco and Crespo—Slim and Curly. They harvested
the coconuts, bananas and avocado, and looked after the animals. Flaco was thin, slow and sunny. Crespo was malevolent and knotty, with bulging exophthalmic eyes. He kept
his machete polished and keen, and always looked ready to
start slicing something or someone into pieces. I soon realized that he didn't bear an especial grudge against me, or
even gringos. It was just people he didn't like.

Crespo apart, I felt blissfully at ease. I had brought nothing with me from the hotel, no clothes, no notebook, not
even a toothbrush. I almost felt I had left my lies behind as
well. The place was totally apart. No roads led here, only a
trail down through the forest. There were of course no
phones or electricity. Drinking water was collected from a
brook near the farm-workers' hut. For washing there was the
sea, or if you wanted *agua dulce*, a washing pool ten minutes
inland. Feeling that my gringo sensibilities required fresh
water, Mama told Flaco to show me the pool. It was a little
grotto, a deep, cool bowl of leafy river-water between two
white, egg-shaped boulders. The sun filtered through over-
hanging foliage and lit up the water a deep, iodine yellow.

Back at the farm Rita was up, same dress, lipstick fading,
hair tousled, pouring a large mug of *tinto*. "You sleep OK?"
she yawned. "Bugs didn't bite you?"

We sat outside the kitchen smoking cigarettes. She spilt
some coffee on her dress. *"Porca madonna!"* The phrase
sounded familiar but odd—it took me a moment to realize it
was Italian. I asked her where she was from. "From round
here." But you speak Italian? "Hey," she smiled, "the
gringo's clever. My father was Italian, from Genoa. I know a
few cuss-words, not much else."

The sun was still soft enough to sit in. Mist rose off a little
stillwater lagoon at the end of the bay. Leoncito basked in
the dust at our feet. Rita seemed disposed to tell her story.

I was right when I'd thought she had a mongrel look. Her father was in fact half-Italian, half-Turkish. Her mother was Colombian, from here on the coast.

"So you're half *costeña* then?"

Rita shrugged. "*Quién sabe?* Papa said she was a *gitana*"—a gypsy—"I never knew her."

Her father came to Colombia in 1944, settled in Barranquilla. "He was a *fascista*," she explained. "He got up to all sorts of tricks in the war. When things got bad in Italy he got out, like the other fascist rats, South America or bust. He always called himself an exile. He had his flags and emblems, his little picture of Mussolini. Wherever we went, there was Il Duce like a little monkey on the wall. Papa didn't like the English one little bit," she added, with a sly smile.

"He had a business in Barranquilla, import–export. No *narcotráfico* in those days, mostly what we call *café calientito*—you know, contraband coffee. I was a little girl, six or seven, when La Violencia came. Papa got mixed up, we had to move out, in exile again. We lived in a lot of places, me and Papa and a great big suitcase. Three years we spent in the Mato Grosso. He was superintendent in a rubber plantation." She shook her head at the memory. "*Mucho sudor, mucho peligro.*" Sweat and danger. "We called that place Hacienda La Calentura"—Fever Ranch—"just like in the song. You know it?" I didn't, so she sang me a verse.

There were other countries, a succession of fever-ranches and tawdry rooming houses, then a couple of teenage years in Buenos Aires, where Papa revived former glories among fellow fascist expatriates and did his bit for the Dirty War. He died of an apoplexy in Asunción, Paraguay. It was the night General Somosa, the exiled Nicaraguan despot, was assassinated in Asunción. There was a curfew, Rita braved it to get a doctor, she was picked up by the police. She got back the next morning and he was dead. "So you see, the bullet that killed the fascist Somosa had Papa's name on it too."

She had drifted back up to the Caribbean, the only home she'd known, picked up with some old childhood friends, who were now running dope out of Barranquilla. "And that was how I met Ariel." The way she said it answered at least one of my questions. Neither Agaton nor Miguelito was her husband, probably no one was, but Ariel was undoubtedly her man.

"Tell me about Ariel."

She laughed. "Ariel will tell you about Ariel. It's like there's lots of Ariels: he'll be someone different for you. He's hard to find, hard to catch. Like we say, *nació de pie*—he was born on his feet."

She spoke lightly, not a trace of menace intended, but I felt the knot tighten again. Which Ariel would he be for me? The one who could smell a rat at a hundred paces?

The sun was hot now. We walked down to the seashore. The pig rooted sullenly through a pile of coconut shells. We strolled through the shallows, Rita bunching her dress, towards the headland we had rounded last evening. Diamond Point, they called it, huge white boulders packed together with a rough green and brown grouting of vegetation. A small thatched hut perched on the top, looking somehow Chinese. Pelicans flew in chevrons, slow, graceful and prehistoric, peeling off for their lethal, vertical dives. The headland was bathed in a bright mist of spray. Everything seemed to quiver, as if in a giant lens.

"I've been living here two years," she said, "off and on. Every day it looks more beautiful." She closed her eyes, put her face back to the sun and squeezed her hands slowly down her cotton dress.

"So this is Ariel's place?" I asked, averting my gaze from this sun-worship.

"No, it is Agaton's. He's lived here all his life. His father drowned a few years ago. There's brothers and sisters: they come back sometimes, but they live in Santa Marta or Riohacha now. There's really only Agaton and his Mama. For years they've worked with a *marimbero* up in the Sierra. They bring the dope down on mules, load it into the boat, take it out to meet a yacht somewhere out there." She gestured off into the Spanish Main, where the pirate ships still await the cargoes of gold.

"So Ariel . . . ?"

"Ariel's the boss now. He handles all the business: a bit of *marimba* still, but mainly the big one, *la perica*. That's Ariel's specialty. Well, you know that. That's why you're here, no? You want to move some *perica* out."

"Yes, of course."

Enough questions, I thought. We walked on in silence, nearing the headland. A strange marine corpse lay on the wet sand, fish-head poking out of what was less a body than a pouch, a glove-puppet of thorny yellow and white flesh. I bent to examine it. Rita strolled on. Hardly checking her pace, she pulled her dress up over her head, dropped it in the sand and walked into the sea wearing nothing but a pair of pale blue pants.

Life may have left a few scorch-marks on her face, but her body was in its prime, plump perhaps, but tall, ripe and strong. The water was warm and clear. She struck off strongly towards the headland, and I followed.

The sea slapped heavily against most of the promontory, but there was a little inlet where the water was green and calm. Rita had swum in there. She floated propped between two rocks, half in the water, breasts lolling, basking like a voluptuous mermaid.

I had felt the currents tugging as I swam. "You don't want to go too far out," she said. I had seen a gringo nearly drown once, up the coast at Cañaveral. He swam out through the breakers and couldn't get back. He was only a few metres from the shore, but he was the wrong side of the current. The waves shut like a door behind him. The fishermen have a rope they throw out, with coconut shells to make it float. He was lucky: he just got hold of it in time. When he came out he was grey all over, naked and grey.

After we had rested a bit, Rita said, "I'll show you the boat, the one that takes the *perica*."

"Ariel's boat?"

She nodded. "Speedboat. He bought it last year, for the longer runs. You know Agaton's fishing boat, it's called *El Problema*. So Ariel calls his speedboat *La Solución*! Come on.

We can climb over the headland further down. They keep it in the cove the other side."

She swam off back towards the bay, pale blue rump bobbing above deep blue water. As she waded the last few yards up onto the rocks, I saw her stumble and pitch into the water. A faint yelp of pain carried back over the wide roar of the breakers. Then she was up again, hobbling out, falling heavily onto the sand.

I called, "What's happened?"

"*Erizo! Hijo de puta erizo! Mierda! Que pica!*"

I had no idea what *erizo* meant, but as I came out of the water I saw her craning her foot round to look at the sole, and I saw the long black quills embedded there, and I realized that *erizo* meant a sea-urchin, and that Rita had stepped on one.

The only thing to do with urchin's spines is to pull them out one by one. They're strong and slightly barbed, and it's a painful business. She leaned back on her elbows in the sand. I cradled her calloused foot and began to work. She bit her lip with the pain. The grimace turned to a wicked laugh, then back again as another purple-tipped quill came out. I ministered away like some exotic shoe-shop assistant. She squirmed and moaned and giggled, predatory and submissive. The sun beat down. The waves roared. The temperature needle edged towards red. Another wince of pain, eyes holding mine, limbs pressing. "Don't stop now, gringo, do it some more." Coarse sand was smeared over her breasts. Her big thighs twitched, widened. Wet blue cotton, shadowed and fringed with crow-black hairs. A man could disappear in there and never be seen again. Inside the cocaine underworld! No one would know, just the *gitana* and me, and the incurious pelicans.

Wrong again. Straightening for a moment to wipe the sweat from my eyes, a flash of brightness turned my head. The sun dazzled off a polished blade. On the headland above us, in the doorway of the Chinese hut, staring intently down at us, stood the misshapen figure of Crespo.

Rita followed my gaze. "*Testa di cazza,*" she swore in her

Genoese fascist Italian. "That creep never leaves me alone."
She was pulling away, disentangling herself, leaving me like
this. She shouted up at him, *"Zapatero, a tus zapatos!"*—cobbler to your shoes: in other words, mind your own business—
but he made no sign of hearing her. She pulled out the last
few spines herself and started hobbling back up the bay to
where her fallen dress lay like an old memory. When I
looked up to Diamond Point again, Crespo had vanished. I
crawled off into the sea and cooled myself down for a while.

This might be difficult, I thought, following the distant,
hopping figure of Rita back to the *finca*. This could be taken
very amiss. Oh yes, Don Ariel, I saw them with my own
pop-eyes, the gringo playing peek-a-boo with your woman on
the sand.

In fact Ariel did not arrive that day. No one seemed surprised, least of all me. In Colombia patience is not so much a
virtue as a survival instinct. Rita ignored me all afternoon.
Waldino was getting irritable—the absence of street life, the
loss of his watch, the worry about getting the station-wagon
back safely to Santa Marta. He sat in the shade, slapping at
the sand-fleas, and read his way doggedly through a month-
old *Diario del Caribe*.

As evening fell on my first twenty-four hours at Sea Breeze
Farm, Rita brought a handful of *punto rojo* buds from a sack
of the stuff in an outshed. She rolled a cigar-sized splif in a
piece of newspaper. She leaned over the back of my chair,
musky and close, and put it in my mouth. "Maybe this makes
you sleep tonight," she breathed, "maybe not."

Waldino struggled up out of the hammock, eased his trousers out of his crotch with ungainly scooping movements.
Two *papagallo* parrots passed overhead, ochre and turquoise
in the last light, and then the frogs started.

22

A FRIEND IN RIOHACHA

The next day, around midday, Agaton and Miguelito returned, having sold their catch at dawn in Santa Marta. We lunched on swordfish fried in coconut oil. Two or three hours later, in the laziest part of the lazy day, a barrage of barking from the farm dogs announced two visitors. They came down the forest trail behind the *finca*, two men, one elderly and light-footed, with long, lank grey hair under a dirty Panama, the other young, stocky, curly-headed.

The older man was greeted warmly by everyone there. Waldino knew him as well, and he introduced me. "This is Garman. He's a very good friend of Ariel's, isn't that right, *viejo?*"

Garman said to me, "The gringos call me Herman." He had a faraway smile, full of big, broken teeth. There was something sharp and mischievous in his eyes. I guessed he was a half-breed: not one of the Sierra tribes—the squat, dark Kogui and Arhuaco, descendants of the Tairona—but perhaps half Chibcha. He carried a fine woven *mochila* bag slung crosswise. I liked him immediately.

They brought bad news concerning the *cosecha* of marijuana which I had heard talk of on the first night. There had been one of the periodic US-funded army forays into the Sierra. A plantation had been burned. It was OK, the *marimbero* had a dozen others. They would harvest one of these in a few days' time. The consignment would be here in a week or so. Twelve *arrobas*—300 lb—as arranged. These few fragments I gathered, hovering at the edge of the conversation, then Herman and Agaton went off to speak more privately, in the part of the *finca* where no one went unless invited.

Of the younger man I felt less sure. His eyes were the unexpected blue one sometimes meets here. They were not mischievous, but stoned and wild, with a porcelain shine in the iris. His name was Juancho. He worked for the *marimbero* full-time—Herman's connections were vaguer and more senior. Juancho was the *catador*, the taster, who sampled and graded the marijuana crop. I suppose there are worse jobs. He had grown the thumb-nail of his right hand out long, and drilled a small hole through the projecting nail. This served him as a roach-holder, for use when the reefer burnt too low to handle. I never heard him say much beyond a brief commendation or disapproval. He used the English word "full" in the *costeño* slang sense of "very." Anything he liked was "full *chevere*" or "full *vacano,*" even occasionally "maximum full *chevere.*" Anything that displeased him was dismissed with *"que vaina"* (this word means scabbard—the vanilla tree bears pods shaped like "little scabbards"—but the phrase means "What a drag") or *"que zanahoria"* (literally a carrot, otherwise "What a waste of time"). Perhaps these oracular verdicts were part of the technical jargon of the Colombian *marimba*-taster.

It was a little later that Waldino and I learned something that touched us more nearly. Herman had seen Ariel in Riohacha—to give him this same news about the delay in the dope-consignment: Ariel would contact the mother-ship by radio—and Ariel had said that he would not be back down at Finca Las Brisas for another two or three days. He had business to see to in Riohacha, and with no consignment coming down from the Sierra he had no reason to hurry back.

My first feeling was one of relief. I'd been wondering a lot about Ariel, the hidden centre round which all this wheeled, the specialist cocaine-runner, the one who'd been born on his feet. He sounded sharp, too sharp for my shoddy scams.

Waldino was not pleased. *"Que vaina,"* he whined, catching the phrase off Juancho. "This is very bad, Charlie. We *must* see Ariel, talk this through."

"Oh well," I said philosophically. "I'm pretty happy, Waldino. I've seen the set-up, met the people. It all seems very tight to me. Perhaps we could discuss a few points with Agaton. I think that'll be enough."

"No, Charlie. That's not right. Ariel's the boss, he takes the decisions. And I tell you this—if Ariel finds out you've been here *without* meeting him, he'll be pretty sore. He wouldn't like that at all. It's like, now you've been here, now you're one of us, he's got to see *you*, check *you* out. *Me entiendes?*"

Leaving me to ponder this new and cheerless perspective, he went off to discuss with Herman and Agaton. A few minutes later he returned. He looked grubby and greasy: the simple life did not sit easily on him. But he'd clearly hatched something. "It's OK, Charlie. It's all fixed. We go tomorrow morning, with Garman. He'll take us to Ariel in Riohacha. Man, that guy's hard to pin down."

We set off early the next morning—Herman, Waldino, Juancho and me—through the diaphanous shade of the palm grove, past the banana trees dulled with dew, past the shack which housed the dwarf Crespo, past the washing pool, and into the forest. I carried the prints on my body, I could feel them all the way—on my left palm Agaton's hard handshake, on my lips Rita's wet, close, momentary kiss, tongue and all. *Hasta la vista, gringo!*

The trail was clear but narrow. Herman took the lead, looking fresh and easy. He seemed to have a whole repertoire of gaits to choose from. We climbed steeply and soon we could look back over the bay, and the tree-tops, and the huddle of thatched roofs beneath the palms, all tricked up in the morning sun like a snapshot of paradise. As we walked the landscape seemed to modulate. Now it was shady and soft, the path rocky and rutted, leaf-mould beneath our feet giving off the powdery brown smell of an English woodland. Then we changed height, or rounded a bend, and it was all bright, spiky, lush and tropical. Blue *morpho* butterflies, strange leaves with pink, teat-like appendages, and the busy, robotic columns of ants carrying sawn-off squares of leaf.

We stopped in a clearing to rest and take water, a glade of tropical trees, immensely tall, groping for the light: cotton-woods, *anattos*, the delicate spreading tree called Mulatto's Ear. A strange, deep gurgling sound, like some crazy under-water siren, whirled through the forest. Herman and Juancho knew it so well they didn't even look up. Howler monkeys, I learned. Little red fellows with beards. Juancho uttered the longest sentence I had heard from him: "Best way to get co-conuts down: throw rocks up at the monkeys, they throw coconuts down at you."

Juancho pushed off into the underbrush to attend to a call of nature. When he came back five minutes later he was cursing. *"Garapatas! Maximum vaina!"* He asked me for a cigarette—I was the only one with any tobacco. "Light it for me," he said. To my surprise he then turned his back on us, and pulled his jeans down. He wore no underpants. On his buttocks I saw half a dozen small brown bumps, like sinister little nuts, clamped to his flesh. Ticks. Juancho had squatted too near a bush with ticks in it. The cigarette was to burn them away. If you try to pull a tick off you with your fingers, you're in for trouble. The tick has burrowed its little snout right into you, to get the blood, and if you pull the body it breaks away from the head. This remains under your flesh and quickly festers in the heat, and if you haven't got the right chemicals, it has to be dug out with a knife-point. The application of heat—a cigarette, a candle, a glowing ember, held as close to the skin as is bearable—will shrivel the ticks out of you, one by one.

After another hour we came quite suddenly out of the trees and found ourselves on the dusty verge of the Troncal de Caribe, running east to Riohacha, west to Santa Marta. The blacktop shimmered, slightly raised off the verge, but seemingly about to melt back down into it. Three vultures flapped up lazily from the squashed corpse of an iguana.

We turned right, westward back towards Santa Marta, but only for a few hundred metres. We came to a small wooden roadhouse with a Coca-Cola sign, a cluster of huts by a stream. Here Herman had a pick-up parked. We said goodbye to Juancho, who would go on to Palomino, then up into the Sierra by foot. As we drove off towards Riohacha, I looked out of the window at the place where the trail had come out on to the road. It was hardly there at all, a momentary gap in the trees, unmarked and, unless you knew exactly where to look, invisible. The way back to Sea Breeze Farm was as secret as the way back to yesterday.

We crossed a steel section-bridge over Quebrada las Lágrimas, the Brook of Tears. A sign announced we were entering a Yellow Fever Zone. The truck chugged along, warm wind blowing through the open windows, Herman a picture of contentment at the wheel. The landscape grew harsher, drier, paler, and then we were over the state-line and into the Guajira.

There are few reasons for going to the Guajira, and I was going for the most common one: to do business with a smuggler. When the word "cocaine" first trembled on Malcolm's lips, he was all but handing me a ticket to the Guajira.

The Guajira peninsula juts like a snout into the Caribbean, 150 miles long and no more than 30 miles wide at its narrowest point, guarding the Venezuela Gulf and Lake Maracaibo, and terminating at Punta Gallinas, Chicken Point, the northernmost tip of South America. Apart from a few minor hillocks towards the tip, it is as flat as a runway, a hot, arid spit of rock, sparsely dusted with scrub and thorn. There are just two towns of note, Riohacha—the department's capital—and Maicao. The rest of the peninsula is populated by semi-nomadic, goat-herding Indians, by vast flocks of flamingos up around Cabo de la Vela, and by a shifting army of *contrabandistas*, who use its inhospitable spaces for their airstrips and its deserted shorelines for the boats. The Guajira is one big hideaway, an old-style badlands. The police are virtually non-existent outside Riohacha. Every now and then the army goes in to seize and burn, but the smugglers soon sprout up again, like the tough scrub of the *monte*. The police and judiciary are entirely bought off. The Guajiros have a catch-phrase: *Plata o piombo*—silver or lead? Given this choice, most officials take the money rather than the bullet.

On the outskirts of Riohacha, Herman pulled up beside a big concrete building, baking under a cloudless blue sky. It was the new bus terminal. Waldino said, "You get out here, Charlie." For one blank moment I thought they were putting me on a bus back to Santa Marta. But he continued, hairy arm pointing across me, "You go on down that road there. It takes you downtown. You can take a look around Riohacha, get some lunch. We'll come and find you later."

They hadn't said anything about this arrangement. He must have worked it out with Herman. I was suddenly piqued. "For Christ's sake, Waldino, what is this? Is this guy the Pope, or what?"

"It is better this way," he said silkily. "I can explain about you, get the little problems out of the way. Then you can discuss things with Ariel, nice and simple. It's the way we do things, that's all."

Herman smiled, taking no part, always quiet and vigilant. I shrugged. After all these weeks I could wait a few more hours. "Where and when?" I sighed.

"There's a bar on the waterfront called Los Cocos. You be there at—" His naked wrist was uninformative: he tutted petulantly. "Be there at sundown, Charlie. Around 6. Someone will come."

I walked down a wide, littered, tumbledown street—wood walls, tin roofs, lopsided telegraph poles—and through a warren of market stalls. A truck filled with Indians nosed through the crowds—"El Mestizo," bound for the Manaure salt-flats up the peninsula. The Indian women sat among their sacks of fruit and grain. Their fine, flowing dresses, brightly patterned, looked African. Their handsome faces, aquiline and high-boned, were smeared with the dark brown vegetable dye they call *putti*. The Indian men were half and half: *mestizos* down to the waist, sporting hats, sunglasses and short-sleeved shirts; below, nothing but the traditional loincloth—*nurcti*, in their language—knotted up tightly between their legs.

It was siesta-time. Downtown the streets were narrow and silent. They seemed to lead nowhere in particular: a hot town square where no one walked, a scalded seafront without a beach. A few skyscrapers—banks, apartments: monuments to drug-money—protruded above the low white houses. A long wooden jetty snaked out, a fisherman or two, a gang of workmen repairing a winch, a police launch lying off. In a stand of palm trees were three big, open-sided bars, more or less the town's social centre. One of these was the meeting-point, Los Cocos.

I took a drink at the bar next to it. The waiter was drunk. He wore a yachting cap too small for him. I asked for a Cuba Libre: he brought me whisky. There was no rum, he said. I asked him what kind of whisky it was. As I suspected from the bouquet, it was one of the bootleg brands, House of Lords—raw corn-liquor, flavoured with essence of cough lozenge, packaged with a marvellously off-target sense of Scottishness. Another brand is called Glenn, spelt like the American astronaut. I told him I didn't want it. A shot of 140-proof Tizer was something I didn't need right now. He replaced it with aguardiente.

"Why you here anyway?" he slurred suspiciously.

I trotted out the touristic formulae. Doing a quick *vuelta* of the Guajira. *Para conocer la región.*

"There's nothing to see here," he said, sitting down beside me. "We are underdeveloped. Once we were rich with pearls here. The pirates came to loot the town. Now we've only got two things in Riohacha."

"And what are they?"

"*La droga y la muerte!*"

Drugs and death. It was hard to believe it, but I knew it was true. In the old newspaper at Sea Breeze Farm there had been a new item: a couple of minor *traficantes* gunned down in one of these side-streets. The report said that this brought the tally of drug-related deaths in Riohacha to 145 so far this year. The newspaper was dated mid-March. A rough average of two a night.

"You see the fat man over there?" the waiter was saying. I saw him: crisp white shirt unbuttoned, heavy bandages showing underneath, arm in a sling. "We say: He did that falling down the mountain." He made a pistol with two fingers and a thumb, mouthed the shots. *Pow! Pow!* "There are no mountains in the Guajira, my friend."

Customers were banging on the tables for service. The waiter happily cursed at them. He drained his glass. "Don't stay out too late!" he said, and skipped off. He grabbed one of the drinkers by the neck in mock strangulation. Shouts, laughter, more hammering on the rusty table-tops. I drained my aguardiente and left.

I walked some more round the meagre streets. Was this fly-blown little place really the gun-slinging gangster town of cocaine myth? Was there going to be some Jekyll and Hyde transformation after dark, or was this it? I was in the geographic heart of the cocaine racket, and it was dead.

It was Herman who came for me at Los Cocos. We drove through the dusk to a house on the outskirts of Riohacha. A featureless, vaguely suburban street: low houses among shrubs, expensive American cars, tall TV aerials pointing inland. Here, unlike in the centre of town, I got the whiff of big money behind the bland façades. There were lights in some of the houses, but none where we pulled up. Close to, the house was shabby, with a small withered garden in front, and peeling shutters. We walked down the side of the house. Round the back was a verandah. I saw coils of rope, a couple of broken chairs, a hanging bowl with cactus in it. This was no one's home. People came here for a while, then went away again, leaving the shutters to creak in the breeze.

We went in through a screen-door. In the passageway I saw two lit rooms. The one to the left was obviously a kitchen: I could hear the clatter of plates, water being poured. Herman led me down towards the other. I heard low voices, two men, but as Herman pushed open the door and ushered me through, the voices stopped and I entered in silence.

The room was lit by two kerosene lamps which threw big, expressive shadows on the walls. It was hardly furnished at all: a few hard chairs looking like they'd been lifted from a café, a table, Venetian blinds. Everything else—and there was a lot—lay stacked around anyhow, very new-looking, in transit. I saw a TV, ghetto-blaster stereos, electric fans, crates of drink, shiny boat-tackle, and some kind of harpoon-gun for big game fishing. It looked like someone had been out that morning with the express purpose of spending $10,000 as quickly as possible. Leaning against the wall, pinned to hardboard, I saw a navigational map of the Caribbean. This was well-thumbed and annotated, not new at all.

The man sitting behind the table was lean and good-looking. I guessed his age at about thirty-five. The remains of a meal—fish, rice, Aguila beer—lay beside him. A cigarette burned in the ashtray. His arms rested loosely on the table-top. He batted a small tin of toothpicks idly from hand to hand and he watched me with what seemed, for the moment, friendly curiosity.

The other man was Waldino, sitting in one of the chairs, little legs neatly crossed. His comfy posture said in body-language: "Well, here you are, I brought you here, you're on your own now." What he actually said was, "Charlie, I want you to meet Ariel. Ariel, this is the inglés, Charlie."

Ariel rose to shake hands, rangy and confident. His palm was calloused. Not a trace of dampness, though the air inside the room was still. He had a healthy sheen of sun on his face, a sailor's tan, sea-wrinkles round the eyes. He had a couple of days' stubble. He was clearly tired, but he looked like someone who fed on tiredness. He wore a loose, short-sleeved shirt, blue jeans and beach shoes. He looked good. If he wasn't a smuggler he might have been a seafront gigolo, or a gambler looking for a game.

Herman brought three beers in, then left us. "I'm sorry,"

said Ariel. "We have no electricity tonight. The beer is warm."

I was seated, my cigarette was lit, and not a word of small-talk could be found in my head. Ariel sat back, waiting. I shot a glance at Waldino, but he seemed to have nestled down into his beard. He wouldn't look at me, and I knew it was up to me to call the first shot.

"Waldino has . . ." I began. Because the room was still, because my throat was dry, it came out in a cracked whisper, and I had to cough and start again. "Waldino has told you about me?"

"Of course. He had told me all about you, Inglés."

"Excellent." There was another pause. "So, as you know, I—"

He cut in suavely. "You're asking him for 10 kilos, but you haven't got the money yet."

It seemed a bald summary of all I'd laboured over, but I couldn't dispute it. The voice, though brisk, still seemed friendly enough. I said, "The money is agreed, of course. Two hundred thousand including transportation. Waldino has shown you the telegram?" I looked again at Waldino, but he was still hibernating.

Ariel just said, "Ah yes. The telegram."

He was watching me. Blue eyes again, *garzitos*. The telegram didn't count for much, the eyes said. If my pitch was genuine, the cable was genuine. If I was lying, the cable was a lie. Circular evidence in a very linear game.

It was all I had. I blundered on. "My associates in London need to know everything about the move before they arrange for the money to be drafted to me."

"OK," he said, the soul of reasonableness. "You've seen my *finca* by the sea. You've seen my men. Agaton: a very strong man, my boatman. You've seen . . ." There was a chilly humour in his eye. I thought he was going to say "my woman," but he let it trail off. "You've seen enough, no?"

"Yes, I think I've seen enough. There's just a few points of information, a few details to clear up, and then . . ."

He came back quickly. "You're right, Inglés. You're right." He lit a cigarette, took a drag, then let it stand in the ashtray. The smoke threaded up, grey and blue. I was just about to start in with some questions, when he said: "First thing to clear up, Inglés, is this. How do we know you're not a u-c?"

I didn't understand at first, but I knew the tone had subtly changed. "*Que no eres oo-si?*" Waldino couldn't ignore my startled face this time. He looked pained, as if he had to remedy some social gaffe I'd unwittingly committed. "U-c, Charlie," he said softly. "*Agente narcótico.*"

A high, mirthless laugh broke from me. "Jesus! Do I look like a policeman?"

Waldino shook his head, furtively reassuring me, but Ariel said, in a bored voice, "A lot of policemen don't look like policemen, Inglés. That's their job."

"So how do I know that *you're* not a narc?" I said.

"You don't. You have to trust me. Trust all the way: that's the bottom line when you're smuggling. You know that."

"I trust you, Ariel, of course."

"Sure you do." His voice had hardly changed throughout this little crisis. It was still friendly, coaxing, feline. He wore his hair swept back, but it flopped forward over his forehead, and when he pushed it back he looked haggard for a moment. Then he smiled and said, "OK, Inglés, I'll tell you how it all works." Waldino, signalling the release of tension, got up and stretched, and paced the room a bit.

"Our move is up to Aruba," said Ariel, easing into a familiar routine. This is the westernmost of the islands of the Dutch Antilles, Aruba, Bonaire and Curaçao—the ABCs, as they're called. "The island is 400 kilometres from Finca Las Brisas, four days in the speedboat, open sea all the way. I have my partner in Aruba, my cousin. He's a very big wheel in Oranjestad." The Dutch name sounded odd in nasal *costeño* Spanish. "You know Aruba, Inglés? No? Plenty of hot money in Aruba. My cousin's got free-shops on Nassaustraat, and also he has a big agave plantation. He supplies agave oil to big cosmetics companies in the Netherlands. They use agave oil to make suntan lotion, to make all you *blancitos* nice and brown like us, OK? That's how the *coco* goes over. It goes with the agave oil. My cousin has a man on the ship to nurse it through the other side."

He got up and walked over to the corner, picked up an untidy pile of paper, riffled the pages. "I got documents here: shipping lines, freight bills, everything. My cousin sends the agave shipment out every six weeks, a regular order. Just as soon as you put your money on the table we can map the whole thing for you. Precise dates, times of shipment. We can tell you the merchandise will be at this hotel, on this street in Amsterdam, at this hour precisely. Inglés, we'll even tell you what the weather will be. It'll be raining. It always rains in Europe, no?"

"Never stops, Ariel, except when it snows."

"We'll make it snow all night! So—you go back to Santa Marta and cable your friends. Tell them everything AOK on the move. We've done this run twenty times, smooth as stone. Different volumes, different clients. It's worked every time."

The spiel over, he sprawled back in his chair and lit another cigarette. Waldino made an "O" with his thumb and forefinger. "I told you, Charlie. This is the best."

Ariel smoked deep. Sometimes he had a wheeze in his lungs, a sudden hacking cough that caught him, made him wince with pain. It was like a chink in his armour. He said reflectively, "I've been in this business twenty-five years. When I was selling cigarettes along the beach bars in Santa Marta, I had a little secret box of *marimba*, ready-rolled." He leaned forward, a caricature of furtiveness. "Psst! Meester! You wanna cigarette-a-make-you-deezy?" He shook his head. "I sold it at a peso a shot then, now it's 200,000 US all the way to Europe. It's still the same game."

He dumped the pile of shipping papers back on the floor. As they landed they nudged another pile of odds and ends, and off the top of this something small but heavy, wrapped in a cloth, fell to the floor. The cloth parted, and out poked what was unmistakably the black snout of a hand-gun.

Ariel saw my eyes flinch. He laughed. "Don't worry, Inglés. It's not pointing at you tonight!" He picked it up, cradled it affectionately in his hand for a moment. "Seven millimetres," he said, "only little. Everyone carries a friend in Riohacha, Inglés. We say: *Gata con guantes no caza ratones.*"

He wrapped the gun back up and replaced it. A cat with gloves on doesn't catch any rats. Thus far and no further, I thought. Time to start talking myself out. Ariel's claws would be long and sharp.

"There's one other thing, Charlie," said Waldino, studying the bubbles in his beer bottle. "Ariel and I have talked this over, and—"

Ariel cut in, born on his feet and still running. "We've decided that I will *supply* the merchandise as well. Waldino had made other arrangements, but this is better, no?" He cocked an eye at Waldino, who nodded vigorously. How easily he had slipped into the henchman's role, I thought.

"The price will be the same," Ariel continued. "Two hundred all in. I have a very good source, just come onstream. *Perica de primera calidad,* on its way to the States. I have 5 kilos on order. This is spoken for—I have another move going out of Santa Marta soon. I'll mark 10 kilos down for you, Inglés, if you get the money. You can have 15 if you want, 20 . . ."

I assured him that 10 would be enough. I asked him about this stuff.

"It comes up from Bogotá. We pick it up in Barranquilla. They call this Snow White cocaine."

"Jesus."

Two pairs of eyes narrowed. "You know something about this, Inglés?"

"Know it? Jesus. It's only the best damn cocaine I've ever tasted. Someone gave me a *muestra* in Bogotá."

Ariel gave a thin smile. "You get around, Inglés, no?" He had noted it down, everything was filed away. "So," he said, concluding the business. "Once we get the dollars we're there. Am I right?"

"We're there, Ariel, we're there."

It all linked up. My confused stumblings had actually unearthed a whole pipeline. I could trace my phantom 10 kilos of cocaine all the way—Huanaco leaves from the Yungas of Bolivia, mulched with kerosene and acid into cocaine paste, smuggled up through the jungles of Peru to the Colombian border near Leticia, flown up to the Hacienda Alaska in the southern *llanos*, elaborated by a German cook into prime cocaine hydrochloride, trucked up in cattle wagons to the San Felipe slaughter-house in Bogotá, distributed through Rafael Vallejo's Transcarne meat network, offloaded in Barranquilla, driven down the Troncal de Caribe, carried down the trail to Sea Breeze Farm, loaded into a speedboat called *La Solución*, ferried by Agaton and Miguelito to the island of Aruba, delivered to a businessman in Oranjestad, packaged up in a cargo of agave essence, nursed across the Atlantic by a bent crewman on a Dutch cargo ship, picked up in a hotel room in Amsterdam, spirited to London via any number of mule-runs, wholesaled, brokered, buffed, diluted, filtered through the ounce-dealers and gram-merchants, thirty thousand grams of one-in-three, sixty thousand hungry nostrils twitching, a hundred thousand toots at the parties that really matter, the suave new *soirées* where as likely as not you'll see Malcolm himself, jawing with some beautiful literary agent from New York, who's wishing he'd shut up about this super book on the cocaine trade, and let her get her nose down into that sweet white candy.

23

BAD MOVES

Two days later I was sitting in the Bar Mamatoca in San Martín, the dockside *barrio* of Santa Marta. It was the twilight hour, *entre dos luces*. The bar was half-empty, the music turned up too loud. There were no street lights in this part of town, and soon the low, sand-coloured walls opposite faded from view. Inside the Mamatoca, a pair of bare 25-watt bulbs served to illuminate the evening's business and cast a dim, not very welcoming pool of light on the sidewalk. I could tell the two men were still standing there across the street, because I could see the red tips of their cigarettes. Their presence made me uneasy.

I had got a message from Waldino to meet him here. When I got here there was only Ariel, whom I had not expected to see at all. It was getting pretty close to the day of my sudden disappearance from Santa Marta. I had sent off another cable to Malcolm, just to keep Waldino happy. "ALL SYSTEMS CHECKED PROCEED IMMEDIATELY." I had a few days' grace—"These big financial moves take time, Waldino"—before it started to become apparent that there was no 10-kilo order, no big London *capo*, no 200,000 US, no reason at all why I should have been poking my pink gringo nose into their private business. By that time I would be miles away, perhaps even sitting on a plane bound for London. According to my plans, in fact, this was going to be my last night in Santa Marta, and I felt a stab of nerves when I saw that it was Ariel I was going to spend it with.

We sat drinking *tintos*. The *tinto* keeps you sharp, Ariel said. He was looking smarter than when I'd seen him before: loose white jacket, open shirt, pointed black slip-on shoes. There was a pallor of tension under his weathered skin. He was still and watchful, energy-saving. The *contrabandista* had business tonight, and he wanted some help with it.

We were waiting for Waldino and Rita, he explained. With them, he hoped, would be a Swedish seaman—his name was actually Sven, but he spoke of him simply as Sueco, the Swede, just as I was always Inglés, the Englishman. The Swede's ship, the *Nordic Star*, had docked in Santa Marta that afternoon. The Swede did not speak Spanish, but he did speak passable English, and this was where I came in. "You must help us talk to him," Ariel said. "We have a proposition for him. He may need a little persuasion." I didn't like that term at all. I wondered what tools of persuasion Ariel was carrying. Money and guns—software and hardware, as Gus put it. There was room for both in the loose white jacket.

While we waited Ariel spelt out the situation. The music was loud enough, and the lights dim enough, to ensure total privacy as we talked. This was doubtless part of the service Bar Mamatoca provided for its clientele. I had the feeling that everyone there was setting up a deal, waiting for a mark, portioning out a take. Dodginess pervaded the place like a smell.

This was the move out of Santa Marta he had spoken of the other night, the one for which he had 5 kilos of Snow White cocaine ordered up. He'd done this move half a dozen times before, without a whisper of trouble. The container ship *Nordic Star* called in at Santa Marta once every two or three months, homeward bound for Goteborg, having already visited Houston and Panama. On its last few voyages home it had unwittingly carried back 5-kilo consignments of cocaine supplied by Ariel. The coke was eventually bound for Hamburg. That was where the order originated. Ariel had nothing but praise for the efficiency of Los Tedescos, the Germans, who had set the business up. They had their man—the Swede—aboard the ship. They paid good prices and they paid up-front: the Swede handed over in dollars, in exchange for the package of coke. *"No tapucos"*—no jiggery-pokery—that was what Ariel liked about this move. He wasn't a man, as he put it, to go looking for three-legged cats.

The lynch-pin of Ariel's side of the operation was a *winchero* who worked at the docks. He it was who ferried the *perica* into the restricted port area. He brought it through the checkpoint in a compartment under the pillion of his motor-bike. Once inside it was a piece of cake for the *winchero*, in the course of his legitimate work, to meet up with the Swede inside the boat, near the loading area, and exchange the packages of drugs and dollars. So slickly had this run in the past that Ariel had not even met the Swede. He knew him by sight, because it was part of the arrangement that the Swede should come onshore, on the night the *Nordic Star* docked, and take a turn or two, natural enough, along the waterfront bars. If he was wearing a red bandanna round his neck that meant everything was cool—he had the money, and would await the drop at the prearranged time. The time was always 11:30 a.m.—half an hour before the end of the morning shift—on the day after the ship docked. Sometimes the ship stayed in port a day, sometimes two days, but Ariel's *winchero* would either be unloading or loading at this time. On every occasion, the Swede had been wearing his neck-erchief, and the meet had been made, smooth as clockwork.

The previous night, however, disaster had struck. The *winchero* had got involved in a fight over a bar-girl. A man had been knifed to death, and the *winchero* was languishing in the town jail. Ariel had considered going straight down to the Comisario to try and bail him out, but he had decided this would be costly—back-handers all round—and could well lead to awkward questions. The best course of action, he concluded, would be to target on the Swede. The Swede must be persuaded that he himself must carry the *mercancia* on to the boat.

To this end Waldino and Rita were out on the beach drag,

trawling for the Swede. They would bring him here, and we would explain to him, nice and easy, that there'd been a little change in the plans.

So we waited, Ariel chain-smoking, languid in manner but watchful as a cat. People drifted in and out of the pool of light on the sidewalk. A hooker stared in, cast her hook, got no bites, and walked on. La Loca got up from time to time, with a sudden petulant hiss. There was a thin drift of sand under the bar-stools. I watched the *muchacha* pecking at it with her witch's broom. She swept it out on to the street, and the wind blew it straight back in. I could still see a shadowy figure against the opposite wall, cigarette burning. I mentioned this to Ariel, but he shook his head, said "*No importa,*" and ordered more coffee. The music pounded on, an old Rafael Escalona song—

> Ay mi vida, ay mi vida,
> Soy un hombre perdido . . .

I've been through this movie before, I thought. Just a few blocks away, just a few years away, talking someone through a cocaine deal, and one never learns, does one, and here I am again, torqued up on *tinto*, dust in my throat, and a dim foreboding in my gut that if history really does repeat itself, this time round it's tragedy's turn. But there was no time to grapple with this, because here came Waldino, and a step or two behind him, with Rita on his arm, was the Swede.

The Swede was not what you would call classic mule material. Mules tend to be neat and inconspicuous, like Rosalita in her specs. The imperative of camouflage is ingrained in their souls. The Swede was about as inconspicuous as a bear at a tea-party. He may not quite have stood six foot six and weighed two forty-five, but he was generally built along the lines of Big Bad John. He was a good head taller than anyone else in the bar and was further marked out by his extreme blondness. A blond curly beard half-covered his face, and more hair came sprouting up like reinforcements out of the neck of his denim work-shirt. Lurking amid this undergrowth was the red neckerchief that signalled "All Clear."

Waldino chivvied him respectfully towards a seat. I could tell he was completely fazed by the man's size. He came about up to the Swede's breast-pocket, out of which a pouch of Dutch black-shag tobacco poked. Rita too kept darting glances at him, biting her lip, with that droll, intrigued look of hers. In fact everyone at the bar was staring at him. If it wasn't for the music, a silence would have fallen, like in Westerns when the baddie shoulders through the swing-doors into the saloon.

It was clear that the Swede was not at all well-pleased. He looked as if he felt like uprooting a few pine trees. Installing him at our table, on a chair not intended for a man of his size, Waldino hurried off to the bar to order beers. He glanced at Ariel as he passed, and shot his black, piggy eyes heavenwards.

Ariel played it very cool. He let the Swede simmer down a bit and get his bearings, and then he rose slightly to shake hands. The Swede's big, gnarled paw, with engine oil worked deep into the grain of the skin, completely engulfed Ariel's hand. Ariel introduced himself as Manuel. The Swede scrutinized him solemnly and answered with a deep, sonorous grunt, which I realized was the name Sven. When it was my turn to introduce myself I called myself Frank. I don't know why.

Ariel motioned me to begin. The Swede's cold blue eyes peeked out at me from his sailor's wrinkles. "You speak English, Sven?" I asked.

"Yaw. I am speaking English OK."

"Good. Our friends here have a problem. The man who brings in the merchandise is out of action."

"So." He nodded slowly. Rita giggled at our curious Northern cadences.

"So they . . ."

"So they must find another man focking quick."

I had already suggested this to Ariel. It was not possible, he said. "I don't think they can do that, Sven. These things take time to set up, even here in Santa Marta. There must be complete trust, as I'm sure you . . ."

"So."

"So . . . they are hoping you will carry the merchandise aboard yourself."

He banged his bottle down on the table—it was already empty—and shook his grizzled head. "No deal. You tell these focking people it's no deal. The gear comes on to the boat, I'll be there with the dollars. But I don't do no focking carrying."

The interview continued much in this fashion for a while. The Swede was implacable. The grunt of "So" rolled down like a boulder to block every avenue that Ariel could suggest. Waldino followed the conversation like a tennis match, nodding brightly at the end of each sentence, darting deferential glances at the Swede. I saw the little man's thirst for revenge alight in his eye. Ariel tried various tacks. It was to all our advantage that the deal went through, he said. The Swede just shrugged. Then out came the money, $500 rolled in a tight wad in his fist. He flashed it at the Swede like a cardsharp. The Swede remained mountainously negative as the carrot grew, and at $2,000 Ariel gave up.

The Swede's argument, reasonable enough, was that he kept himself strictly offshore. His role in the operation began and ended in Europe. He was paid in kronor, in Goteborg. He took his risks aboard a Swedish ship, and when spiriting the drugs off the boat past Swedish port police and customs. He wanted as little as possible to do with the Colombian end. He didn't like Santa Marta, any more than he liked any other South American ports, Barranquilla, Buenaventura, Guayaquil, Valparaiso. They were all the same, gutters of sweat and treachery, filled with con-artists and with peculiarly virulent strains of clap. He had the pay-offs clearly balanced in his mind. If he got busted aboard the *Nordic Star*, or in Goteborg, OK, it was trouble, but it was trouble he could live with. No previous record, wife and two kids. He'd be going on conditional discharge, or at worst a few months in an open prison, all very cosy, free association and smorgasbord every Sunday.

Ariel's final bid was that he could get the *perica* inside the port area, though not on the boat. It could be thrown over the perimeter fence at a certain point he knew. All the Swede would have to do was pick it up the next morning, and walk it back on to the ship. No checkpoints, no problem. What could be simpler than that?

But no. The Swede didn't like that either. It was too dangerous for him. What if someone had seen it? He would be walking into a trap. Also, it was too complicated to organize payment. He was under orders never to part with the money until he had got the cocaine. He was adamant. It was clear he wasn't going to deviate one inch from the prescribed routine. Ariel had just one crumb of comfort. The *Nordic Star* would be undergoing a few minor repairs tomorrow, and wouldn't be leaving port until Thursday evening, nearly forty-eight hours from now. Ariel had until Thursday morning to find someone to ferry the *perica* aboard the *Nordic Star*. The Swede would be waiting, at the usual place, at 11.30 on Thursday. No merchandise, no money.

He stomped off through the dwarfish doorway of the Mamatoca. Ariel sauntered after him and leant there, watching him go. Then he called softly across the street. The man I had seen standing there came over. Ariel moved out of the light. They talked briefly. I saw the man pocketing money as he left, and I realized that Ariel had put him there to watch his back all through the meeting.

The following day—so close to the end, just about to pull up the ladder and disappear forever—I made the slip I had feared all along. It was a hot, still day with many flies. The rains were not far off, the air drooped over the roofs. Ariel and Waldino, philosophical about the stubbornness of the Swede, had gone off to Barranquilla to pick up the 5 kilos of Snow White. They seemed confident that they would find a way of getting the merchandise on board the *Nordic Star*.

I was planning to leave Santa Marta at 6 that evening: I

had already bought a bus ticket. They would not be back in town till midnight, they said. It seemed ideal. When they called by at the Corona that morning—Waldino had a little *muestra* of basuko to give me, in the hopes of further interesting my "associates"—I secretly knew I was saying goodbye for the last time.

I felt bad about it, I had to admit. I was leaving town with a story of sorts in my bag, but with a very nasty taste in my mouth. I had come to respect these people in their way—Ariel the boss, Waldino the pirate, Rita the gypsy, Agaton the pilot. As the song says, "To live outside the law you must be honest." I was the dishonest law-abider. These are your cocaine smugglers, Malcolm. No. 1 Public Enemy, traders in misery and corruption. You wanted the truth and all I've done is tell them lies.

I spent most of the day writing at my table at the Corona, pausing from time to time for the refreshments so vital for serious work in the tropics—fruit, bread, beer and basuko. The afternoon wore on. The door and the long, shuttered window stood open on to the balcony. No breeze stirred the sapodilla trees. Omar was down in his den, dozing over the latest issue of *Adelita*. Music from his radio rested lightly on the pillowy air. The Zuleta brothers, with "El Viejo" on squeeze-box.

I was just thinking about starting to get my bag packed up, when out of the stillness came a voice at my window. A familiar voice: "Charlie. *Qué tal?*"

I started like a guilty thing. "Waldino! Ariel! *Qué tal?*" I hadn't heard them coming, and—more to the point—they weren't supposed to *be* here. Waldino had clearly said they were going to pick up the cocaine in Barranquilla that evening, and they wouldn't be back in Santa Marta till midnight. But here they were, Waldino leaning at the window, Ariel sauntering in through the door, hands in pockets, eyebrows genially raised over cold blue eyes, and here was I, with papers, notebooks and news-clippings strewn around the table, the incriminating tools of the trade, the snoop at work on his gleanings.

"I thought you were in Barranquilla," I laughed, hastily rising from the desk.

"We made the pick-up sooner than expected," said Waldino, scratching his beard. "We got back quickly. We're going to have another go at the Swede tonight. We want you to come."

Ariel strolled around, idly appraising the room and its contents. He was at his most dangerous when he was slow and easy like this. He could spring out of this mood like a jack from a box. His gaze fell on the cluttered writing table.

"Beer? *Sucito?*" I babbled, moving between Ariel and the desk. "You must be tired."

Waldino said "*Como no?*" and swung his tubby frame over the low sill. He landed in the room with a little sigh. Ariel just shook his head, still looking at the desk. They want to keep everything off the record, I thought. Reasonable enough. I picked up the newspaper with the basuko and tobacco on it.

"You're working, Inglés? We're disturbing you?" Ariel's voice was colourless. He used the formal, third person "you."

"No, no. Sure you won't have a beer, Ariel?"

"But you are writing, I think?"

"No, well—yes. Just a couple of letters." I waved an airmail envelope at him. It was empty and unaddressed, and seemed flimsy evidence.

"Letters, Inglés?" The voice had hardened. Waldino had begun some inconsequential chat—an obscene comparison, to do with holes, between the road to Barranquilla and the women of that town—but he stopped in mid-flow to look at Ariel. Ariel, dispensing now with any social niceties, riffled through the scattered papers on my desk. He squinted at my notebook. He couldn't understand the words but I could see he was beginning to understand the general drift.

"So who you writing to, Inglés?"

"That's my business."

He looked me in the eye for the first time, and said softly, "No, Inglés. It's our business. We're partners, remember?" Waldino was standing at his shoulders now, the henchman's position. His brows were knitted in puzzlement. He it was who spotted the publisher's Letter of Introduction, peeping out of a pile of papers under the ashtray, his magpie eye alighting on the glimpse of tasteful green letter-heading. He extricated it with his stubby fingers, holding it up by the corner, as if it were valuable and fragile. "*A Quien Se Interese.*" To whom it concerns . . .

They both read the letter, with its ornate courtesies and cringing subjunctives. They took it in slowly. Waldino ran his fingers over the publisher's logo, to see if it was embossed or offset. Everything has its price, even at these critical stages.

"*El autor británico . . .*" said Ariel thoughtfully. "This is very interesting."

"I can explain," I said.

"You should have told us, *hombre,*" said Waldino. He shook his head at me reproachfully, almost pityingly, as if I had spoiled everything with a fatal blunder. "We're your friends, Charlie. You should have told us."

"I thought you asked too many questions," mused Ariel. "Rita said so too. You gringos are always asking questions. *Cómo se llama éste? Porqué el diablo eso?* But you . . ." He shot an angry glance at Waldino—Waldino whose job it was to check my credentials, Waldino who had introduced me to Ariel's set-up, Waldino on whose back I had ridden into Sea Breeze Farm. "Hey, stupid," he said to him. "You brought in a flea in your beard, and now we're all going to itch." He turned back to me. "So you are writing a story about us? You are going to tell the world about Finca las Brisas, about the *Nordic Star.* We're going to be *estrellas,* Waldino. Big stars. I'm not sure we like this."

"I can explain," I said again. My mind raced and got nowhere.

"No need," said Ariel sharply. "I don't want to hear. We don't like your sort. In our business we say, *Zapatero, a tus zapatos!*" Cobbler, to your shoes: in other words, eyes down and mind your own business.

He let the letter fall from his fingers. The ceiling fan

caught it. It floated off the table and landed on the floor at my feet. This was a very bad moment. They were entitled to take it badly. Somewhere in my life someone had said, "It's one thing to lose, it's another thing to cheat and lose." That was about the size of it: I had cheated and lost.

Then Ariel laughed. *"Carajo! Eres un zorro, no?"* Waldino looked at him in surprise. Yes, Ariel was definitely smiling, calling me a crafty fox, shaking his head in disbelief. Ariel put his hand to his forehead and massaged along the wrinkles as if so much disbelief had given him a headache. He said *"Carajo!"* again, called me some more names, and said wearily, "Roll us a *sucito*, then. I want to discuss this with my *compañero* here."

He jabbed Waldino on the shoulder, motioning him back out onto the balcony. I was uncomfortably reminded of the *bingero* at El Molino, jabbing the *costeño* off onto the sidewalk. Ariel too would be carrying a friend under his jacket. Waldino, nonplussed, decidedly one jump behind, shot me another glare of reproach and trotted out after the *contrabandista*. They closed the door, pushed shut the shutters on the window. I stood in the empty, half-darkened room, straining to catch the urgent, hissed conference out on the balcony. Looking down I found I was still carrying my newspaper tray of basuko in both hands, like some ridiculous butler, and even as I looked, my hands started shaking like leaves on a tree.

They came back in. Waldino looked chastened. He closed the door behind him and leant against it. Ariel advanced. Everything felt suddenly close and claustrophobic. I was trying to read the look on his face. I smelt the smuggler's tang on him: salt and sweat, one part sea, one part fear. "You know what a lot of my friends would say about this business?" I shook my head. "They'd say it was time to check your oil, Inglés." I stared at him uncomprehendingly. He made a graphic gesture, and I quickly understood that *mediando el aceite* meant sticking a knife into someone's belly, like a dipstick into the oil-sump. He let this possibility hang in the air for a moment. Waldino looked at the ceiling fan, rubbed his beard non-committally. Somewhere below I heard Omar discussing a football match with one of the *porteros*. Unión de Magdalena was playing Junior de Barranquilla on Sunday, a *costeño* local derby. Ariel continued: "But we've got a better idea, no?" He cocked his head at Waldino, who hastened to agree. "Oh yes, Don Ariel, we've got a wonderful idea." I looked from one to the other. The bastards are enjoying this, I thought.

"This problem of ours, Charlie," said Waldino. "As you know, we—"

Ariel cut in. "You will take our *perica* on to the *Nordic Star* tomorrow," he said.

I sat down heavily on the bed. They weren't going to kill me, they were going to co-opt me.

24

PICK-UP AT WHARF THREE

The fateful morning dawned pink and grey. Soon Ariel was at the door, unshaven, speedy, bringing an all-night smell of stale tobacco and beer into the room. The *perica* was in place, he said. He had thrown it over the perimeter fence a couple of hours earlier. "She's ready and waiting for you, Inglés. Legs wide open." He slapped me on the back. The last strand of hope that I had clung to through the night—the possibility that something would go wrong with the drop—was gone.

He dumped a large carrier bag on the bed. In it was a brand new "executive" brief-case, purchased that morning from Waldino's stationery store off 5th Avenue. Black imitation leather, gold-plate fittings, combination locks, made in Taiwan.

"You sure it's big enough?" I asked.

"Open it, Inglés." Inside were five kilo-bags of sugar. They fitted snugly in the fake velour upholstery.

We ran through the layout one last time. The sketch-map Ariel had drawn the previous night was already grubby with handling. I knew the layout of the docks by heart. The harbour was roughly triangular. When I came in through the check-point, the two main covered *bodegas* would be on my left, the grain silo on my right. Up in the apex of the triangle was Wharf Three, used for shallow draught boats. Off to the side of Wharf Three, over the rail track, was a generating plant. This was the Spot Marked X: between the back

of the *generador* and the perimeter fence lay 5 kilos of pure
Snow White cocaine, "ready and waiting." How I got myself
to the generator, and how I got myself and the cocaine into
the *Nordic Star*, were my problem. We ran through the directions for once I was on board the boat: up the gangway, right
down the passage, through the swing-doors, second door on
the left. That was where the Swede would be waiting, in the
john. He would be there with the money at 11.30 precisely.
He would wait for ten minutes, no more. The timing was
critical.

Ariel took out the sugar and packed it into the carrier bag.
He had only borrowed the sugar, he explained. No need to
incur unnecessary expenses. Into the brief-case I piled notebooks, business cards, calculator, passport and the wretched
Letter of Introduction. All the tools of the *bona fide* researcher. A whole lot of little truths around one big lie . . .

Under a beating sun, in a newly laundered white shirt, I
sallied forth from the Corona, a man about his business. I
went up to the stationer's and bought a clipboard to complete my business researcher's kit. I cut back across the cathedral square, light bouncing off the white walls. In the
shade of a mango tree an old man sat on a fruit-crate. He
chewed reflectively on a slice of sugar-cane. How I envied
him his ease.

I walked down 10th Street. There was the ex-Fruit Palace,
El Progreso. I had a bit of time to spare. I stopped to take a
jugo there for old times' sake, but checked myself at the doorway. Today of all days, let the shade of Harvey rest. Let me
not end up in the hen-house today.

I crossed the bleak sandy stretches around the railway station. My shirt was already wet with sweat, and my hand
sticky round the plastic handle of the brief-case. La Loca
whipped up the dust into my eyes. I bought a *tinto* from an
itinerant seller. He carried two thermos flasks strung round
his neck, one with *tinto*, the other with cinnamon tea. I
could turn round now, take a taxi to the airport, cash in my
last few dollars, and run all the way to Bogotá with my tail

between my legs. But some obscure sense of mission kept me going. I owed it to them.

The sea was picture postcard blue, and here I was at the Terminal Marítimo de Santa Marta, about to make my small contribution to the *otra economía*.

The first stage was easy enough. At the Harbour Police station I presented my letter of introduction and my business card to an acned young cadet at the desk. As instructed by Ariel, I asked him to present these to the Commandante, who would issue me with a pass to enter the docks. A few minutes later, I was duly ushered down a corridor, to a door which read "Vice-Commandante Policia Portuaria, Departamento de Seguridad," with a name below it that was almost as long. A tall man in naval uniform was writing at the desk, a cigarette-holder between his teeth. My card and letter lay on the neat, polished desk. He rose courteously, and we shook hands. His arms were thin, brown and hairless.

"*Entonces, señor.* You are writing a book about our country."

"Yes, Vice-Commandante."

"And you wish to visit the port area. For what purpose exactly?"

He took out his cigarette-holder. He held it in his delicate fingers and scrutinized me. I trotted out my spiel: *informe económico*, foreign trade statistics, port expansion programme. I larded in a few oblique compliments about the vital significance of this thriving port to Colombia's national development. The word *desarrollo*—development—has an almost mystic ring here. He listened politely. He fingered the letter-heading, just as Waldino had done yesterday.

I threw in a couple of polite questions about the Harbour Police. He told me he was in charge of some 150 officers and marines. "We keep a very tight control here. Perhaps you are aware, there are many . . . bad elements here in Santa Marta. Much contraband, *narcotráfico.*"

Sweat pricked my back. My throat was dry. I nodded gravely.

"You will wish to see Señor Bustamente," he said, jotting the name down on his note-pad. "He is Director of Operations. He will have the details you need." He explained how I might find him. He reached into a shallow wooden tray on his desk and drew out a small, mimeographed docket. He wrote on it my passport number and name. He stamped it and handed it to me. He clicked his heels as we shook hands. "I hope your visit will be of benefit to you," he said.

Two minutes later I was at the checkpoint. I presented my pass, a *permiso provisional*. The guard frisked me cursorily. He gave the contents of my brief-case a quick once-over and waved me through. It was 10.15 a.m. and I was inside the docks.

I saw the *Nordic Star* straight away and strolled over to join a knot of people watching the loading. The ship loomed over us like a blue steel rock-face. They were trucking containers of coffee into the loading bay. I wandered around, clutching my clipboard, looking vaguely official. I had no idea how I was going to get myself into the ship itself, but that was for later. Right now the important thing seemed to be to get myself noticed, to *establish* myself—a vague but thoroughly legitimate presence, jotting notes on his clipboard from time to time. The first duty of shoplifters, snoops and smugglers: to become a part of the landscape. A few seamen were lounging over the railings high above. I couldn't spot the Swede, and I didn't really want to.

I found Señor Bustamente in one of the big covered warehouses—Bodega No. 2, according to Ariel's map. He was, as his name somehow foretold, a large, fat, expansive man. He said he would be delighted to answer a few questions. After he had finished his business we walked back through the *bodega*. Thousands of sacks of pale, unroasted coffee were piled everywhere: the port loads 170,000 tonnes of coffee a year, he told me. We went up some concrete steps into a cluttered little office. A secretary in a tartan skirt brought us *tintos*. I plied him with questions. We discussed the containerization programme, the length of port rail-track, the 5,250 square metres of covered storage. We flourished our calculators to convert deadweight tonnes into ordinary tonnes. He regaled me on the subject of *diversificación económica*, as instanced by the declining proportion of bananas in the exports from the port. Twenty years ago, 98 per cent of products exported from Santa Marta were bananas; last year it was only 16 per cent.

Every interview reaches a natural plateau, after which one can either coast down through the formalities and take one's leave, or overstay one's welcome with more questions. Just as we were reaching this point, I introduced the subject of the *Nordic Star*.

"Just to get the feel of a typical day here, Señor Bustamente. Perhaps you could tell me a bit about the ships in dock today. The biggest would be . . ."

"The *Nordic Star*. Swedish container ship. Three thousand six hundred tonnes, unloaded the day before yesterday: paper, industrial machinery, chemical products. Today we are loading. Coffee, bananas, melons, textiles."

"How long will that take?"

"We shall be finished this afternoon. We are operating, as I said, our new roll-on roll-off system."

"Ah yes, the roll-on roll-off system. This is most interesting for my study. I wonder, would it be possible to observe this in action?"

Of course it would, he said, glad of a chance of shaking me off.

We strolled down together. As we watched the loading I racked my brains for questions, last-minute points, nebulous patter—anything to keep him there at my side, so everyone could see me enjoying an amiable but businesslike chat with El Jefe Director. Finally I could cloy him with small-talk no longer. We shook hands and he returned to the *bodega*.

I checked my watch. It was time to move on to my next "appointment," the pick-up at Wharf Three. I set off purposefully: always look like you're going somewhere, Ariel had said. I passed the harbour rail depot. Men were unloading sacks of grain on to an overhead track. These were winched up towards the vast IDEMA grain silos. Twenty silos, capacity 32,000 tonnes: I ground out these recently gleaned facts under my breath, repeating them like a mantra, because at this point the most important person to convince of my credibility was me. The sun was like a weight on the top of my head. My heart beat wildly. I could still turn back. The moment of reckoning could be delayed. Which was worse—the Harbour Police fingering my collar for drug-running, or Ariel checking my oil in some dark, piss-ridden alley in San Martín? It was not a question I could answer. The only thing to do was to keep on walking.

I was up to Wharf Three, in the northern corner of the harbour, by 11 o'clock. The layout was just as Ariel had described it. Looking away from the waterfront, across a wide open patio with parked cars and containers in it, I could see the narrow-gauge track that ran all the way round from the far side of the harbour, Wharf Four, under the shadow of Punta Betín. My eye followed the curve of the track to the point where it reached nearest to the perimeter fence, and there it was—the generating plant, a couple of low breeze-block buildings and a cat's cradle of high-voltage transformers. Behind it the ground rose steeply: a couple of chalky-coloured tumps, with a rough sand track running between them, for trucks carrying cargo to and from the Punta Betín wharf. From that road, at about 4 o'clock this morning, Ariel had slithered down to the perimeter fence and tossed over the cocaine, wrapped in an old sack. Unless it had been spotted by an unusually vigilant guard, it should still be there, between the generator and the fence, just another bit of rubbish in another cranny, with the single vital difference that, once reclaimed and transported to its destination, this particular bit of rubbish would be worth a quarter of a million dollars.

I now had to leave the busy thoroughfare of the wharfs and warehouses, where my presence was unremarkable, and head into the no-man's-land of the open patio. With every step I took, my cover became more and more meaningless. I was heading towards the edge of the dock area. There would be no one to interview there, no possible reason for a researcher to be bending his busy steps that way. I had got to the edge of the patio when a group of workmen suddenly appeared from among the freight trucks and started walking towards me. After a moment of frozen panic I did the only thing I could think of, which was to stand myself up against a pile of planking and pretend I was taking a pee. They passed quite close by me, but didn't make any comment. When they were gone I got myself in among the freight trucks. My main worry now was any patrolling guards around the fence, and anyone who happened to be at the generator itself. I peeked out from among the box-cars. A couple of dusty trucks were rolling along the road above the fence, but no one was to be seen. As I made the last 50 yards between the rail track and the generator, there was nothing in my mind except the rushing of my blood and the pumping of my heart. I had no story to spin, no cover to wear. I was in the real smuggler's spotlight, where the only kind of camouflage is not being seen.

I made it without mishap to the appointed spot behind the generator. I spotted the sack immediately, lying among a thin scattering of other detritus. It was an excellent spot for a drop, certainly. There was only a few feet between the building and the fence. Behind the fence, the embankment shelved up steeply. Huddled in there I was hidden both from the road outside and from the rest of the docks.

I knelt down beside the sack and pulled out the polythene package inside it. It was at this point that the first major hitch occurred. The sack had landed on a nest of broken *gaseosa* bottles. Five kilos, thrown up and over a 12-foot fence, lands with quite a bump, and by sheer bad luck a shard of glass on a standing bottle had pierced straight through the burlap sacking and—as I discovered when I took the package out—straight through the polythene as well. Cocaine poured out of the rent like spilt salt. I struggled to fit the package into my brief-case. I was clumsy, and the package sagged. The tear in the polythene lengthened. Several hundred dollars' worth of *perica* wafted off on the breeze. Cursing, I manhandled the drugs into the case. It was a tight fit—Bustamente had given me a few brochures and photocopies, and I had to jettison a couple to get the stuff in. The white dust was everywhere, sticking to my sweat-drenched shirt and arms, and to the fake velour inside the case. It was a horrible mess. Even without the brochures, the case was difficult to shut. As I forced it, one of the hinges at the back snapped. When it was at last shut, it had a lopsided, suspiciously full look. It would have to do. I dusted off the coating of cocaine from the case and from my clothes. My hands had got grimed with something oily among the rubbish, and in dusting myself down I smeared the oil on my white shirt.

I straightened up and leant against the wall, quivering like a cur, panting with heat and fear. I felt very ragged. I cursed Ariel, the Swede, cheap Taiwanese brief-cases, and bloody Malcolm with his bright ideas.

It was 11.25 by the time I was back at the *Nordic Star*. I had just a few minutes, fifteen at the most, to get myself inside the belly of the boat for my rendezvous with the Swede. This was the last and possibly the stickiest part of the whole operation. I was carrying now, staring at ten years without option in the delightful purlieus of the town jail. I slid back into the knot of people. It is a sociological law in Colombia: wherever there are people working there are always at least as many standing around watching. They were loading *cajas* of bananas now, 20-kilo wooden crates, green bananas that would ripen on the voyage. I glanced around furtively. No one seemed to have noticed my presence or my absence. I let myself cool down a bit.

I steadied myself to make my move. Nonchalantly up the gangplank, clipboard in hand, prayer on my lips that no one would challenge me. Then I saw, to my dismay, the bulky figure of Señor Bustamente bearing down on me. With him was a small, saturnine man sporting a florid kipper tie. Guilt and fear surged up my gut. Surely it was written all over me: flushed and sweating, smudged with dust and oil, my brief-case bulging suspiciously. I could feel the incriminating weight of it in my hand. I stood my ground—I had nowhere else to go.

It seemed to be all right. Bustamente was beaming cordially, and the little man he was introducing to me, whom for a moment of black resignation I took to be a narcotics agent, was in fact the Port Systems Manager. "I was just telling Señor Lino about you," said Bustamente. "I think he can fill you in on some of those details about the port expansion programme." I shook hands with Señor Lino. A twinge of distaste crossed his face as he felt my damp, dirty palm.

I was well and truly trapped. Little Señor Lino waxed lyrical about the *desarrollo portuario*, from its widest ramification to its smallest cubic metric detail. I dutifully jotted notes on my clipboard. I looked at my watch: 11.35. The Swede would be waiting already. I had five minutes at the most. I couldn't just say, "Excuse me, thank you very much," and walk up the gangplank on to the boat. The only thing to do was to try and ease the conversation to a full stop, and hope they would leave me. At a suitable lull, therefore, I slipped the clipboard under my arm, put my pen back in my breast-pocket, picked up my brief-case, and assumed that sullen, introverted politeness with which the Englishman signals his withdrawal from company. I hovered in vain. Another Englishman would have taken the hint but Colombians are made of sterner stuff. It was ironic really—I had sweated small-talk to detain Bustamente here half an hour ago, and now that I was praying he would leave me alone, he stuck to me like a burr. He radiated the relaxed bonhomie of a man whose morning's work is done. He dug his hands deep into his pockets as he talked.

Then I noticed something that made my blood run cold. Out of a corner of my brief-case, where the lid sagged away slightly round the broken hinge, a thin stream of cocaine was leaking out. A little conical pile had formed on the ground already. I moved to cover it with my foot. The powder continued to pour, implacably, like flour from a punctured sack. Anyone watching us could have seen it: Bustamente or Lino might see it any minute. La Loca gave a sudden warning hiss.

Sweet Jesus, I thought, if the wind starts throwing it around they can't fail to spot it. These were senior officials at one of the world's major smuggling centres. I did not think they would have much difficulty identifying the substance once it started blowing in their faces.

Still talking, on automatic pilot, I shifted the brief-case under my arm, and with a swift, uncomfortable manoeuvre, cupped my hand under the leaking corner. I felt the cocaine pour into my palm. My hosts droned on, I hopped from foot to foot in agony, and every now and then, camouflaged by whatever twitch, cough or conversational banality I could muster, I moved my hand behind my back to loose another small cargo of cocaine into the air.

The philosophers say that life begins beyond despair. I was about to break down completely, sob out my confession, the whole sorry story from the Fruit Palace till now, when someone called to Bustamente from inside the loading area of the ship. One of the banana crates had been damaged. The man wore blue overalls with "Texaco" on the breast pocket, and thick padded gloves. He wanted Bustamente to look at the crate: official procedure for damaged goods, and so on. Busta-mente walked up the gangplank, into the ship's belly. Lino followed. There was nothing more natural than for me to follow also, firmly cradling the case under my arm. Inside, the ship hummed dully. There was much shouting and bang-ing. Fork-lift trucks nipped in and out. They drive them like they drive their buses, I thought. Bustamente examined the crate. A smell of mashed banana brought a strange, mis-placed memory of childhood teas.

11.38, two minutes to go. Only a few yards separated me from the Swede, from my burning desire to get rid of the illicit chemical. I had a brainwave. I broke in urgently on their conversation. "Excuse me, *señor*. Is there a bathroom I could use?"

"Of course," said Bustamente. He started directing me back out of the ship, round the back of the coffee warehouse.

"No, no," I cried. He stopped, looking puzzled. I made a

grimace of apology, fidgeted unhappily, and said, "It is very urgent. *Malo del estómago.*"

The man in the overalls laughed. He called out to one of the loaders.

"Show the gentleman up to the *baño*, quickly," he said. I heard them tittering sympathetically behind me, as I trotted up the stairs behind my escort. We followed the route Ariel had explained. The swing-doors closed behind us, softening the noise of the loading bay to a hush. I thanked the man, and lurched into the john at 11.40 precisely.

The Swedish john was spotless, but someone had been sick into one of the basins. There were fire-buckets on the wall, and rails to steady oneself by above the urinals. I thought the place was empty at first. I thought I'd missed the rendezvous. Then I saw that one of the cubicles, the furthest from the door, was occupied. I sidled up to the wash-basin opposite it. I wanted to knock on the door, or call out for the Swede, but if it wasn't him I'd look pretty silly. I ran some water, made noises with the liquid soap-dispenser. As I splashed my hands, I gradually crouched down further and further, till I could see the feet of the man in the lavatory. They were certainly big enough to be the Swede's: heavy-duty black boots. Why hadn't I been really cool and noticed what boots the Swede had been wearing at the Mamatoca? Now I saw the boots shifting. I straightened up sharply, and just as I did so, the broad blond brow of the Swede peeped cautiously over the door of the cubicle. Our eyes met.

"It's you," he growled. He straightened to his full height. His beard jutted over the top of the door. He looked like he was in one of those fairground booths where you extrude your head through a comic backcloth. "You're late," he added.

"For Christ's sake hurry up," I hissed. "I've got people waiting downstairs."

"What focking people?"

"What people? Never mind what people. Let's do it, for God's sake."

"Pass the case in. Keep washing your hands."

I handed it over the door. "Be very careful," I said. "The *perica* is coming out. The polythene got torn."

"So." There was silence for a moment. "It don't open," said the face over the door.

"Shit! I forgot—the combination. Six-six-six."

There was another agonizing silence from inside the cubicle, as the Swede's ursine paws fumbled with the wheels of the combination locks. He seemed to take ages. Someone was drilling metal deep in the bowels of the ship. It jarred my head. The Swede bent in concentration and emitted a low, grumpy rumble of Swedish, which seemed to be full of "fee" and "farn" and other phrases you probably wouldn't find in *Swedish for Beginners*.

I heard one catch spring, then the other, and even as I was saying again, "Be careful," I heard him curse and I saw the fine white powder floating down in spots on his black boots.

"I can't take this focking gear, man," he said in an angry half-whisper. "This right up the focking spout. I can't pay you for this. I don't know how much is here."

He was shutting the case up again. "Oh God!" I cried. "Look—give me less money. Give me half. Surely you can give me half."

"No focking deal. I am not permitted to open the envelope. It's all or nothing. This is a very tight business, man. I got the money for 5 kilos. This is damaged cargo. You must take it back."

"Back? Back where?" He pushed the case over the door. I tried to shove it back at him. He raised a huge fist, swore evilly at me. I staggered back, clutching the case. Cocaine was smeared all over the shiny black plastic. I had to get back down below. Bustamente would be wondering where I was. I thought of just jettisoning the case there and then, but of course I couldn't. It had all my papers in it, for a start. And I couldn't leave the cocaine either. What was my friend Ariel going to say if I turned up without the drugs *or* the money? Checking the oil wouldn't be in it. He would roast me alive.

Frantically I started rubbing and sweeping at the cocaine dust on the case. Without thinking, I did what everyone does when they have cocaine dust on their fingers. I kept putting my hands to my nose and snuffling up the dust like snuff. I did this half a dozen times. The case was clean, but as I lurched back out into the corridor, I realized I had made yet another false move. This was pure Snow White, remember. Not a trace of cut, not a footstep in the snow. As I pushed back through the swing-doors, I was 10 foot tall with a face made of ice. Coming down the steps I couldn't even feel my feet. I was dancing on air, and I still had a brief-case crammed full of the stuff.

"Better?" asked Bustamente with a broad grin. I nodded and leered. The fork-lift trucks had taken on the aspect of dodgem cars. The noise was appalling. The three men were still talking, just as before. They didn't seem to have noticed anything amiss. They laughed knowing masculine laughs about the gastric perils of Santa Marta. My ploy certainly had the virtue of realism. Few gringos escape the local strain of Montezuma's Revenge. At the end of the long dry season the water supply is at its deadliest. You can almost smell the rats up the taps.

The conversation continued. Perpendicular forces seemed to be straining forth from my skull. Yet, incredibly, I could hear the talk being punctuated by a familiar, stilted gringo accent, which was saying "Sí" and "No" and even "Claro, hombre" at all the right moments.

I failed to understand the noise at first. Was someone screaming in my ear? No, it was the lunch-time siren cranking up for its wail. There was a general bustle out of the boat. Trucks were parked, gloves were peeled off. Bustamente's hand was on my shoulder, gently steering me down on to the wharf, talking all the while with Lino. I let myself be led. I didn't know, I didn't care, where we were going. One survival instinct throbbed away inside the mêlée. Stick with El Jefe Director—don't let him out of your sight. We joined the stream of loaders and *wincheros*, sailors and secretaries, making their way out through the check-point. This is it, go with the crowd. Everyone was showing passes as they left. Thankfully I still had my pass ready, fastened under the clipboard. In a moment of inspiration I asked Bustamente his thoughts about Sunday's football match, the local derby between Santa Marta and Barranquilla. He was wonderfully opinionated on the subject, and we were chattering away as I passed through the check-point.

I stepped out the other side like a drowning man touching *terra firma*. It was then that I felt the hand on my shoulder.

I wheeled round, took in the soldierly uniform, the rifle strapped on the shoulder. The phantom of liberty dispersed in the hot sea winds. The guard was holding out his hand. Of course, he wanted the case. I was just about to hand it over. Everything had become strangely limpid—perhaps I was about to get an instant replay of my life and times, like you do when you drown. But all the guard said was, "Your pass, *señor*. You must hand in your pass. It is only a *permiso provisional.*"

"Of course, of course." My hands shook as I took the pass out from under the clip. The guard said, "Excuse me," with a little bow, more to Bustamente than me. I saw his eyes flicker down over the brief-case, but he didn't ask to look into it. No one would be crazy enough to smuggle cocaine *into* Colombia.

Waldino was waiting at the corner, with a clear view of the check-point. He skulked there while I said goodbye to Bustamente and Lino, then he motioned me over and bustled around me with questions. "You got the money, Charlie? Who were those people you were talking to? What happened, Charlie?"

I couldn't say anything. Strange pharmaceutical juices clogged my throat. I opened and shut my mouth like a goldfish.

He peered into my crazed eyes. "What's happening, *hermano*?" He was beginning to sound worried. I started walking towards the beach drag. He pulled at my arm. "Hey, no, Charlie. We must go to the Mamatoca. Ariel is waiting."

I shook my head. "Corona," I croaked. I walked on. Waldino skipped around me, so confused by my behaviour that he didn't try to persuade me. We turned into 10th Street. Waldino kept looking around nervously. "I don't think Ariel will like this," he whinged. "I said I would bring you to the Mamatoca."

A voice from a doorway hailed us. "*Señor! Qué tal, pues?*" Waldino hadn't answered. It must have been me he was addressing. I focused on a vaguely familiar face. It was the owner of the Restaurante El Progreso, the Fruit Palace as was. We were standing outside the familiar cedarwood door. "Did you find your friend Julio?" the man asked.

I was coming round now. Things were beginning to resume their rightful position. The egg-man was ringing his bell a block away, a crowd of schoolgirls in blue and white uniforms were laughing on the corner. "I need a drink," I said. The man stepped out of the doorway to let us enter.

The quiet, midday calm of the Fruit Palace soothed me, and two straight rums put back a little of what the morning had taken out. There were just two other people in the café. The *señora*, wearing the same turquoise dress as before, served them with huge platters of steak and kidney-beans. By the third rum I felt ready to tell my story. But now it was Waldino's turn to demur. He put his finger to his lips, and jerked his head at the diners. "*Wincheros,*" he mouthed. "Don't say anything."

He called for music, and under the cover of Juancho Rois singing "La Gordita" I told him the whole sorry story about the lost coke and the failed deal. At each revelation he sank into deeper gloom. When I had finished he slumped back in the chair and spat out the word "*Coño!*"

"Christ, Waldino, I don't see what I could—"

"Hey, *hermano*. I don't mean you. I mean that *hijo de puta* Swede."

We left the Progreso, ditched the brief-case back at the Corona, and went off to find Ariel at the Mamatoca. His reaction was much the same as Waldino's. I had done my best. These things happen in the uncertain world of contraband. It was the Swede's fault: he should have been prepared to haggle a bit. The main point was that I'd saved the whole thing from disaster by bringing the *perica* out more or less intact. OK, they'd lost a few grams, perhaps even a kilo, but this was Snow White—dynamite *perica*. They could buff it up a bit with talc or borax, make up the weight, and get the same good price elsewhere. They came back with me to the hotel and took the stuff away.

I lay on my bed for a while, watching the ceiling fan. Then I packed my bags, paid off my bill and walked off through the siesta-heavy streets to the bus station.

25

INDIAN COUNTRY

I had one more trip to make on this half-cocked odyssey. I thought of it as a way of forgetting, of washing all the drugs and lies away. It was a trip I'd wanted to make when I was first in Colombia, and never had, and I was determined to do it this time before my money ran out and my batteries went dead. I was going up into the mountain Indian territories of the Sierra Nevada.

The Sierra Nevada de Santa Marta is the highest coastal range of mountains in the world. It is not actually part of the Andes, being separated from the northernmost spur of the Andean Cordilleras by the valley of the Rio Cesar. In shape it is roughly triangular, with each side about 100 miles long. The base of the triangle is to the north, running parallel with the Caribbean coastline between Santa Marta and Riohacha. This northern face is the sheerest, coming right down to the sea in those steep, densely forested foothills I had seen behind Sea Breeze Farm. On a clear day you can see the snow peaks while paddling in the Caribbean. At the shortest point the mountains rise from sea-level to over 19,000 feet in 28 miles, a gradient only surpassed by the Himalayas. It is very hard to get into the Sierra from the north, however. The trails are arduous and easy to lose, and once you get lost in the *macizo* you are very likely to wander into someone's marijuana plantation, where they tend to shoot first and ask questions later. It is supposedly possible to hire a Kogui guide in one of the coastal villages, but I had been warned against this. Most self-respecting Koguis have as little to do with the white man as possible, and those that do hang around the *mestizo* villages are reputed to be drunkards and thieves.

The best way to get up into the Sierra, I was told, was from the south-east, where the slopes rise more gently. The Indians of this corner of the Sierra are the Arhuaco. These are the most numerous of the mountain tribes—about 15,000 of them live in small, nucleated settlements in the high valleys of the south and east. The Arhuaco are marginally more acclimatized to the white man than the fiercely isolationist Kogui who live on the northern slopes.

Both tribes are the remnants of the Tairona culture which flourished for perhaps 1,000 years on the Caribbean coastlands before the Spaniards arrived in the early sixteenth century. The Tairona were primarily farmers. They cultivated maize, beans, yucca and other staples on irrigated fields and terraces that one of the Spanish *cronistas* compared to those of Lombardy and Etruria. They fished the Caribbean for tuna, snapper and *ojo gordo*. They wore cotton, kept bees, drank *chicha* and chewed coca leaves. Their ceramics and stone-work were decorated with elaborate figures—warriors in feathered headdresses, monstrous fanged humanoids, jaguars, snakes, bats, foxes, birds, turtles and crocodiles. The jaguar was of particular significance to the Tairona. Jaguar skulls hung in the doorways of their ceremonial houses, and the Kogui still dedicate their ceremonial houses to a jaguar-god, Cashinducua.

Of greatest interest to the colonizing Spaniards, the Tairona were master gold-workers. Some early sources say that the name Tairona actually meant "smithy." Their technology was sophisticated, including the lost-wax method. A vigorous vein of phallic and sexual representation enabled the Spaniards to plunder in the name of godliness and cleanliness. The Chronicler Gonzales Fernández de Oviedo saw a Tairona gold piece weighing 20 pesos, which depicted "one man mounted upon another in that diabolical act of Sodom." The worthy Fernández was pleased to relate that he had smashed this "jewel of the devil" to smithereens at the smelting-house in Darién.

The Spaniards bartered—axes, tools, knives, combs, beads, shirts, coloured hats, wine and gunpowder, in return for gold. But the Tairona were fierce, proud and cunning, and through the sixteenth century the coastal foothills of the Sierra were the scene of bitter skirmish warfare. In 1599 the governor of Santa Marta, Juan Guiral Velon, led a final campaign of attrition. The chiefs were hanged and burned, and the great Tairona townships—Taironaca, Posigueca, Betoma—were put to the torch. The last remnants of the tribe—those not killed, or rounded up for baptism and slave-labour in the Spanish *encomiendas*—retreated to the higher slopes of the Sierra, to valleys too distant and inaccessible for the Spaniards to follow. It was a hollow victory for the gold-hungry *colonos*. The jungle reclaimed the abandoned terraces and temples, and covered the intricate pathways that connected the villages, and guarded the Tairona gold even more jealously than the Indians themselves had.

Since then other settlers have lapped around the lower edges of the Sierra: banana-growers and coffee-planters during the boom years at the beginning of the century, political refugees from La Violencia in the 1950s, and most recently the marijuana planters. Hard-bitten treasure-hunters—the *guaqueros*—still comb the rugged mountain jungles in search of lost temples and burial sites. But none of the *mestizo* settlements have penetrated any higher than 5,000 feet. The heart of the Sierra remains Indian country, and the descendants of the Tairona—Arhuacos, Koguis and a small tribe called the Arsarios—continue their old ways undisturbed. To the average *mestizo*, the Indians represent poverty and underdevelopment and not much else. They are *gente baja*, low people. The Indians respond to this with their ancient, disconcerting, stone-like gaze, and their inner conviction that apart from the minor inconvenience of colonization, the continent still entirely belongs to them. Anyone who has ventured much into South America will know the feeling that there is another pulse, another country, just beneath and behind the surface. You're walking on solid earth, you're confident of what your wisdom is worth, and then suddenly you're falling into the cunningly concealed pit of the past.

The way into the Arhuaco domain is from Valledupar, a cowboy town in the Cesar valley, five hours by bus from Santa Marta. At the bus station off 22nd Street I put coins into the blind man's cup. He grinned like a monkey and turned his moon-glasses up at me. *"Que vaya usted con Dios."* I took a last look at the lazy, rakish streets of Santa Marta. Goodbye to the fruit palaces, the smugglers' lore, the gold-toothed piratical smiles.

The bus rolled out past San Pedro Alejandrino, where Bolívar died a broken man, along the shores of the Ciénaga Grande, and south along the valley road through banana groves and wide, untidy cotton-fields. The towns all down the road are built around the big rivers that flow down the western slopes of the Sierra. One of these is Aracataca, birthplace of "Gabo"—Gabriel García Márquez, Colombia's Nobel Prize-winning novelist and cultural folk hero. Aracataca is the Macondo of Márquez's stories, the little village where South America's rickety dreams and exotic despairs are played over and over in miniature. There wasn't much there. Just another dusty grid of pastel streets, another steel bridge, another grey river with women slapping their washing in the shallows. The bus stopped on the outskirts for a few minutes. I saw a café called April Mornings. There were the sun-baked almond trees that Márquez writes of. I heard the train whistle blow. Every day the train comes through on its journey between Santa Marta and Bogotá. It comes at no particular time: *llega cuando llega.* There are no timetables in Colombia, only rumours. The sound of it seemed to plunge the village still deeper into its sleepy, melancholy isolation. Aracataca is only an hour or two from Santa Marta. It is close to the foothills of the Sierra, close to lagoons of the Ciénaga, close to the fertile plains of the Magdalena. Yet the feel of it is somewhere far, far from everything. The streets petered out into banana groves and scruffy *potreros* where mules dozed. The bus rolled southward, depositing another layer of dust on the roadside scrub.

Valledupar was full of jeeps, and cowboys with big straw hats and shiny wrist-watches. The Hotel Comercio—"*ambiente distinguido y familiar*"—was two rows of small blue rooms looking on to a thin strip of courtyard. The ceiling fan worked, the bed was comfortable, and there was running water at the end of the yard. The room was windowless, only a ventilator in fleur-de-lys shapes cut in the stone wall, so one left the door open for light and air. Men in vests, back from the day's work, took it in turns at the tap. The atmosphere was easy and friendly. The place was more or less par for the course for $2 a night, and I liked it a lot better than some I have stayed in for 200.

Twilight settled over the bars and flophouses round the bus station. Most of the street traders had gone now, but the tarts were out in force, black and white, fat and thin, *chulitas* and *monitas*, raddled old pikes and fresh young pickerels. They lounged outside the murky little *residencias*, where the room-numbers were painted on a blackboard to facilitate quick turnover. The tariffs showed so much for the night, so much for a *ratito*, a little while. The dwarfish wooden rooms were hardly big enough to hold a bed. Accordion music poured out on to the streets. Valledupar claims itself as the home of the *vallenato*—the Colombian accordion dance-song, stomps or ballads according to taste—though this is hotly disputed by Guajiros. The accordions seem to be a legacy of German immigrants, grafted on to the Afro-rhythms of *costeño* music. The legendary maestro of the *vallenato* was known as Francisco El Hombre, Frankey the Man. The devil challenged this Paganini of the squeeze-box to a duel and lost.

In the morning I set off to obtain my permits. One has to get permission from the local office of the DAS—Departamento Administrativo de Seguridad—before travelling up into the Sierra. It is a "controlled" area, and anyone found there without authorization is liable to be suspected of marijuana or guerrilla connections. In an old side-street off the main plaza, peeping out among piles of identity cards and forms, a neat small man wrote down my particulars in a neat small hand. Next I toiled out to the Casa Indígena, the government office which administers Indian affairs, on the edge of town. Without a letter of introduction from them, I was assured, I would be refused entry into Arhuaco territory. A letter was typed up, even outdoing Malcolm's in its baroque lardings and formalities. It was addressed to the Arhuaco chief in person, Don Luis Napoleón Torres.

I was at last prepared, administratively if not spiritually, to journey up into the Sierra. From Valledupar there were trucks or jeeps up to Pueblo Bello, the last *mestizo* village, 3,600 feet up, and from there a road of sorts led on up to the chief village of the Arhuacos. This is known on the maps as San Sebastián de Rábago, but to the Arhuacos themselves, it is Nebusimague.

Transport to Pueblo Bello left from a small truck-park behind the market. I found a jeep that was going. It would leave when it was full. While I waited I bought some iguana eggs from a simian little man. They were strung from his fruit stall like necklaces. Individually they look like nuts, or like little bones, off-white and oblong, ballooning slightly at either end. The shell is rubbery, hard to tear. Cut with a sharp knife in the indented middle, it reveals at either end two small, rich, yellow yolks. These will give you strength, *señor*, he assured me, and from the sinewy movement of his forearm and the leering of his lips, I gathered they would also do wonders for my sexual prowess. I also bought bread, a *paso de bananos*—a hefty wad of pressed banana wrapped in dried palm leaves—some mangoes and crisp, red, gingery-tasting *peritas*.

When we finally left the market there were ten passengers squeezed into the Nissan Patrol jeep, and when we turned off the main road on to the dirt track that led to Pueblo Bello, a mulatto in a straw hat waved us down and amid general grumbling he too was packed in. The driver charged 200 pesos for the ride to Pueblo Bello. He reckoned on 2,000 pesos going up, 1,500 coming down: two of the four-hour round trips a day would net him about $100 less petrol and maintenance. The road was pitted and cratered. We edged through fords. There were occasional glimpses of blue mountains beyond. The talk was of Venezuela, the land of oil and money, and of the rise and fall of the bolivar. Valledupar was five hours from the Venezuelan border, close enough to support a range of black market currency and import businesses. The number plates on the jeep were Venezuelan.

The driver's ears stuck out beneath his baseball cap. He asked me why I was going to Pueblo Bello. "There's nothing there," he told me. I said I was going on to San Sebastián.

"What for?" he asked.

I trotted out the traveller's formula. *"Para conocer la región."* To get to know the area.

"I know it," he said, addressing his friend in the back, the one in the string vest reading *Selecciones de Reader's Digest,* "and it's horrible. *Muy feo."*

The *mestizo* has little contact and less sympathy with the Indians. Amid his contempt is a vein of puzzled fear of people so wilfully underdeveloped, so indifferent to the civilized things in life. The feeling is mutual. To the Arhuaco the white man is *bunaci,* the bringer of disease and ill-fortune to the native Indians.

Pueblo Bello, the furthest reach of *mestizo* colonization on this flank of the Sierra Nevada, was not well-named. I stood in the dust by the roadside, surveying the thin line of habitation down the village's one and only street. It was lunchtime. The doors were shut, the street empty. A bitch peed in the dust and two attendant dogs licked it up. The jeep's passengers seemed to have merged instantly into the surroundings. I found a *tienda* and had a couple of beers. The owner was slumped in a seat, radiating a profound boredom. He made me sleepy just to look at him. Machetes hung from a beam, in leather sheaths with long tassles. A boy served me. He asked me about England. How much would his *moto*—a Yamaha 175, parked outside the store—have cost in England?

The driver had smugly told me I had certainly missed the

daily jeep up to San Sebastián, but I stuck to my belief that if one stumbles on optimistically enough something generally turns up. I asked the boy if he thought there might be any trucks going up there. He didn't like to say "No," so he said, "Yes, tomorrow morning." I asked him if he knew anyone who hired out mules or horses. He didn't. He praised the village hotel, El Hogar de Mamá. I bought a can of sardines and a half of aguardiente, and set off down the street. I had no intention of staying at Mamá's Place, or anywhere else in this glum little one-horse town. This was not what I came to the Sierra for. If no one would take me to San Sebastián I would walk there. It was about 15 miles, I reckoned. I asked the way at the village police station. Two young soldiers were sitting on the verandah, their heavy black boots on the railing. They couldn't believe I was going to walk there. "Eight hours at least," they told me. If I didn't pick up a truck, I would have to camp on the way and then pick up the jeep the next morning.

I shook off the last scruffy parcels and plots of Pueblo Bello. No one had a mule for hire. I lunched on bread and iguana eggs by the side of a river, and set off. The road snaked off into the distance, a sand-coloured scrawl slowly winding upwards through tough, rocky terrain. The mountains were hard and pale, with a patchy down of esparto grass, but the watercourses that ran down the folds of the hill were braided with tropical greenery.

I soon passed beneath a large sign, strung between two concrete posts. "RESERVA TERRITORIAL INDIGENA," it announced. From here on out it was Indian country, where even the Colombians are foreigners.

An hour later I was squatting exhausted on a clump of cootch-grass. The sun was still high overhead. I was drenched in sweat, my mouth caked with dust. The valley below me showed I had come some way, but it was a hard uphill slog. Everywhere I looked the ground was hard and dry, and the only places where there was any shelter were the steep, boulder-strewn streams. It was not a hospitable sight.

Then down on the trail below, I saw a woman riding a mule uphill towards me. When the figure came into view round the final bend, I saw that it was not a woman at all, but a handsome young Indian with long black hair. He wore the traditional Arhuaco dress—a white woollen *manta*, or blanket, turned back at the shoulders so it fell in one fold, front and back, like a tunic, held at the waist by a belt of *fique* fibre. He wore trousers of the same coarse wool, and leather sandals. On his head, instead of the traditional *tutosome*—a woollen hat like an elongated fez—he wore a black cowboy hat.

He stopped to talk. "You are going to Nebusimague?" he asked. I said I was. He looked up at the sun and said it was too far to walk before dark.

"I'm going to sleep in the *monte*," I said. He looked at me disbelievingly. I asked if there was water up ahead—I didn't want to get caught in a dry stretch when it got dark. He said there were some rivers, though it was very dry for a while. He said he was thirsty himself, and I fetched my water bottle. As he drank I saw him wince with displeasure—it was river water, and I had added some sterilizing tablets. The taste was obviously very strong to him, though he was too polite to say anything. He spoke in a pleasant, lilting voice. His Spanish was fluent, but had a formality, a carefulness in placing the words, that showed it was not his first language. I had not yet heard the strange, sussurating tones of Iki, the Arhuaco language.

After a bit he asked, in his polite, precise way, *"Quiere usted montar?"*

"But the mule can't take both of us," I said, making a show of reluctance, though there was nothing I would have liked better.

He laughed. "No. You ride," he said, and climbed off the mule.

This is the genius of Colombia. One moment you're sitting in the dust, red-faced and gasping. The next you're up on a high-pommelled saddle, feeling the powerful grace of the mule beneath you, as he pulls steadily up the steep, rutted track.

The young Arhuaco's name was Victor—they all use Castilian names—and he was eighteen years old. He had been down in Pueblo Bello, selling maize and buying provisions. He had got 1,000 pesos for a mule-load of corn. He jogged alongside the mule, not at all out of breath despite the steepness. I thought it must be chewing coca that gave him such sprightliness. I asked him. He said, "No, I am not married."

I assumed he had misunderstood my question, so I asked again. He explained that it was forbidden for an Arhuaco to use coca until he was married. "Only men may take coca," he said. "Not boys, not women, not girls. Only men."

We climbed and climbed. The mule's name was Rosario. Sweat-suds flecked his brown neck. Victor answered my remarks with a jolly "*Sí, no?*"—"It is, isn't it?" For long stretches we travelled in silence, with only the measured fall of Rosario's hooves, the creaking of the saddle and a low undertone of grunts and whistles from Victor to keep the mule going. He pulled switches from the scrub-trees by the track to twitch at Rosario's backside. There was no sight of Pueblo Bello when I looked back. The mountains seemed to close like a door behind us. We breasted the Alguacil Plateau, at nearly 9,500 feet the highest point on the journey to Nebusimague. A kind of swallow with an immensely long tail flitted past us. I asked Victor what it was called. He deliberated carefully. "*Turi,*" he said. I later learned this was simply the Iki word for "bird." We came down from the plateau through a shady gorge of high trees and stopped to rest in a clearing. A few round, grass-thatched huts were scattered in the valley below. I reached into my bag for bread and *paso de bananos*. I handed them to Victor, meaning for him to tear a bit off each. He gave a radiant "Thank you!", stuffed the loaf into his *mochila* bag and ate his way through the entire *paso*. I hadn't the gall to stop him, after his kindness to me. He presumably thought it was some kind of payment. "Delicious," he said, tossing away the empty bark wrapping.

We took a precipitous short-cut which sliced off a wide elbow of the road. Rosario slithered on the stones. Twice my *campesino* hat came off, to Victor's amusement. The sky flushed pink. The evening star—*Virakoku* in Iki—appeared. Victor produced a torch from his bag. We stopped to drink at a small pool, Victor slapping the water up to his mouth with swift, flat-palmed movements, the mule shifting and snuffling, seeming to breathe the water up through his velvety nose.

We must have gone on about two more hours in the dark, taking it in turns on the mule, stumbling on the rocks. My feet hurt. I felt like giving up, but Victor kept saying we were *al llegar*, almost there. Then I heard the sound of dogs on the breeze, and I found we were walking beside a stretch of dry-stone wall, and there were plots of maize and cane by the roadside, and now Victor quietly said, "We're here." I wouldn't have known it. I knew it wasn't going to be like arriving in an ordinary Colombian village at night—a lit square, a few bars, hurricane lamps—but I hadn't been ready for this utter stillness. In the darkness I could just make out the stone wall which encircled the village. Low thatched roofs huddled within it, humped like sleeping animals in a pen.

"We must go round to the other gate," said Victor. "You are a stranger," he added.

A knot of young Arhuaco men were hanging around the main gate—the eastern end of the village. Victor spoke with them in Iki, and then one of them said to me, "Please enter." The gate was barred shut. It had a little thatch roof like a churchyard lych-gate. The way in was by a smooth, notched log leaning against the wall. I followed Victor up this gangplank, over the wall and into Nebusimague.

26

NEBUSIMAGUE

Once inside the village I could see firelight in some doorways, and knots of people standing around. Everyone seemed to be whispering, rustling. There were no hard sounds. No metal, no traffic, no music. I saw the moon, big and low over a black flank of mountain. The smell of wood-smoke filled the air.

We were somewhere in the centre of the village. Victor and some friends were horsing around like big children. He was more or less ignoring me now. Someone had gone off to get Chief Napoleón, so I could present him with my letter of introduction from the Casa Indígena in Valledupar. In the meantime, I gathered, I was something of a stateless person. I wished there was a bar to merge into, time to take stock behind a couple of beers. I slumped exhausted, feeling about as local as a fish in a tree. The strange lunar village twittered and rustled around me.

After a bit I was beckoned over to meet a small, weasel-faced man. A thick quid of coca distended his cheek. He shone his torch in my face. He was polite but brusque. He was not Chief Napoleón, I learned, but one of the village administrators. He demanded my letter and read it aloud by torchlight. Don Napoleón was not available at present, he said. I must present myself to him tomorrow morning. He gave me to understand that upright, honest people didn't come skulking into the village after dark like this.

I was, I realized, a bit of a nuisance. I had not expected to find a hotel in Nebusimague, but had imagined there would be some kind of village hostel for *viajeros*. There was none. Where was I going to sleep? I said vaguely, *"En el monte,"* gesturing out to the countryside beyond. There was a twitter of mirth as this was relayed to the crowd by the weasel-faced man. I wanted to explain that I had a sleeping-bag in my pack, but I couldn't remember the Spanish word for it. I feebly rendered it as *una bolsa para dormir*. The weasel's eyes narrowed still further. Not content with slipping into town like a thief in the night, I was now proposing to sleep the night in a sack. "Show me this *bolsa*," he said. I duly hauled out my scarlet sleeping-bag. Torches were turned on it. It was thumbed, scrutinized and discussed like a hank of wool at the market. "It has feathers in it," I explained. The word *plumas* flitted to and fro among the crowd.

Things seemed to relax a little. We all trooped off into one of the houses. A group sat and squatted around a glowing wood *candela*—the central fire which always burns in the house. The room was thick with smoke. There was a brief conference. I was to be allotted a small empty house about ten minutes' walk back down the valley. The weasel shook my hand and told me to present myself at the *casa de convención* tomorrow morning. I was escorted down to the house by four young Arhuacos.

The grass outside the house was already wet with dew. I ate a moonlit supper of iguana eggs, *ersatz* sardines and aguardiente, and fell into a dreamless sleep.

The following day I met Chief Napoleón. There was nothing much to mark him out as the *cacique*, only that his clothes were bright white, rather than the muted cream wool worn by everyone else. He was rather a disappointment: small, fussy and saturnine. He did not look at me while the weasel explained about me. For the time being I was no more than an administrative problem, an item on the parish agenda for the morning.

We filed off into the *casa de convención*, a long rectangular building in the centre of the village. It was dark inside. There were benches along the wall and rails of knotty wood. Chief Napoleón's desk stood in the corner, before the only window. He put on a pair of horn-rimmed glasses. They gave him a comic schoolmaster look, with the fez-like *tutosome* instead of a mortar-board. An absurd pun on "Arhuaco" and "Whacko" flitted through my confused mind. The weasel gave him the letter from the Casa Indígena. He read through it, breathily mumbling the words to himself, squinting through his specs, holding the paper up to the light of the window. In that bright little rectangle there were children's faces, and a brilliant blue sky and buff-coloured adobe walls. The meeting-house was quite full now. The men greeted one another, each doling out a little helping of coca leaves into the other's *mochila* bag. All the men carried their coca kit: a *mochila* full of the crisp, dried leaves, and an hour-glass gourd, called a *poporo*, which contains the powdered lime necessary to activate the stimulant principles of the coca leaf. The Arhuacos get their lime from burnt and powdered sea-shells. Elsewhere in South America other sources—quick-lime, or the ash of qinoa or carob—are used.

Having read my letter, Chief Napoleón made what sounded like a well-rehearsed speech on the evils of visitors and tourists. "We see a lot of requests like this," he said, jabbing a stubby finger at the letter. "Tourists come to look at us. Doctors and students make reports on us. People photograph us." He spoke the word "photograph" as if it were some social disease. "We see no benefit," he continued. "We, *el pueblo indígena*, receive nothing. They come, they take, they go."

I stood there with my hands behind my back, like a scolded schoolboy, saying, "I understand, *señor*, I understand," radiating useless waves of liberal sentiment. Then the chief started on about visitors violating the mountains and the lakes of the Sierra, the places sacred to the Arhuaco. I protested that I had no intention of violating anything. I was just beginning to get irritable. I had had no breakfast, my head was dizzy with hunger and the rare mountain air, and I had had enough of this hectoring. The weasel, sitting on the chair opposite the desk, cut in. "We are a peaceful people, *señor*. In your country there is much violence." He made a gun with his fingers and shot at me. "Many pistols, many problems!" There was a murmur of laughter from the silent gathering, placidly masticating their plugs of coca. There were a few women in white cotton dresses tied with black woollen belts, but most of the audience were men. I told the weasel he had got it wrong. In Inglaterra everything was *muy tranquilo*, not at all like the Estados Unidos. This distinction is a fine one at the best of times—people are not always sure where England is, and as the Yankee gringos all speak *inglés*, someone describing himself as *inglés* must surely be a Yankee gringo. Here the distinction was meaningless anyway. Violence, haste and rapacity are indissolubly associated with any white man, the *"bunaci"* as they call us.

Now Chief Napoleón was holding forth again. I heard the word "tariff," and felt that at last we might be getting to the nub. Indeed we were. "Contribution to the community . . . exploitation . . . inconvenience . . . *bunaci* . . . we charge 500 pesos *por cabeza.*"

Under the watchful eye of the assembly, I paid over a 500-peso bill to Napoleón. He briskly sorted it away in an old ledger, where I saw one or two other bills. The mood now perceptibly softened. Napoleón conferred gruffly with the weasel, and then he announced in a loud, orotund voice that I was to be granted the freedom of Nebusimague for eight days. After certain formalities I would be free to walk around, and . . . He couldn't apparently think of anything else I might want to do, so he just added "and so on," and spat a gob of green coca-cud onto the dirt floor.

The weasel was dispatched to relay the chief's ruling to the Inspector of Indigenous Police, a *mestizo* called Torres whom I had briefly met that morning. Chief Napoleón waved me brusquely into the chair. He shuffled papers on his desk. His ease with paper and pen was a manifestation of his power in this mainly illiterate community. He seemed to be expecting me to interview him. Now that I was legitimized he was quite friendly. He had been *cacique* of the Arhuacos for seven years, I learned. The position is not hereditary: the chief is elected by the tribal council of *cabildos*. Nebusimague is the tribal capital and administrative centre, with a permanent population of about 200. The majority of the Arhuacos, some 15,000 in all, live scattered through the territories in small villages in the high valleys on the southern and eastern flanks of the Sierra. Arhuaco territory is divided into eighteen regions, each of them supporting about eighty families. Frequent tribal conventions and ceremonial gatherings were held at Nebusimague. I had, in fact, just missed one. "And do many people come?" I asked. He gave a comic "Ooooh!" *à la* Frankie Howerd, and spat once more on the floor, a precise little gob as after cleaning one's teeth. "Many, many people. They come from Atikimakeka, from Kurakata, from Nemecina, from Circuyunka . . ." The list was cut short by the return of the weasel. He bore in a sheet of headed paper, with the legend "Confederación Indígena Tayrona" styled in red and black.

The tribal red tape was not yet exhausted. I sat for ages while Inspector Torres, a sullen *mestizo* with a thick black moustache and bad catarrh, typed up my letter of authorization. More formalities, more subjunctives: that I might sojourn in this place and travel onwards through the Sierra, trusting that the indigenous authorities would collaborate with me to ensure my journey through this region might be tranquil and secure. I bore the fruit of his literary labours back to the *casa de convención*, where it was duly signed by Chief Napoleón, by Comisario Manuel Chaparra, and by Cabildo Otoniel Mejia, each signature being rubber-stamped by the busy weasel.

"Now you are free," said the weasel. "But you must be sure to obey our laws," he added, "or we will put you in a hut with no food or water." My stomach gurgled nervously. "Are you strong?" he asked, and gripped my arm to feel the muscle, and again there was a discreet mumble of laughter round the dark room.

As I left, I turned to say "*Hasta luego*" to Chief Napoleón and the weasel, and back came a ringing chorus of "*Hasta luego*" from everyone in the building. It came quite unexpectedly, out of the gloom, like the sudden chime of a big deep bell. It wiped away all the hassles of the morning. I stepped into the clean mountain air, with the sun bouncing off the stone walls, and I reflected that it had taken a while to obtain my passport into Arhuaco lands, because it was a kind of passport into another time.

From the back of my house, which looked south across a marshy stretch to wooded slopes, I could see a cluster of huts. The smoke seeped out of the thatched roofs, so they seemed to be steaming in the morning sun. In one of these live Valentín, an Arhuaco of about thirty years old, short, flat-faced, with long black glossy hair. He was a sunny character and liked to talk, unlike most of these passive, introspective people. His face would split into a wide grin, showing discoloured teeth. As is common with the Arhuaco, Valentín and his family had three homes, each with its own little plot of a hectare or two. One was higher up, near the *páramo* north of Nebusimague. There he cultivated cold-climate crops: potato, manioc, beans. At the lower *finca* he had cane, bananas, maize and coca.

From Valentín I learned a little about the use of coca among the Arhuaco. They do not actually call it "coca," which is a Spanish derivation from the Quechua word *kuka*. They call it *hayu*. As I had learned from Victor, only married men are permitted to use the leaf. When a young Arhuaco is to be married, he undergoes a period of instruction and initiation under the tutelage of a *mame*, an Arhuaco priest. Valentín would tell me little of this, but I gathered that the strength and endurance afforded by chewing coca leaves were linked with the manliness and virility of the adult male. During this ceremony the *mame* gives the young man his *poporo*, the small, hour-glass-shaped calabash gourd in which he keeps the lime-powder. The Arhuaco guards his *poporo* jealously. It is the symbol of his initiation—an *amuleto*, Valentín called it. The action of the lime-dipper in the gourd is sexual, and this too is part of the initiation.

Nebusimague stands nearly 8,000 feet above sea-level. At some times of the year there are night-frosts, and this means that coca cannot be cultivated here. Coca thrives in the lush, hot, semi-tropical valleys of the *tierra templada*, the middle altitude region between 2,000 and 6,000 feet. It can be cultivated down in the tropical lowlands—it is used, for instance, by some Amazonian tribes—but it is essentially a mountain plant. According to Valentín, "life is too easy" for the coca plant grown in the lowlands. In the intense and humid heat it produces dense foliage, but the leaves have little potency. Lower-altitude plantations are also prey to a butterfly, the *ulo*, whose larvae feed on the leaf, and to various destructive lichens. The best situation for a *cocal*, Valentín said, is as high up in the hills as possible, while still retaining the necessary warmth. A young coca plant produces eighteen months to two years after planting. It is said that a well-tended plant, once established, will outlive the *coquero*.

I remembered seeing coca in the Peruvian Andes, growing on small hillside terraces—*cocales*—or in the wild. An untended coca shrub will grow to about 12 feet, though for cultivation it is generally pruned down to 3 to 6 feet. The cut-back bush is known as a *pajarito*, a little bird. The coca bush—*Erythroxylum coca*—is a slim, graceful plant, bearing small, creamy-white flowers, or bright scarlet fruits like a cranberry. The leaves are smooth, oval, lanceolate, about an inch or two long according to species. The two main strains of coca used for cocaine production are the Bolivian Huanaco leaf and the Peruvian Trujillo leaf. The coca cultivated in the Sierra Nevada is a relative of the Trujillo, a strain of the species known to botanists as *Erythroxylum novogranatense*. The leaves of this are small, and the cocaine content is somewhat sweetened by an admixture of other alkaloids.

Valentín harvested his coca bushes just once a year. The leaves are ready, he said, when they take on a faint yellowish tint, and when they harden so that they snap when folded. Coca grown at lower altitudes can be harvested up to three times a year, but most Arhuaco plots were up at the higher altitude limit for the plant. Though there is only one actual harvest, leaves are also gathered when the bushes are pruned. This mini-harvest is humorously called *la quita calzón*—literally, the coca bush has its trousers taken off. At harvest, Valentín and his family reckon to pick one *arroba* of leaves a day. There are five of them doing the picking, so each is expected to harvest about 5 lb of leaves a day. The leaves, always picked one by one, are gathered in woollen blankets. They are laid out to dry in the sun on slabs of stone next to the farmhouse. If conditions are right, the early morning's harvest will be fully dried by the end of the day. Fast drying seals in the stimulant alkaloids, and *coca del dia* is the most highly prized leaf. Once dried, the leaves are crisp and brittle. Then they are piled into heaps, and left for two or three days. This makes them sweat, and they regain some pliability and moisture. After this they are sun-dried again, very quickly, before being packed up. All of this is a delicate operation. If the initial drying has taken too long, the leaf will be brownish and brittle. If it has been sweated too long, it will be greyish and musty, and have a mildewed look, a *caspa* or dandruff, as Valentín put it. For storage the coca leaves are first pressed with wood weights, then wrapped in banana leaves, and bound up in sacking or rough wool. Properly dried and packed, and stored in cool, dry conditions, the coca leaf keeps its strength for a year, lasting the *coquero* until the next harvest.

The Arhuaco keeps his daily supply of leaves in a *mochila* bag, usually woven for him by his wife. He chews throughout the day. The leaf suppresses hunger and relieves tiredness. As Valentín simply put it, the coca "*cuida del cuerpo*"—it takes care of his body. It is a kind of freedom from the prickings of the flesh.

The correct quantity for a *mascada*, a mouthful of coca, is the amount you can balance on three fingers. This is put in the mouth, moistened with saliva, and held in the cheek. Lime is added by means of a long thin spatula, the *sokane*, which is poked into the gourd containing the lime-powder. The powder adheres to the moistened end of the *sokane* and is tamped into the coca quid in the cheek. When the spatula is taken out of the narrow-necked gourd, it is always rubbed against the rim. In time this produces a bowl-shaped encrustation, greenish-yellow, around the rim of the gourd. Valentín called this *la calavera*, the "skull" of the *poporo*. If this crumbles or cracks, it is an omen of death or imminent disgrace.

I asked Valentín if he would sell me some coca leaves. This was such bad form that he pretended he hadn't heard. One evening, however, he gave me a small heap of leaves and a pile of powder. This was a gesture of friendship, and would have been disapproved of by the more conventional Arhuaco. He apologized that they were not the best. The finest leaves are olive-green, smooth, almost glossy, with a soft, slightly spongy texture. These were paler and drier, but they smelt good—a slightly metallic odour, but soft and aromatic, like a form of tea.

To taste, the leaf is bitter. The higher the cocaine content—usually about 1 per cent by weight—the sharper the leaf. Actually the first impression of taking coca is the unpleasantness of stuffing a handful of dried leaves into one's mouth. But once moistened with saliva they form a quid which sits snugly between the gums and the cheek. As I had no *sokane*, I had to use an ordinary stick to poke the lime in, again not very tasty. The effects of a *mascada* come on gently, scarcely noticeable until you learn to recognize them. Your mouth is numbed where the quid sits. You salivate a lot. You are not hungry, nor thirsty, nor tired. You are cool and buoyant. Chewing coca is not a "high" as such, not a "drug experience." It is more of a load lightener. Valentín's phrase was just right—the coca "takes care of" your body. One might quantify the effect by comparing it to a strong cup of black coffee, except that the mode of ingestion makes it smoother, longer and more elastic than a caffeine-hit. After about half an hour the effects of your quid will be exhausted: the process is repeated and a new handful of leaves is added. An Arhuaco might consume 2 ounces of leaves daily. Depending on the potency of the leaves, this is the equivalent of between a quarter and half a gram of pure cocaine a day.

27

SIERRA MEDICINE

There were two ways of getting myself back down to Valledupar. The first and simplest was to return the way I had
come, through Pueblo Bello. The other way was to strike out
through the mountains to another *mestizo* village, Chemesquemena, about 25 miles north-east of Nebusimague. The
trail to Chemesquemena, I was reliably informed, was clear
to follow and very beautiful. All you had to do was keep with
the rivers—follow the San Sebastián river upstream, cross
the watershed, pick up the Los Mangos river, follow it east
until it joins the Guatapuri river, then turn north and follow
the Guatapuri as far as Chemesquemena. What could be simpler?

Late one afternoon I suddenly decided to go. I would camp
the night somewhere near Nebusimague, and strike out the
following day. I said goodbye to Valentín. He assured me I
would be in Chemesquemena in two days' time. That night I
slept beneath a giant caracoli tree beside the San Sebastián
river. The river was swollen and blackened after the previous
day's rains. I slept fitfully and dreamt of familiar faces. Waking to the spiky, unfamiliar skyline, the rushing of the river,
the moving moon, it seemed impossible to believe that this
was the reality, and the people I knew so well were the
dream. At sunrise I breakfasted on bread and *panela*, and
after an hour of quite steep walking I stood high up on the
watershed, looking down on the breathtaking panorama of
the canyon below, dense cloud forest in its hollows, pale

brown *ico* grass on the upper ridges. Occasional tiny grass-roofed huts clung to the skirts of the slopes, and all along the south side of the valley I could see the trail running off east-wards, mile upon mile into the morning haze.

The path wound down through the cloud forest: thin silver waterfalls, luxuriant hanging plants, blue morpho butterflies the size of bats, orioles and tanagers flitting in the branches high above. As I sat to rest I saw a mule train beginning the descent above me. The leader was an old man, followed by three mules, one of them carrying a little girl, then a young Arhuaco with a rifle, and then the women, always following behind. The men greeted me gruffly and confirmed that I was on the right path for Chemesquemena. The women didn't look up, just called back "*Buenos días*" in their quavery, flut-ing voices. Each carried a bundle on her back, with the strap tied round her forehead. The dark, saturnine look which sits so handsomely on the Arhuaco men does not become the women, who tend to be squat and dumpy. Later I met a young boy and his sister coming up the other way, their mule carrying net sacks filled with oranges. They were bringing these up from the *tierra templada* to Nebusimague. They had slept the night by the trail. The boy said he was twenty, but he looked no more than twelve.

Soon the path came out of the forest canopy and wound along the slope. The river roared below. This was a hot, rocky stretch, and I was glad when the path finally dipped back down into the shade of the greenery. I swam, ate some lunch and crossed the Los Mangos river over a neat wood and concrete bridge. The builder's signature—Jorge Los Rios, George of the River—was etched in the concrete. I picked windfall mangoes and set off for the afternoon's trek.

During the afternoon the character of the day began to change. Beware smugness and self-congratulation. If I'd thought this was just a pleasant hike through breathtaking scenery, the Sierra was about to prove me wrong. The first thing I noticed was that the trail, though fairly level, seemed to be getting harder and harder. I found myself panting and drooping. I stopped frequently for water and fruit, and each time starting off again was more effortful. I was also confused about the trail. When I crossed the Rio Los Mangos, I had thought I would pick up the Guatapuri river and head north-wards, but consulting my compass I found I was still going east. The trail, which in the morning had been fairly busy, was now deserted, so I had no way of knowing if I was right.

I soon realized why I was feeling so feeble. The air over the buff-coloured peaks was massing, grey and charged. The brief stretches of woodland round the feeder rivers seemed strangely silent. There was no doubt about it: a storm was gathering. I heard the thunder ricochet up along the ridges. The first fat drops spat on to the dusty track, and within seconds it had turned into a downpour. I was on a high, bare stretch of the trail. There was nowhere to shelter, I had no waterproof gear to put on, and by the time I reached some trees I was drenched. I huddled for a few minutes under some bushes, but the rain was too strong and pounded through unabated. There was no point in sitting there, so on I went. The path had turned into a rivulet of mud and leaves. The feeder streams that had purled down the rocks a few mo-ments earlier were now running faster and louder. Water poured off the brim of my hat. I cursed my unpreparedness.

Suddenly, in front of me, I saw a little dog scampering along the trail, and when it cut off left, down a wooded slope, I followed it, thinking it must be leading me some-where, perhaps to a farm where I could beg shelter until the storm subsided. Then just as suddenly as it appeared the dog vanished, and I found myself teetering at the edge of a gorge, staring down at the boiling waters of Los Mangos 50 feet below. I hacked back up the slope, slithering in the mud, and rejoined the trail. The only thing was to keep on going, until either the rain stopped or I came upon some kind of shelter. After a while even this option was closed off. The trail wound down into tall woodland, and disappeared en-tirely beneath the swollen waters of a feeder river. I stood there, uncertain. I knew there must be stepping stones under the water: all the feeder rivers I had crossed had had some kind of ford. I felt gingerly for the first stone, the rush of the water grabbed my foot, and I fell. For a moment I thought I was going to be swept away, thrown like a soft tomato against one of those big boulders, but I managed to fall slightly backwards and get a grip on some rocks. The few parts of me the rain had not reached were now completely drenched. I crawled out and lay on the bank, shivering. The trail was blocked, the light was fading fast, and the storm showed no sign of letting up.

Then I spotted, down in a hollow of the woods, what I'd been looking for all along: a cave. When I got to it I saw it was not really a cave, just an arrangement of rocks, but it was space enough for a half-drowned rat to crawl into. I pulled off my wet clothes and wormed into my sleeping-bag. The accommodation was meagre, wedged against dank rock, half-sitting, half-lying. The light had gone completely now. I took a few slugs of aguardiente. It looked like it was going to be a long hard night.

I don't know how long I sat there—probably not much more than an hour. I listened to the roar of the river. I hurled futile, Lear-like curses at the elements. I wished I was back in Santa Marta, eating red snapper at El Molino. Then I began to notice a subtle addition to the noise. The raging of water outside the cave was now counterpointed by another, softer, liquid sound. For a moment this seemed comforting, a childhood memory of water filling up a stone sink. But what sink? The sink was the cave. Swivelling round I found water pouring steadily through the back of the rock. It had been coming in for a while before I had heard it. The cave was awash. Unknown to me, my sleeping bag had been quietly soaking up water. The cave was too small to stand up in. I had to drag myself out in my sleeping-bag, floundering like some preposterous mermaid. There was a big humped rock a few yards from the cave: I must make for that, higher ground. I scrabbled some belongings together from the cave and set off for the rock. I promptly sank up to my thighs in a morass of mud and leaves. My boots were unlaced, and I walked clean out of one of them as I forded this mulch.

After three journeys I was up on the rock with my things

scattered around me. Thankfully my torch still worked. Everything else was in a pitiful condition. Bread, fruit and *panela* squashed into a mulch of protein, cigarettes and matches beyond redemption, sleeping-bag leaden with water. My world seemed to have shrunk to tiny, primitive proportions—the cave, the morass, the rock.

Water was still dripping off the trees, but I was aware that the rain had stopped. I considered my options. I couldn't stay here, wet and shivering on the rock. I couldn't go on across the swollen river. The only thing to do was turn back, in the hope of finding some shelter, someone to take me in. I squeezed everything into my bag with difficulty. It seemed to weigh twice as much as before. My ropy old walking boots had suffered badly. The one I had lost in the morass had come completely unstitched and flapped dismally as I walked.

Back on the trail I was amazed at how quickly the storm-waters had been soaked up. The soil was thin, the foliage thirsty, the streams well-channelled. The land had drunk up the water, and now the trail was mostly as dry and firm as it had been that afternoon. The storm had come and gone, and I alone on that hillside was unable to cope with it.

After about half an hour I recognized the stretch of woodland where I had followed the little dog off the trail. Maybe there *was* a house around somewhere. I took the same side-path I had slid down before, and found a fork in it I had not seen previously. This led back round the side of the slope, running more or less parallel with the trail, but hidden from it. In a few minutes I came out into a small grassy clearing. There, sitting in the moonlight, was a small farmyard, and the round thatched hump of an Arhuaco house, lying in the fold of the hill.

I stood irresolutely at the gate. All was silent, except the distant river in the gorge below. A dead hog's plum tree stood in the farmyard. I saw what looked like a mound of old blankets lying in the yard, a few feet from the entrance to the hut. As I got nearer I saw there were two figures asleep beneath the blankets, children I supposed from the size of them. The moon was bright, the dusty yard as mysteriously dry as the trail. I went up and tapped one of them on the shoulder. The figure started up. It was not a child, but a small, squat, very ugly man with matted black hair, who might have been anything between forty and four hundred years old.

I stuttered forth my supplication. I was caught in the storm, I needed shelter, I would gladly pay.

"You are wet," he said in gruff Spanish. He woke the woman beside him, spoke to her in Iki. She climbed out of the blankets, without much obvious enthusiasm, and shuffled off inside. "You may sleep here," said the little man. He told me to hang my wet things on the rails of the corral that ran down one side of the farmyard. A pair of small white *cebu* cows stared at me. In another part of the corral I saw a mule and a horse. Chickens, small pigs and a dog or two were loose in the farmyard. I asked the old man if he had any matches. He said he had the *candela* going inside the hut. He went in and lit me a cigarette. I lit another off it, for him to smoke. He took it out of politeness, but coughed and spat when he smoked it, and threw it away.

I asked him if it would rain again.

He shook his head. "The rains have gone on," he said, gesturing east. We stood in silence for a while. There were rustlings in the farmyard, a night bird calling. I wanted to ask why he was sleeping out in the yard, but this seemed improper. He said, "The rains always come at the full moon."

I looked up, ashamed that I hadn't noticed. Full moon in the Sierra. If you were after purification, this was surely it.

I slept naked in the farmyard, among pigs and toads, with a cow-hide mat beneath me and a woollen blanket on top. The blanket reeked with a redolent compound of wood-smoke, horse-sweat and old clothes. A small brindled pig lay in the dust, snuffling and shifting in its sleep. The ridges of the mat bit my back, and the fleas bit everywhere else, but I have never felt so snug in my life. I was touched with grati-tude to the little farmer—who, like some good dwarf in a

Grimm fairy tale—had offered his humble hospitality to a stranger lost in the storm.

At dawn a cock crowed, old and wheezy, like a rusty door being forced open. In the east the sun was glinting pink on the mountain tops, in the west the moon was still precise and bright. I saw that the little pig had died in the night. Around its body, as it shifted in the grip of its fever, its trotters had traced a perfect circle in the dirt. Everything seemed charged with a strange, hermetic significance.

Dew sparkled on my mangy belongings hanging on the corral. The little farmer appeared up the path, leading a mule carrying two *cestas* of maize. He was travelling up to Nebusimague today. He beckoned me into his dark, smoky hut. His wife fanned the *candela*. A blackened pot sat on the glowing wood. A mess of greyish pottage bubbled sluggishly. I breakfasted on a bowlful of gruel, which seemed to taste of little else than the layers of black wood-carbon on the bowl. It was doubtless maize.

Their children stared at me, their dogs growled at me. The little man and his wife bent over their wood dishes, ladling the gruel in with their hands. Nothing was said.

I loaded my damp gear into my bag. The old Arhuaco stood watching me, while his mule munched on cane-stems before taking the trail for Nebusimague. He explained carefully how I should recognize the point where I must ford the Los Mangos, in order to pick up the northbound trail along the Guatapuri. As I was sorting my bedraggled clothes, I came upon the bag of coca leaves given me by Valentín. They were a sorry sight, blackened and mulched against the side of the bag. The scrap of newspaper containing the lime-powder had disintegrated.

"You need coca," said the farmer. He got me to hold out my towel. He dipped his hand in his *mochila* and deposited fresh green leaves on the towel. "You need *yotinwe.*" I found some paper, and he sprinkled a small heap of the creamy powder out of his calabash. "You have a journey. You need medicine for your journey."

I thanked him profusely. He laughed and said something unintelligible in Iki. I said, "I do not understand Iki."

He translated into his rough Spanish, "Do not thank me, thank God. God gives it."

I offered him money, making it clear it was not for the coca, but for his hospitality. He refused. I pressed him, saying he had been my "hotel" for the night. He didn't seem to understand the word. I walked with him back up the trail. The air was clean and bright, and carried the sound of the river.

We shook hands. He was going west. I was going east. I thanked him all over again. He said, "The *bunaci* will do the same for me if I am lost."

"I hope so."

I set off down the trail, one boot flapping open like a vaudeville tramp's. I walked for a day and a half, living on Spam and windfall mangoes, chewing the old man's coca, spitting green spit. I swam in the big rivers, and slept beneath a giant caracoli, and in the morning woke to find a blue hummingbird hovering near my head like the spirit of a departed ancestor. The mountains were full of portents: thundering before a storm, sunlit while it was still cool in the valley. Ten o'clock, *bunaci* time, was when the sun was first starting to toast you. Midday was the hour of the lizard. On my third day out of Nebusimague, at midday, I made one last ascent on a rocky stretch and found myself on a real dirt-road, with real tyre marks leading down to a bridge—not one of those horizontal thickets of woven wood the Arhuacos build, which look like they've grown across the river, but real tawdry steel. On the other side, sun bouncing off the tin roofs, stood Chemesquemena.

I slumped exhausted at the village store, Señora Rosada's. The villagers spoke of her in the hushed tones that the Indians might reserve for their *mame* shamans. She sat eating a plate of yucca and rice, and spearing sardines straight out of the can with her pen-knife. I bought Pepsi and cigarettes—there was mysteriously no beer—and sat in a chair for the first time in a week. The houses were wooden with hammocks slung inside.

Solon, a big, handsome man in a wide-brimmed straw hat, drove the daily truck down to Valledupar. I slept in a hammock at his family's house. His sister gave her son reading lessons by torchlight. It seemed I had only just dropped off to sleep when I heard Solon's truck outside, blaring his horn, ready for the four o'clock departure. Down the dark road, into the wind, the mealy taste of dust in my mouth. Bowls of mist in the valleys at dawn. After three hours we hit a proper road. There was a police road-check, a *retén*. They had everyone out of the truck, checked papers, searched bags, and finally waved us through, back over the invisible border into the twentieth century.

There followed the long, hot bus-haul south to Bogotá. I was tired and careless, the old farmer's coca leaves did not travel well. They sweated in the hotlands, and when I unpacked them in Bogotá they smelt like compost, and the first specks of mildew could be seen on them. *Coca caspada*. It was as if they were sickening for the Sierra. I could believe it. I could believe anything by now.

I nearly chucked them away, but I didn't. They were a gift, a memento, evidence that I hadn't been dreaming. Now they're sitting on the customs man's desk. They're what this story, this whole business, is about. Behind all the greed and the violence, the need to make laws and the itch to break them, there is just this handful of leaves, medicine for the journey.

AUTHOR'S NOTE

Many people contributed to this story, some knowingly, some not. Almost all who appear in it do so with their names changed, and for obvious reasons some of them would not feel much thanked if I gave their real names now.

For particular help and encouragement before, during and after my trip to Colombia in 1983 I would like to thank the following: Luz Marina Vallejo, Ana, Dario, Raúl, Jaime and Estella Vallejo, Ana Rita and Juan Contreras, Nydia and Kevin Scanlan, Luis Murcia, David Godwin, Andrew Baldwin, Tony and Blanca Hutchings, Mary Ensor, Elena Vitterli, Giovanni, Alejandra Duarte, José and Olivia at Los Idolos, Omar Parodi, Jaime Conde Danies, Marc Gerstein, Chuck Pinsky, Garman Daza, Harvey and Clavia Aronson, and Alastair Macdonald.

The mention of their names carries no suggestion of their involvement in, or approval of, cocaine. This book is not a tract for or against the trafficking of drugs. It is simply a story.

I know that I owe some sort of apology to the people of Colombia, because like everyone I talk of little else but their *mala fama*. I can only say that the book grew—if at an odd angle—out of my love for Colombia, and for the warmth, wit and honesty of its people.

About The Author

Freelance journalist, author and researcher, Charles Nicholl was born in London in 1950. His work has appeared in *Rolling Stone*, *The New Statesman*, *Time Out*, and *The Spectator*. He is the author of a book about Elizabethan alchemy, *The Chemical Theatre* (1980) and a biography of the pamphleteer Tom Nashe, *A Cup of News* (1984).